In Desert and Wilderness

IN DESERT AND WILDERNESS

WORKS OF

Henryk Sienkiewicz

———

In Desert and Wilderness

With Fire and Sword

The Deluge. *2 vols.*

Pan Michael

Children of the Soil

"Quo Vadis"

Sielanka, A Forest Picture

The Knights of the Cross

Without Dogma

Whirlpools

On the Field of Glory

Let Us Follow Him

Henryk Sienkiewicz.

IN DESERT
AND WILDERNESS

BY

HENRYK SIENKIEWICZ

AUTHOR OF "WITH FIRE AND SWORD," "QUO VADIS,"
"WHIRLPOOLS," ETC.

TRANSLATED FROM THE POLISH BY

MAX A. DREZMAL

BOSTON
LITTLE, BROWN, AND COMPANY
1912

Published, February, 1912

THE UNIVERSITY PRESS, CAMBRIDGE, U.S A.

PART FIRST

IN DESERT AND WILDERNESS

I

"Do you know, Nell," said Staś Tarkowski to his friend, a little English girl, "that yesterday the police came and arrested the wife of Smain, the overseer, and her three children, — that Fatma who several times called at the office to see your father and mine."

And little Nell, resembling a beautiful picture, raised her greenish eyes to Stas and asked with mingled surprise and fright:

"Did they take her to prison?"

"No, but they will not let her go to the Sudân and an official has arrived who will see that she does not move a step out of Port Said."

"Why?"

Stas, who was fourteen years old and who loved his eight-year-old companion very much, but looked upon her as a mere child, said with a conceited air:

"When you reach my age, you will know everything which happens, not only along the Canal from Port Said to Suez, but in all Egypt. Have you ever heard of the Mahdi?"

"I heard that he is ugly and naughty."

The boy smiled compassionately.

"I do not know whether he is ugly. The Sudânese claim that he is handsome. But the word 'naughty,' about a man who has murdered so many people, could he used only by a little girl, eight years old, in dresses — oh — reaching the knees."

"Papa told me so and papa knows best."

"He told you so because otherwise you would not understand. He would not express himself to me in that way. The Mahdi is worse than a whole shoal of crocodiles. Do you understand? That is a nice expression for me. 'Naughty!' They talk that way to babes."

But, observing the little girl's clouded face, he became silent and afterwards said:

"Nell, you know I did not want to cause you any unpleasantness. The time will come when you will be fourteen. I certainly promise you that."

"Aha!" she replied with a worried look, "but if before that time the Mahdi should dash into Port Said and eat me."

"The Mahdi is not a cannibal, so he does not eat people. He only kills them. He will not dash into Port Said, but even if he did and wanted to murder you, he would first have to do with me."

This declaration with the sniff with which Stas inhaled the air through his nose, did not bode any good for the Mahdi and considerably quieted Nell as to her own person.

"I know," she answered, "you would not let him harm me. But why do they not allow Fatma to leave Port Said?"

"Because Fatma is a cousin of the Mahdi. Her husband, Smain, made an offer to the Egyptian Government at Cairo to go to the Sudân, where the Mahdi is staying, and secure the liberty of all Europeans who have fallen into his hands."

"Then Smain is a good man?"

"Wait! Your papa and my papa, who knew Smain thoroughly, did not have any confidence in him and warned Nubar Pasha not to trust him. But the Government agreed to send Smain and Smain remained over half a year with the Mahdi. The prisoners not only did not return, but news has come from Khartûm that the Mahdists are treating them more and more cruelly, and that Smain, having taken money from the Government, has become a traitor. He joined the Mahdi's army and has been appointed an emir. The people say that in that terrible battle in which General Hicks fell, Smain commanded the Mahdi's artillery and that he probably taught the Mahdists how to handle the cannon, which before that time they, as savage people, could not do. But now Smain is anxious to get his wife and children out of Egypt. So when Fatma, who evidently knew in advance what Smain was going to do, wanted secretly to leave Port Said, the Government arrested her with the children."

"But what good are Fatma and her children to the Government?"

"The Government will say to the Mahdi, — 'Give us the prisoners and we will surrender Fatma' — "

For the time the conversation was interrupted because the attention of Stas was attracted by birds flying from the direction of Echtum om Farag towards Lake Menzaleh. They flew quite low and in the clear atmosphere could be plainly seen some pelicans with curved napes, slowly moving immense wings. Stas at once began to imitate their flight. So with head upraised, he ran a score of paces along the dyke, waving his outstretched arms.

"Look!" suddenly exclaimed Nell. "Flamingoes are also flying."

Stas stood still in a moment, as actually behind the pelicans, but somewhat higher, could be seen, suspended in the sky, two great red and purple flowers, as it were.

"Flamingoes! flamingoes! Before night they return to their haunts on the little islands," the boy said. "Oh, if I only had a rifle!"

"Why should you want to shoot at them?"

"Girls don't understand such things. But let us go far-ther; we may see more of them."

Saying this he took the girl's hand and together they strolled towards the first wharf beyond Port Said. Dinah, a negress and at one time nurse of little Nell, closely followed them. They walked on the embankment which separated the waters of Lake Menzaleh from the Canal, through which at that time a big English steamer, in charge of a pilot, floated. The night was approaching. The sun still stood quite high but was rolling in the direction of the lake. The salty waters of the latter began to glitter with gold and throb with the reflection of peacock feathers. On the Arabian bank as far as the eye could reach, stretched a tawny, sandy desert — dull, portentous, lifeless. Between the glassy, as if half-dead, heaven and the immense, wrinkled sands there was not a trace of a living being. While on the Canal life seethed, boats bustled about, the whistles of steamers resounded, and above Menzaleh flocks of mews and wild ducks scintillated in the sunlight, yonder, on the Arabian bank, it appeared as if it were the region of death. Only in proportion as the sun, descending, became ruddier and ruddier did the sands begin to assume that lily hue which the heath in Polish forests has in autumn.

The children, walking towards the wharf, saw a few more flamingoes, which pleased their eyes. After this Dinah announced that Nell must return home. In Egypt, after days which even in winter are often scorching, very cold nights follow, and as Nell's health demanded great care, her father, Mr. Rawlinson, would not allow her to be near the water after sunset. They, therefore, returned to the city, on the outskirts of which, near the Canal, stood Mr. Raw-linson's villa, and by the time the sun plunged into the sea they were in the house. Soon, the engineer Tarkowski,

Stas' father, who was invited to dinner arrived, and the whole company, together with a French lady, Nell's teacher, Madame Olivier, sat at the table.

Mr. Rawlinson, one of the directors of the Suez Canal Company, and Ladislaus Tarkowski, senior engineer of the same company, lived for many years upon terms of the closest intimacy. Both were widowers, but Pani Tarkowski, by birth a French lady, died at the time Stas came into the world, while Nell's mother died of consumption in Helwan when the girl was three years old. Both widowers lived in neighboring houses in Port Said, and owing to their duties met daily. A common misfortune drew them still closer to each other and strengthened the ties of friendship previously formed. Mr. Rawlinson loved Stas as his own son, while Pan Tarkowski would have jumped into fire and water for little Nell. After finishing their daily work the most agreeable recreation for them was to talk about the children, their education and future. During such conversations it frequently happened that Mr. Rawlinson would praise the ability, energy, and bravery of Stas and Pan Tarkowski would grow enthusiastic over the sweetness and angelic countenance of Nell. And the one and the other spoke the truth. Stas was a trifle conceited and a trifle boastful, but diligent in his lessons, and the teachers in the English school in Port Said, which he attended, credited him with uncommon abilities. As to courage and resourcefulness, he inherited them from his father, for Pan Tarkowski possessed these qualities in an eminent degree and in a large measure owed to them his present position.

In the year 1863 he fought for eleven months without cessation. Afterwards, wounded, taken into captivity, and condemned to Siberia, he escaped from the interior of Russia and made his way to foreign lands. Before he entered into the insurrection he was a qualified engineer; nevertheless he devoted a year to the study of hydraulics. Later he secured a position at the Canal and in the course of a few years, when his expert knowledge, energy, and industry became known, he assumed the important position of senior engineer.

Stas was born, bred, and reached his fourteenth year in Port Said on the Canal; in consequence of which the engineers called him the child of the desert. At a later period, when he was attending school, he sometimes, during the vacation season and holidays, accompanied his father or Mr. Rawlinson on trips, which their duty required them to make from Port Said to Suez to inspect the work on the embankment or the dredging of the channel of the Canal. He knew everybody — the engineers and custom-house officials as well as the laborers, Arabs and negroes. He bustled about and insinuated himself everywhere, appearing where least expected; he made long excursions on the embankment, rowed in a boat over Menzalch, venturing at times far and wide. He crossed over to the Arabian bank and mounting the first horse he met, or in the absence of a horse, a camel, or even a donkey, he would imitate Farys [1] on the desert; in a word, as Pan Tarkowski expressed it, "he was always popping up somewhere," and every moment free from his studies he passed on the water.

His father did not oppose this, as he knew that rowing, horseback riding, and continual life in the fresh air strengthened his health and developed resourcefulness within him. In fact, Stas was taller and stronger than most boys of his age. It was enough to glance at his eyes to surmise that in case of any adventure he would sin more from too much audacity than from timidity. In his fourteenth year, he was one of the best swimmers in Port Said, which meant

[1] Farys, the hero of Adam Mickiewicz's Oriental poem of the same name. — *Translator's note.*

not a little, for the Arabs and negroes swim like fishes. Shooting from carbines of a small caliber, and only with cartridges, for wild ducks and Egyptian geese, he acquired an unerring eye and steady hand. His dream was to hunt the big animals sometime in Central Africa. He therefore eagerly listened to the narratives of the Sudânese working on the Canal, who in their native land had encountered big, thick-skinned, and rapacious beasts.

This also had its advantage, for at the same time he learned their languages. It was not enough to excavate the Suez Canal; it was necessary also to maintain it, as otherwise the sands of the deserts, lying on both banks, would fill it up in the course of a year. The grand work of De Lesseps demands continual labor and vigilance. So, too, at the present day, powerful machines, under the supervision of skilled engineers, and thousands of laborers are at work, dredging the channel. At the excavation of the Canal, twenty-five thousand men labored. To-day, owing to the completion of the work and improved new machinery, considerably less are required. Nevertheless, the number is great. Among them the natives of the locality predominate. There is not, however, a lack of Nubians, Sudânese, Somalis, and various negroes coming from the White and Blue Niles, that is, from the region which previous to the Mahdi's insurrection was occupied by the Egyptian Government. Stas lived with all on intimate terms and having, as is usual with Poles, an extraordinary aptitude for languages he became, he himself not knowing how and when, acquainted with many of their dialects. Born in Egypt, he spoke Arabian like an Arab. From the natives of Zanzibar, many of whom worked as firemen on the steam dredges, he learned Kiswahili, a language widely prevalent all over Central Africa. He could even converse with the negroes of the Dinka and Shilluk tribes, residing on the

Nile below Fashoda. Besides this, he spoke fluently English, French, and also Polish, for his father, an ardent patriot, was greatly concerned that his son should know the language of his forefathers. Stas in reality regarded this language as the most beautiful in the world and taught it, not without some success, to little Nell. One thing only he could not accomplish, that she should pronounce his name Stas, and not "Stes." Sometimes, on account of this, a misunderstanding arose between them, which continued until small tears began to glisten in the eyes of the girl. Then "Stes" would beg her pardon and became angry at himself.

He had, however, an annoying habit of speaking slightingly of her eight years and citing by way of contrast his own grave age and experience. He contended that a boy who is finishing his fourteenth year, if he is not fully matured, at least is not a mere child, but on the contrary, is capable of performing all kinds of heroic deeds, especially if he has Polish and French blood. He craved most ardently that sometime an opportunity would occur for such deeds, particularly in defense of Nell. Both invented various dangers and Stas was compelled to answer her questions as to what he would do if, for instance, a crocodile, ten yards long, or a scorpion as big as a dog, should crawl through the window of her home. To both it never occurred for a moment that impending reality would surpass all their fantastic suppositions.

II

IN the meantime, in the house, good news awaited them during the dinner. Messrs. Rawlinson and Tarkowski, as skilled engineers, had been invited a few weeks before, to examine and appraise the work carried on in connection with the whole net-work of canals in the Province of El-Fayûm, in the vicinity of the city of Medinet near Lake Karun, as well as along the Yûsuf and Nile rivers. They were to stay there for about a month and secured furloughs from their company. As the Christmas holidays were approaching, both gentlemen, not desiring to be separated from the children, decided that Stas and Nell should also go to Medinet. Hearing this news the children almost leaped out of their skins from joy. They had already visited the cities lying along the Canal, particularly Ismailia and Suez, and while outside the Canal, Alexandria and Cairo, near which they viewed the great pyramids and the Sphinx. But these were short trips, while the expedition to Medinet el-Fayûm required a whole day's travel by railway, southward along the Nile and then westward from El-Wasta towards the Libyan Desert. Stas knew Medinet from the narratives of younger engineers and tourists who went there to hunt for various kinds of water-fowls as well as desert wolves and hyenas. He knew that it was a separate, great oasis lying off the west bank of the Nile but not dependent upon its inundations and having its water system formed by Lake Karun through Bahr Yûsuf and a whole chain of small canals. Those who had seen this oasis said that although that region belonged to Egypt, nevertheless, being separated from it by a desert, it formed a distinct whole. Only the Yûsuf River connects, one might say with a thin blue thread, that locality with the valley of the Nile. The great abundance of water, fertility of soil, and luxuriant vegetation made an earthly paradise of it, while the extensive ruins of the city of Crocodilopolis drew thither hundreds of curious tourists. Stas, however, was attracted mainly by the shores of Lake Karun, with its swarms of birds and its wolf-hunts on the desert hills of Gebel el-Sedment.

But his vacation began a few days later, and as the inspection of the work on the canals was an urgent matter and the gentlemen could not lose any time, it was arranged that they should leave without delay, while the children, with Madame Olivier, were to depart a week later. Nell and Stas had a desire to leave at once, but Stas did not dare to make the request. Instead they began to ask questions about various matters relative to the journey, and with new outbursts of joy received the news that they would not live in uncomfortable hotels kept by Greeks, but in tents furnished by the Cook Tourists' Agency. This is the customary arrangement of tourists who leave Cairo for a lengthy stay at Medinet. Cook furnishes tents, servants, cooks, supplies of provisions, horses, donkeys, camels, and guides; so the tourist does not have to bother about anything. This, indeed, is quite an expensive mode of traveling; but Messrs. Tarkowski and Rawlinson did not have to take that into account as all expenses were borne by the Egyptian Government, which invited them, as experts, to inspect and appraise the work on the canals. Nell, who, above everything in the world, loved riding on a camel, obtained a promise from her father that she should have a separate "hump-backed saddle horse" on which, together with Madame Olivier, or Dinah, and sometimes with Stas, she could participate in the excursions to the nearer localities of the desert and to Karun. Pan Tarkowski promised Stas that he would allow him some nights to go after wolves, and if he brought a good report from school he would get a genuine English short rifle and the necessary equipment for a hunter. As Stas was confident that he would succeed, he at once began to regard himself as the owner of a short rifle and promised himself to perform various astonishing and immortal feats with it.

On such projects and conversation the dinner passed for the overjoyed children. But somewhat less eagerness for the contemplated journey was displayed by Madame Olivier who was loath to leave the comfortable villa in Port Said and who was frightened at the thought of living for several weeks in a tent, and particularly at the plan of excursions on camel-back. It happened that she had already tried this mode of riding several times and these attempts ended unfortunately. Once the camel rose too soon, before she was well seated in the saddle, and as a result she rolled off his back onto the ground. Another time, the dromedary, not belonging to the light-footed variety, jolted her so that two days elapsed before she recovered; in a word, although Nell, after two or three pleasure-rides which Mr. Rawlinson permitted her to take, declared that there was nothing more delightful in the world, in the same measure only painful recollections remained for Madame Olivier. She said that this was good enough for Arabs or for a chit like Nell, who could not be jolted any more than a fly which should alight upon a camel's hump, but not for persons dignified, and not too light, and having at the same time a certain proneness to unbearable sea-sickness.

But as to Medinet el-Fayûm she had other fears. Now in Port Said as well as in Alexandria, Cairo, and in the whole of Egypt nothing was the subject of more discussion than the Mahdi's insurrection and the cruelties of the dervishes. Madame Olivier, not knowing exactly where Medinet was situated, became alarmed as to whether it was not too near the Mahdists, and finally began to question Mr. Rawlinson about it.

But he only smiled and said:

"The Mahdi at this moment is besieging Khartûm in which General Gordon is defending himself. Does Madame know how far it is from Medinet to Khartûm?"

"I have no idea."

"About as far as from here to Sicily," explained Pan Tarkowski.

"Just about," corroborated Stas. "Khartûm lies where the White and Blue Niles meet and form one river. We are separated from it by the immense expanse of Egypt and the whole of Nubia."

Afterwards he wanted to add that even if Medinet should be closer to the regions overrun by the insurgents, he, of course, would be there with his short rifle; but recalling that for similar bragging he sometimes received a sharp reproof from his father, he became silent.

The older members of the party, however, began to talk of the Mahdi and the insurrection, for this was the most important matter affecting Egypt. The news from Khartûm was bad. The wild hordes already had been besieging the city for a month and a half and the Egyptian and English governments were acting slowly. The relief expedition had barely started and it was generally feared that notwithstanding the fame, bravery, and ability of Gordon this important city would fall into the hands of the barbarians. This was the opinion of Pan Tarkowski, who suspected that England in her soul desired that the Mahdi should wrest it from Egypt in order to retake it later from him and make this vast region an English possession. He did not, however, share this suspicion with Mr. Rawlinson as he did not want to offend his patriotic feelings.

Towards the close of the dinner Stas began to ask why the Egyptian Government had annexed all the country lying south of Nubia, particularly Kordofân, Darfur, and the Sudân as far as Lake Albert Nyanza and deprived the natives there of their liberty. Mr. Rawlinson explained that whatever was done by the Egyptian Government was done at the request of England which extended a protectorate over Egypt and in reality ruled her as Egypt herself desired.

"The Egyptian Government did not deprive anybody of his liberty," he said, "but restored it to hundreds of thousands and perhaps to millions of people. In Kordofân, in Darfur and in the Sudân there were not during the past years any independent States. Only here and there some petty ruler laid claim to some lands and took possession of them by force in spite of the will of the residents. They were mainly inhabited by independent Arab-negro tribes, that is, by people having the blood of both races. These tribes lived in a state of incessant warfare. They attacked each other and seized horses, camels, cattle, and, above all, slaves; besides, they perpetrated numerous atrocities. But the worst were the ivory and slave hunters. They formed a separate class, to which belonged nearly all the chiefs of the tribes and the richer traders. They made armed expeditions into the interior of Africa, appropriating everywhere ivory tusks, and carried away thousands of people: men, women, and children. In addition they destroyed villages and

settlements, devastated fields, shed streams of blood, and
slaughtered without pity all who resisted. In the southern
portion of the Sudân, Darfur, and Kordofân, as well as the
region beyond the Upper Nile as far as the lake they depopulated some localities entirely. But the Arabian bands
made their incursions farther and farther so that Central
Africa became a land of tears and blood. Now England
which, as you know, pursues slave-dealers all over the
world, consented that the Egyptian Government should
annex Kordofân, Darfur, and the Sudân. This was the only
method to compel these pillagers to abandon their abominable trade and the only way to hold them in restraint. The
unfortunate negroes breathed more freely; the depredations ceased and the people began to live under tolerable
laws. But such a state of affairs did not please the
traders, so when Mohammed Ahmed, known to-day as
'the Mahdi,' appeared among them and proclaimed a
holy war on the pretext that the true faith of Mahomet
was perishing, all rushed like one man to arms; and so
that terrible war has been kindled in which thus far the
Egyptians have met with such poor success. The Mahdi
has defeated the forces of the Government in every battle.
He has occupied Kordofân, Darfur, and the Sudân; his
hordes at present are laying a siege to Khartûm and are
advancing to the north as far as the frontiers of Nubia."

"Can they advance as far as Egypt?" asked Stas.

"No," answered Mr. Rawlinson. "The Mahdi announces, indeed, that he will conquer the whole world,
but he is a wild man who has no conception of anything.
He never will take Egypt, as England would not permit it."

"If, however, the Egyptian troops are completely
routed?"

"Then would appear the English armies which no one
has ever overcome."

"And why did England permit the Mahdi to occupy so much territory?"

"How do you know that she has permitted it?" replied Mr. Rawlinson. "England is never in a hurry because she is eternal."

Further conversation was interrupted by a negro servant, who announced that Fatma Smain had arrived and begged for an audience.

Women in the East are occupied exclusively with household affairs and seldom leave the harems. Only the poorer ones go to the market or work in the fields, as the wives of the fellahs, the Egyptian peasants, do; but these at such times veil their faces. Though in the Sudân, from which region Fatma came, this custom was not observed, and though she had come to Mr. Rawlinson's office previously, nevertheless, her arrival, particularly at such a late hour and at a private house, evoked surprise.

"We shall learn something new about Smain," said Pan Tarkowski.

"Yes," answered Mr. Rawlinson, giving at the same time a signal to the servant to usher Fatma in.

Accordingly, after a while there entered a tall, young Sudânese woman with countenance entirely unveiled, complexion very dark, and eyes beautiful but wild, and a trifle ominous. Entering, she at once prostrated herself, and when Mr. Rawlinson ordered her to rise, she raised herself but remained on her knees.

"Sidi," she said, "May Allah bless thee, thy posterity, thy home, and thy flocks!"

"What do you want?" asked the engineer.

"Mercy, help, and succor in misfortune, oh, sir! I am imprisoned in Port Said and destruction hangs over me and my children."

"You say that you are imprisoned, and yet you could come here, and in the night-time at that."

"I have been escorted by the police who day and night watch my house, and I know that they have an order to cut off our heads soon!"

"Speak like a rational woman," answered Mr. Rawlinson, shrugging his shoulders. "You are not in the Sudân, but in Egypt where no one is executed without a trial. So you may be certain that not a hair will fall from your head or the heads of your children."

But she began to implore him to intercede for her yet once more with the Government, to procure permission for her to go to Smain.

"Englishmen as great as you are, sir," she said, "can do everything. The Government in Cairo thinks that Smain is a traitor, but that is false. There visited me yesterday Arabian merchants, who arrived from Suâkin, and before that they bought gums and ivory in the Sudân, and they informed me that Smain is lying sick at El-Fasher and is calling for me and the children to bless them —"

"All this is your fabrication, Fatma," interrupted Mr. Rawlinson.

But she began to swear by Allah that she spoke the truth, and afterwards said that if Smain got well, he undoubtedly would ransom all the Christian captives; and if he should die, she, as a relative of the leader of the dervishes, could obtain access to him easily and would secure whatever she wished. Let them only allow her to leave, for her heart will leap out of her bosom from longing for her husband. In what had she, ill-fated woman, offended the Government or the Khedive? Was it her fault or could she be held accountable because she was the relative of the dervish, Mohammed Ahmed?

Fatma did not dare in the presence of the "English

people" to call her relative "the Mahdi," as that meant
the Redeemer of the world. She knew that the Egyptian
Government regarded him as a rebel and an imposter.
But continually striking her forehead and invoking heaven
to witness her innocence and unhappy plight, she began
to weep and at the same time wail mournfully as women
in the East do after losing husbands or sons. Afterwards
she again flung herself with face on the ground, or rather
on the carpet with which the inlaid floor was covered,
and waited in silence.

Nell, who towards the close of the dinner felt a little
sleepy, became thoroughly aroused and, having an upright
little heart, seized her father's hand, and kissing it again
and again, began to beg for Fatma.

"Let papa help her! Do please, papa!"

Fatma, evidently understanding English, exclaimed
amidst her sobs, not removing her face from the carpet:

"May Allah bless thee, bird of paradise, with the joys
of Omayya, oh, star without a blemish!"

However implacable Stas in his soul was towards the
Mahdists, he was moved by Fatma's entreaties and grief.
Besides, Nell interceded for her and he in the end always
wanted that which Nell wished. So after a while he spoke
out, as if to himself but so that all could hear him:

"If I were the Government, I would allow Fatma to
go."

"But as you are not the Government," Pan Tarkowski
said to him, "you would do better not to interfere in that
which does not concern you."

Mr. Rawlinson also had a compassionate soul and
was sensible of Fatma's situation, but certain statements
which she made struck him as being downright falsehoods.
Having almost daily relations with the custom-house at
Ismailia, he well knew that no new cargoes of gums or

ivory were being transported lately through the Canal.
The trade in those wares had ceased almost entirely.
Arabian traders, moreover, could not return from the city
of El-Fasher which lay in the Sudân, as the Mahdists,
as a rule, barred all traders from their territories, and
those whom they captured were despoiled and kept in
captivity. And it was almost a certainty that the statement about Smain's sickness was a falsehood.

But as Nell's little eyes were still looking at her papa
appealingly, he, not desiring to sadden the little girl,
after a while said to Fatma:

"Fatma, I already have written at your request to
the Government, but without result. And now listen.
To-morrow, with this mehendis (engineer) whom you
see here, I leave for Medinet el-Fayûm; on the way we
shall stop one day in Cairo, for the Khedive desires to
confer with us about the canals leading from Bahr Yûsuf
and give us a commission as to the same. During the
conference I shall take care to present your case and try
to secure for you his favor. But I can do nothing more,
nor shall I promise more."

Fatma rose and, extending both hands in sign of gratitude, exclaimed:

"And so I am safe."

"No, Fatma," answered Mr. Rawlinson, "do not speak
of safety for I already told you that death threatens
neither you nor your children. But that the Khedive
will consent to your departure I do not guarantee, for
Smain is not sick but is a traitor, who, having taken money
from the Government, does not at all think of ransoming
the captives from Mohammed Ahmed."

"Smain is innocent, sir, and lies in El-Fasher," reiterated Fatma, "but if even he broke his faith with the
Government, I swear before you, my benefactor, that

if I am allowed to depart I will entreat Mohammed Ahmed until I secure the deliverance of your captives."

"Very well. I promise you once more that I will intercede for you with the Khedive."

Fatma began to prostrate herself.

"Thank you, Sidi! You are not only powerful, but just. And now I entreat that you permit me to serve you as a slave."

"In Egypt no one can be a slave," answered Mr. Rawlinson with a smile. "I have enough servants and cannot avail myself of your services; for, as I told you, we all are leaving for Medinet and perhaps will remain there until Ramazan."

"I know, sir, for the overseer, Chadigi, told me about that. I, when I heard of it, came not only to implore you for help, but also to tell you that two men of my Dongola tribe, Idris and Gebhr, are camel drivers in Medinet and will prostrate themselves before you when you arrive, submitting to your commands themselves and their camels."

"Good, good," answered the director, "but that is the affair of the Cook Agency, not mine."

Fatma, having kissed the hands of the two engineers and the children, departed blessing Nell particularly. Both gentlemen remained silent for a while, after which Mr. Rawlinson said:

"Poor woman! But she lies as only in the East they know how to lie, and even in her declaration of gratitude there is a sound of some false note."

"Undoubtedly," answered Pan Tarkowski; "but to tell the truth, whether Smain betrayed or did not, the Government has no right to detain her in Egypt, as she cannot be held responsible for her husband."

"The Government does not now allow any Sudânese

to leave for Suâkin or Nubia without a special permit; so the prohibition does not affect Fatma alone. Many of them are found in Egypt for they come here for gain. Among them are some who belong to the Dongolese tribe; that is the one from which the Mahdi comes. There are, for instance, besides Fatma, Chadigi and those two camel drivers in Medinet. The Mahdists call the Egyptians Turks and are carrying on a war with them, but among the local Arabs can be found a considerable number of adherents of the Mahdi, who would willingly join him. We must number among them all the fanatics, all the partisans of Arabi Pasha, and many among the poorer classes. They hold it ill of the Government that it yielded entirely to English influence and claim that the religion suffers by it. God knows how many already have escaped across the desert, avoiding the customary sea route to Suâkin. So the Government, having learned that Fatma also wanted to run away, ordered her to be put under surveillance. For her and her children only, as relatives of the Mahdi himself, can an exchange of the captives be effected."

"Do the lower classes in Egypt really favor the Mahdi?"

"The Mahdi has followers even in the army, which perhaps for that reason fights so poorly."

"But how can the Sudânese fly across the desert? Why, that is a thousand miles."

"Nevertheless, by that route slaves were brought into Egypt."

"I should judge that Fatma's children could not endure such a journey."

"That is why she wants to shorten it and ride by way of the sea to Suâkin."

"In any case, she is a poor woman."

With this the conversation concluded.

Twelve hours later "the poor woman," having carefully closeted herself in her house with the son of the overseer Chadigi, whispered to him with knitted brows and a grim glance of her beautiful eyes:

"Chamis, son of Chadigi, here is the money. Go even to-day to Medinet and give to Idris this writing, which the devout dervish Bellali, at my request, wrote to him. The children of the mehendes are good, but if I do not obtain a permit, then there is no other alternative. I know you will not betray me. Remember that you and your father too come from the Dongolese tribe in which was born the great Mahdi."

III

BOTH engineers left the following night for Cairo where they were to visit the British minister plenipotentiary and hold an audience with the viceroy. Stas calculated that this would require two days, and his calculation appeared accurate, for on the third day at night he received from his father, who was already at Medinet, the following message: "The tents are ready. You are to leave the moment your vacation begins. Inform Fatma through Chadigi that we could not accomplish anything for her." A similar message was also received by Madame Olivier who at once, with the assistance of the negress Dinah, began to make preparations for the journey.

The sight of these preparations gladdened the hearts of the children. But suddenly an accident occurred which deranged their plans and seemed likely to prevent their journey. On the day on which Stas' winter vacation began and on the eve of their departure a scorpion stung Madame Olivier during her afternoon nap in the garden. These venomous creatures in Egypt are not usually very dangerous, but in this case the sting might become exceptionally baleful. The scorpion had crawled onto the head-rest of the linen chair and stung Madame Olivier in the neck at a moment when she leaned her head against the rest. As she had suffered lately from erysipelas in the face, fear was entertained that the sickness might recur. A physician was summoned at once, but he arrived two

hours later as he had engagements elsewhere. The neck
and even the face were already swollen, after which fever
appeared, with the usual symptoms of poisoning. The
physician announced that under the circumstances there
could not be any talk of a journey and ordered the patient
to bed. In view of this it seemed highly probable that
the children would be compelled to pass the Christmas
holidays at home. In justice to Nell it must be stated
that in the first moments particularly she thought more
of the sufferings of her teacher than of the lost pleasures
in Medinet. She only wept in corners at the thought of
not seeing her father for a few weeks. Stas did not accept
the accident with the same resignation. He first forwarded a dispatch and afterwards mailed a letter with
an inquiry as to what they were to do. The reply came
in two days. Mr. Rawlinson first communicated with
the physician; having learned from him that immediate
danger was removed and that only a fear of the recurrence
of erysipelas prevented Madame Olivier's departure from
Port Said, he, above all, took precaution that she should
have proper care and nursing, and afterwards sent the
children permission to travel with Dinah. But as Dinah,
notwithstanding her extreme attachment for Nell, was not
able to take care of herself on the railways and in the
hotels, the duties of guide and paymaster during this
trip devolved upon Stas. It can easily be understood
how proud he was of this rôle and with what chivalrous
spirit he assured little Nell that not a hair would fall
from her head, as if in reality the road to Cairo and to
Medinet presented any difficulties or dangers.

All preparations having been completed, the children
started that very day for Ismailia by way of the Canal.
From Ismailia they were to travel by rail to Cairo, where
they were to pass the night. On the following day they

were to ride to Medinet. Leaving Ismailia they saw
Lake Timsâh which Stas already knew, as Pan Tarkowski,
being an ardent sportsman, in moments free from his
duties had taken Stas along with him to hunt for aquatic
birds. Afterwards the road ran along Wâdi Tûmilât
close to the fresh-water canal leading from the Nile to
Ismailia and Suez. This canal had been dug before the
Suez Canal, so that the workingmen working on De Lesseps' grand achievement would not be deprived entirely
of water fit for drinking purposes. But its excavation
had yet another fortunate result, for this region, which
before was a sterile desert, bloomed anew when through
it coursed a strong and life-bringing stream of fresh water.
The children could observe on the left side from the
windows of the coach a wide belt of verdure composed
of meadows on which were pastured horses, camels, and
sheep, and of tilled fields, diversified with maize, millet,
alfalfa, and other varieties of plants used for fodder. On
the bank of the canal could be seen all kinds of wells in
the shape of large wheels with buckets attached, or in the
usual form of well-sweeps, drawing water, which fellahs
laboriously carried to the garden-beds or conveyed in
barrels, on wagons drawn by buffaloes. Over the sprouting
grain pigeons soared, and at times a whole covey of quails
sprang up. On the canal banks, storks and cranes gravely
stalked. In the distance, above the mud hovels of the
fellahs towered, like plumes of feathers, the crowns of date
palms.

On the other hand, on the north side of the railway
there stretched a stark desert, but unlike the one which
lay on the other side of the Suez Canal. That one looked
as level as would the bottom of the sea, from which the
water had disappeared and only wrinkled sand remained,
while here the sand was more yellowish, heaped up as if

in great knolls, covered on the sides with tufts of gray vegetation. Between those knolls, which here and there changed into high hills, lay wide valleys in which from time to time caravans could be seen moving.

From the windows of the car the children could catch sight of heavily loaded camels, walking in a long string, one after another, over the sandy expanse. In front of each camel was an Arab in a black mantle, with a white turban on his head. Little Nell was reminded of the pictures in the Bible, which she had seen at home, representing the Israelites entering Egypt during the times of Joseph. They were exactly the same. Unfortunately she could not see the caravans very well as at the windows on that side of the car sat two English officers, who obstructed her view.

But she had scarcely told this to Stas, when he turned to the officers with a very grave mien and, touching his hat with his finger, said:

"Gentlemen, could you kindly make room for this little Miss who wishes to look at the camels?"

Both officers accepted the suggestion with the same gravity, and one of them not only surrendered his place to the curious Miss but lifted her and placed her in a seat near the window.

And Stas began his lecture:

"This is the ancient land of Goshen, which Pharaoh gave to Joseph for his brother Israelites. At one time in far antiquity a canal of fresh water ran here so that this new one is but a reconstruction of the old. But later it fell into ruin and the country became a desert. Now the soil again is fertile."

"How does the gentleman know this?" asked one of the officers.

"At my age, we know such things," answered Stas;

"and besides, not long ago Professor Sterling gave us a lecture on Wâdi Tûmilât."

Though Stas spoke English quite fluently, his slightly different accent attracted the attention of the other officer, who asked:

"Is the little gentleman an Englishman?"

"Miss Nell, whose father entrusted her to my care on this journey, is little. I am not an Englishman but a Pole and the son of an engineer at the Canal."

The officer, hearing the answer of the pert boy, smiled and said:

"I esteem the Poles. I belong to a regiment of cavalry, which during the times of Napoleon several times fought with the Polish Uhlans, and that tradition until the present day forms its glory and honor."[1]

"I am pleased to form your acquaintance," answered Stas.

The conversation easily proceeded farther, for the officers were evidently amused. It appeared that both were also riding from Port Said to Cairo to see the British minister plenipotentiary and to receive final instructions for a long journey which soon awaited them. The younger one was an army surgeon, while the one who spoke to Stas, Captain Glenn, had an order from his government to proceed from Cairo, via Suez, to Mombasa and assume the government of the entire region adjoining that port and extending as far as the unknown Samburu country.

Stas, who with deep interest read about travels in Africa, knew that Mombasa was situated a few degrees

---

[1] Those regiments of English cavalry which during the times of Napoleon met the Polish cavalry actually pride themselves with that fact at the present time, and every officer speaking of his regiment never fails to say, "We fought with the Poles." See Chevrillon, "Aux Indes."

beyond the equator and that the adjoining country, though already conceded to be within the sphere of English interests, was yet in truth little known; it was utterly wild, full of elephants, giraffes, rhinoceroses, buffaloes, and all kinds of antelopes, which the military, missionary, and trading expeditions always encountered. He also envied Captain Glenn with his whole soul and promised to visit him in Mombasa and go hunting with him for lions and buffaloes.

"Good, but I shall invite you to make the visit with that little Miss," replied Captain Glenn, laughing and pointing at Nell who at that moment left the window and sat beside him.

"Miss Rawlinson has a father," answered Stas, "and I am only her guardian during this journey."

At this the other officer turned quickly around and asked:

"Rawlinson? Is he not one of the directors of the Canal and has he not a brother in Bombay?"

"My uncle lives in Bombay," answered Nell, raising her little finger upwards.

"Then your uncle, darling, is married to my sister. My name is Clary. We are related, and I am really delighted that I met and became acquainted with you, my little dear."

And the surgeon was really delighted. He said that immediately after his arrival at Port Said he inquired for Mr. Rawlinson, but in the offices of the directory he was informed that he had left for the holidays. He expressed also his regret that the steamer which he with Captain Glenn was to take for Mombasa left Suez in a few days, in consequence of which he could not make a hurried visit to Medinet.

He therefore requested Nell to convey his compliments

to her father, and promised to write to her from Mombasa. Both officers now engaged mainly in a conversation with Nell, so that Stas remained a little on the side. At all stations they had a plentiful supply of mandarin oranges, dates, and exquisite sherbet, and, besides by Stas and Nell, these dainties were shared by Dinah, who with all her good qualities was known for her uncommon gluttony.

In this manner the trip to Cairo passed quickly for the children. At the leave-taking the officers kissed Nell's little hands and face, and squeezed Stas' right hand, and at the same time, Captain Glenn, whom the resolute boy pleased very much, said half-jokingly and half-seriously :

"Listen, my boy! Who knows where, when, and under what circumstances we may yet meet in life. Remember, however, that you can always rely upon my good will and assistance."

"And you may likewise rely upon me," Stas answered with a bow full of dignity.

IV

Pan Tarkowski, as well as Mr. Rawlinson, who loved Nell better than his life, was delighted at the arrival of the children. The young pair greeted their parents joyfully, and at once began to look about the tents, which internally were completely fitted up and were ready for the reception of the beloved guests. The tents appeared superb to them; they were double, one was lined with blue and the other with red flannel, overlaid at the bottom with saddle-cloths, and they were as spacious as large rooms. The agency which was concerned about the opinion of the high officials of the Canal Company had spared no effort for their comfort. At first Mr. Rawlinson feared that a lengthy stay under tents might prove injurious to Nell's health, and if he agreed to the arrangement, it was because they could always move to a hotel in case of bad weather. Now, however, having fully investigated everything on the place, he came to the conclusion that days and nights passed in the fresh air would be a hundredfold more beneficial for his only child than a stay in the musty rooms of the small local hotels. Beautiful weather favored this. Medinet, or rather El-Medineh, surrounded by the sandy hills of the Libyan Desert, has a much better climate than Cairo and is not in vain called "the land of roses" Owing to its sheltered position and the plentiful moisture in the air, nights there are not so cold as in other parts of Egypt,

even those lying further south. Winter is simply delightful, and from November the greatest development of the
vegetation begins. Date palms, olive-trees, which on
the whole are scarce in Egypt, fig, orange, mandarin
trees, giant castor-oil plants, pomegranate and various
other southern plants cover this delightful oasis as with
a forest. The gardens are overflowing, as it were, with
a gigantic wave of acacias, elders, and roses, so that at
night every breeze carries their intoxicating scent. Here
one breathes with full breast and "does not wish to die,"
as the residents of the place say.

A similar climate is possessed only by Helwan lying on
the other side of the Nile and considerably farther north,
but Helwan lacks such luxuriant vegetation.

But Helwan awoke sad recollections for Mr. Rawlinson,
for there Nell's mother had died. For this reason he
preferred Medinet, and gazing at present at the glowing countenance of the little girl, he promised to himself
in his soul soon to purchase here land with a garden; to
erect upon it a comfortable English house and spend
in these blissful parts all vacations which he could secure,
and after finishing his service on the Canal, perhaps
even to reside here permanently.

But these were plans of the distant future and not
yet wholly matured. In the meantime the children from
the moment of their arrival moved about everywhere
like flies, desiring even before dinner to see all the tents
as well as the donkeys and camels hired at the place by
the Cook Agency. It appeared that the animals were
on a distant pasture and that they could not see them
until the morrow. However, near Mr. Rawlinson's tent
they observed with pleasure Chamis, the son of Chadigi,
their good acquaintance in Port Said. He was not in
the employ of Cook, and Mr. Rawlinson was somewhat

surprised to meet him in Medinet, but as he had previously employed him to carry his implements, he engaged him at present to run errands and perform all other small services.

The evening dinner was excellent, as the old Copt, who for many years was a cook in the employment of the Cook Agency, was anxious to display his culinary skill.   The children told about the acquaintance they made with the two officers on the way, which was particularly interesting to Mr. Rawlinson, whose brother Richard was married to Dr. Clary's sister and had resided in India for many years.   As it was a childless marriage, this uncle greatly loved his little niece, whom he knew only from photographs, and he had inquired about her in all his letters.   Both fathers were also amused at the invitation which Stas had received from Captain Glenn to visit Mombasa.   The boy took it seriously and positively promised himself that sometime he must pay a visit to his new friend beyond the equator.   Pan Tarkowski then had to explain to him that English officials never remain long in the same locality on account of the deadly climate of Africa, and that before Stas grew up the captain already would hold his tenth position in rotation or would not be on earth at all.

After dinner the whole company went out in front of the tents, where the servants placed the cloth folding-chairs, and for the older gentlemen brought a siphon of soda-water with brandy.   It was already night but unusually warm; as there happened to be full moon it was as bright as in daytime.   The white walls of the city buildings opposite the tents shone greenly; the stars glowed in the sky, and in the air was diffused the scent of roses, acacias, and heliotropes.   The city already was asleep.   In the silence of the night at times could be heard only the loud cries of cranes, herons, and flamingoes flying from beyond the Nile in the direction of Lake Karun. Suddenly, however, there resounded the deep bass bark of a dog which astonished Stas and Nell, for it appeared to come from a tent which they had not visited and which was assigned for saddles, implements, and various traveling paraphernalia.

"That must be an awfully big dog. Let us go and see him," said Stas.

Pan Tarkowski began to laugh and Mr. Rawlinson shook off the ashes of his cigar and said, also laughing:

"Well, it did not do any good to lock him up."

After which he addressed the children:

"Remember, to-morrow is Christmas Eve, and that dog was intended by Pan Tarkowski to be a surprise for Nell, but as the surprise has started to bark, I am compelled to announce it to-day."

Hearing this, Nell climbed in a trice on Pan Tarkowski's knees and embraced his neck and afterwards jumped onto her father's lap.

"Papa, how happy I am! how happy I am!"

Of hugs and kisses there was no end. Finally Nell, finding herself on her own feet, began to gaze in Pan Tarkowski's eyes:

"Pan Tarkowski —"

"What is it, Nell?"

"— As I already know that he is there, can I see him to-night?"

"I knew," exclaimed Mr. Rawlinson, feigning indignation, "that this little fly would not be content with the news itself."

And Pan Tarkowski, turning to the son of Chadigi, said:

"Chamis, bring the dog."

The young Sudânese disappeared behind the kitchen

tent and after a while reappeared, leading a big dog by the collar.

Nell retreated.

"Oh," she exclaimed, seizing her father's hand.

On the other hand, Stas grew enthusiastic.

"But that is a lion, not a dog," he said.

"He is called Saba (lion)," answered Pan Tarkowski. "He belongs to the breed of mastiffs; these are the biggest dogs in the world. This one is only two years old but really is exceedingly large. Don't be afraid, Nell, as he is as gentle as a lamb. Only be brave. Let him go, Chamis."

Chamis let go of the collar with which he had restrained the dog, and the latter, feeling that he was free, began to wag his tail, fawn before Pan Tarkowski with whom he was already well acquainted, and bark joyfully.

The children gazed in the moonlight with admiration on his large round head with hanging lips, on his bulky paws, on his powerful frame, reminding one, in truth, of a lion with the tawny-yellowish color of his body.

"With such a dog one could safely go through Africa," exclaimed Stas.

"Ask him whether he could retrieve a rhinoceros," said Pan Tarkowski.

Saba could not, indeed, answer that question, but instead wagged his tail more and more joyfully and drew near to the group so ingratiatingly that Nell at once ceased to fear him and began to pat him on his head.

"Saba, nice, dear Saba."

Mr. Rawlinson leaned over him, raised his head towards the face of the little girl, and said:

"Saba, look at this little lady. She is your mistress. You must obey and guard her. Do you understand?"

"Wow!" was the basso response of Saba, as if he actually understood what was wanted.

And he understood even better than might have been expected, for taking advantage of the fact that his head was on a level with the little girl's face, as a mark of homage he licked her little nose and cheeks with his broad tongue.

This provoked a general outburst of laughter. Nell had to go to the tent to wash herself. Returning after a quarter of an hour she saw Saba with paws upon the shoulders of Stas, who bent under the weight; the dog was higher by a head.

The time for sleep was approaching, but the little one asked for yet half an hour of play in order to get better acquainted with her new friend. In fact, the acquaintance proceeded so easily that Pan Tarkowski soon placed her in lady fashion on Saba's back and, holding her from fear that she might fall, ordered Stas to lead the dog by the collar. She rode thus a score of paces, after which Stas tried to mount this peculiar "saddle-horse," but the dog sat on his hind legs so that Stas unexpectedly found himself on the sand near the tail.

The children were about to retire when in the distance on the market place, illumined by the moon, appeared two white figures walking towards the tents.

The hitherto gentle Saba began to growl hollowly and threateningly so that Chamis, at Mr. Rawlinson's order, again had to take hold of the collar, and in the meantime two men dressed in white burnooses stood before the tent.

"Who is there?" asked Pan Tarkowski.

"Camel drivers," answered one of the arrivals.

"Ah, Idris and Gebhr? What do you want?"

"We come to ask whether you will need us to-morrow."

"No. To-morrow and the day after are great holidays, during which it is not proper to make excursions. Come on the morning of the third day."

"Thank you, effendi."

"Have you good camels?" asked Mr. Rawlinson.

"Bismillah!" answered Idris; "real saddle-horses with fat humps and as gentle as ha'-ga (lambs). Otherwise Cook would not have employed us."

"Do they jolt much?"

"Gentlemen, you can place a handful of kidney-beans on their backs and not a grain will fall during the fullest speed."

"If one is to exaggerate, then exaggerate after the Arabian fashion," said Pan Tarkowski, laughing.

"Or after the Sudânese," added Mr. Rawlinson.

In the meantime Idris and Gebhr continued to stand like two white columns, gazing attentively at Stas and Nell. The moon illumined their very dark faces, and in its luster they looked as if cast of bronze. The whites of their eyes glittered greenishly from under the turbans.

"Good night to you," said Mr. Rawlinson.

"May Allah watch over you, effendi, in night and in day."

Saying this, they bowed and went away. They were accompanied by a hollow growl, similar to distant thunder, from Saba, whom the two Sudânese apparently did not please.

V

DURING the following days there were no excursions. Instead, on Christmas Eve, when the first star appeared in heaven, a little tree in Mr. Rawlinson's tent, intended for Nell, was illuminated with hundreds of candles. To serve as a Christmas tree there had been taken an arbor vitae, cut in one of the gardens in Medinet; nevertheless, among its branchlets Nell found a profusion of dainties and a splendid doll, which her father had brought from Cairo for her, and Stas, his much desired English short rifle. In addition he received from his father packages containing various hunters' supplies, and a saddle for horseback riding. Nell could not contain herself for joy, while Stas, although he thought that whoever owned a genuine short rifle ought to possess a corresponding dignity, could not restrain himself, and selecting the time when no one was about, walked around the tent on his hands. This knack, taught to him at the Port Said school, he possessed to a surprising degree and with it often amused Nell, who, besides, sincerely envied it in him.

Christmas Eve and the first day of the holidays were passed by the children partly in church services, partly in inspecting the gifts they had received, and in training Saba. The new friend appeared to possess intelligence beyond all expectations. On the very first day he learned to give his paw, retrieve handkerchiefs, which, however, he would not surrender without some resistance, and he understood that cleaning Nell's face with his tongue was an act unworthy of a gentlemanly dog. Nell, holding her fingers at her little nose, gave him various instructions, while he, concurring with motions of his tail, gave her in this manner to understand that he heard with becoming attention and took her lessons to heart. During their strolls over the sandy city square the fame of Saba in Medinet grew with each hour and, even as all fame, began to have its disagreeable side, for it drew a whole swarm of Arabian children. In the beginning they kept at a distance; afterwards, however, emboldened by the gentleness of the "monster," they approached more and more closely, and in the end sat around the tent so that no one could move about with any freedom. Besides, as every Arabian child sucks sugar-cane from morning to night, the children always attract after them legions of flies, which besides being loathsome are noxious, for they spread the Egyptian infection of inflammation of the eyes. For this reason the servants attempted to disperse the children, but Nell stood in their defense and, what is more, distributed among the youngest "helou," that is, sweetmeats, which gained for her their great love but also increased their number.

After three days the joint excursions began; partly on the narrow-gauge railways of which the English had built quite a number in Medinet el-Fayûm, partly on donkeys, and sometimes on camels. It appeared that in· the praises bestowed on those animals by Idris there was indeed a great deal of exaggeration, for not merely kidney-beans but even people could not easily keep on the saddles; but there was also some truth. The camels in reality belonged to the variety known as "hegin," that is, for carrying passengers, and were fed with good durra (the local or Syrian maize) so that the humps were fat and they appeared so willing to speed that it was necessary to check them. The Sudânese, Idris and Gebhr, gained, notwithstanding the wild glitter of their eyes, the confidence and hearts of the company, and this through their great willingness to serve and their extraordinary care over Nell. Gebhr always had a cruel and a trifle bestial expression of face, but Idris, quickly perceiving that that little personage was the eye in the head of the whole company, declared at every opportunity that he cared more for her than for his own soul. Mr. Rawlinson conjectured indeed, that, through Nell, Idris wanted to reach his pocket, but believing at the same time that there was not in the world a person who could not but love his only child, he was grateful to him and did not stint himself in giving "bakshish."

In the course of five days the party visited the near by ruins of the ancient city of Crocodilopolis, where at one time the Egyptians worshipped a deity called Sobk, which had a human form with the head of a crocodile. Afterwards an excursion was made to the Hanar pyramids and the remains of the Labyrinth. The longest trip was on camel-back to Lake Karun. Its northern shore was a stark desert, on which there were ruins of former Egyptian cities, but no trace of life. On the other hand, on the southern shore stretched a fertile country, magnificent, with shores overgrown by heather and reeds and teeming with pelicans, flamingoes, herons, wild geese, and ducks. Only here did Stas find an opportunity for displaying his marksmanship. The shooting from a common rifle as well as from the short rifle was so extraordinary that after every shot could be heard the astonished smacking of the lips of Idris and the Arabian rowers, and the falling of the birds into the water was accompanied by exclamations of "Bismillah" and "Mashallah."

The Arabians assured them that on the opposite desert-

shore were many wolves and hyenas, and that by tossing
amid the sand dunes the carcass of a sheep one might get
within shooting range. In consequence of these assurances Pan Tarkowski and Stas passed two nights on
the desert near the ruins of Dima. But the first sheep
was stolen by Bedouins as soon as the hunters left it;
while the second lured only a lame jackal, which Stas
brought down. Further hunting had to be postponed
as the time had arrived for both engineers to inspect
the works conducted at Bahr Yûsuf near El-Lahûn, southeast from Medinet.

Mr. Rawlinson waited only for the arrival of Madame
Olivier. Unfortunately, in place of her, came a letter
from the physician informing them that the former erysipelas in the face had recurred after the bite, and that
the patient for a long time would be unable to leave Port
Said. The situation actually became distressing. It
was impossible to take with them the children, old Dinah,
the tents, and all the servants, if only for the reason that
the engineers were to be one day here, another there, and
might receive requests to go as far as the great canal of
Ibrâhimiyeh. In view of this, after a short consultation
Mr. Rawlinson decided to leave Nell under the care of
old Dinah and Stas, together with the Italian consular
agent and the local "Mudir" (governor) with whom he
had previously become acquainted. He promised also
to Nell, who grieved to part from her father, that from
all the nearer localities he would with Pan Tarkowski
rush to Medinet, or if they found some noteworthy sight,
would summon the children to them.

"We shall take with us, Chamis," he said, "whom in a
certain case we shall send for you. Let Dinah always
keep Nell's company, but as Nell does with her whatever
she pleases, do you, Stas, watch over both."

"You may be sure, sir," answered Stas, "that I shall watch over Nell, as over my own sister. She has Saba, and I a short rifle, so let any one try to harm her —"

"It is not about that that I am concerned," said Mr. Rawlinson. "Saba and the short rifle will certainly not be necessary for you. You will be so good as to protect her from fatigue and at the same time take care she does not catch cold. I have asked the consul in case she feels unwell to summon a doctor from Cairo immediately. We shall send Chamis here for news as frequently as possible. The Mudir will also visit you. I expect, besides, that our absence will never be very long."

Pan Tarkowski also was not sparing in his admonitions to Stas. He told him that Nell did not require his defense as there was not in Medinet nor in the whole province of El-Fâyum any savage people or wild animals. To think of such things would be ridiculous and unworthy of a boy who had begun his fourteenth year. So he was to be solicitous and heedful only that they did not undertake anything on their own account, and more particularly excursions with Nell on camels, on which a ride was fatiguing.

But Nell, hearing this, made such a sad face that Pan Tarkowski had to placate her.

"Certainly," he said, stroking her hair, "you will ride camels, but with us or towards us, if we send Chamis for you."

"But when alone are we not allowed to make an excursion, even though such a tiny bit of a one?" asked the girl.

And she began to show on her finger about how little an excursion she was concerned. The parents in the end agreed that they could ride on donkeys, not on camels, and not to ruins, where they might easily fall into some hole, but over roads of adjacent fields and towards the gardens beyond the city. The dragoman, together with other Cook servants, was always to accompany the children.

After this both gentlemen departed, but they left for a place near by, Hanaret el-Matka, so that after ten hours they returned to pass the night in Medinet. This was repeated the succeeding few days until they had inspected all the nearest work. Afterwards, when their employment required their presence at more distant places, Chamis arrived in the night time, and early in the following morning took Stas and Nell to those little cities, in which their parents wanted to show them something of interest. The children spent the greater part of the day with their parents and before sunset returned to the camp at Medinet. There were, however, days on which Chamis did not come, and then Nell, notwithstanding the society of Stas, and Saba in whom she continually discovered some new traits, looked with longing for a messenger. In this manner the time passed until Twelfth Night, on the day of which festival both engineers returned to Medinet.

Two days later they went away again, announcing that they left this time for a longer period and in all probability would reach as far as Benisueif, and from there to El-Fachn, where a canal of the same name begins, going far south alongside of the Nile.

Great, therefore, was the astonishment of the children, when on the third day at eleven o'clock in the morning Chamis appeared in Medinet. Stas met him first as he went to the pasturage to look at the camels. Chamis conversed with Idris, and only told Stas that he came for him and Nell and that he would come immediately to the camp to inform them where they, at the request of the older gentlemen, were to go. Stas ran at once with the good news to Nell, whom he found playing with Saba before the tent.

"Do you know — Chamis is here!" he cried from a distance.

And Nell began at once to hop, holding both feet together, as little girls do when skipping the rope.

"We shall go! We shall go!"

"Yes. We shall go, and far."

"Where?" she asked, brushing aside with her little hands a tuft of hair which fell over her eyes.

"I don't know. Chamis said that in a moment he would come here and tell us."

"How do you know it is far?"

"Because I heard Idris say that he and Gebhr would start at once with the camels. That means that we shall go by rail and shall find the camels at the place where our parents will be, and from there we shall make some kind of an excursion."

The tuft of hair, owing to the continual hops, covered again not only Nell's eyes but her whole face, her feet bounding as if they were made of India rubber.

A quarter of an hour later, Chamis came and bowed to both.

"Khanage (young master)," he said, "we leave after three hours by the first train."

"Where are we going?"

"To Gharak el-Sultani, and from there with the older gentlemen on camel-back to Wâdi Rayân."

Stas' heart beat with joy, but at the same time Chamis' words surprised him. He knew that Wâdi Rayân was a great valley among sandy hills rising on the Libyan Desert on the south and southwest of Medinet, while on the other hand Pan Tarkowski and Mr. Rawlinson announced on their departure that they were going in a directly opposite direction, towards the Nile.

"What has happened?" asked Stas. "Then my father and Mr. Rawlinson are not in Benisueif but in El-Gharak?"

"It happened thus," replied Chamis.

"But they ordered us to write to them at El-Fachn."

"In a letter the senior effendi explains why they are in El-Gharak."

And for a while he searched on his person for the letter, after which he exclaimed:

"Oh, Nabi! (prophet) I left the letter in a pouch with the camels. I will run at once before Idris and Gebhr depart."

And he ran towards the camels. In the meantime the children, with Dinah, began to prepare for the journey. As it looked as if the excursion would be a long one, Dinah packed several dresses, some linen, and warmer clothing for Nell. Stas thought of himself, and especially did not forget about the short rifle and cartridges, hoping that among the sand dunes of Wâdi Rayân he might encounter wolves and hyenas.

Chamis did not return until an hour later; he was covered with perspiration and so fatigued that for a while he could not catch his breath.

"I did not find the camels," he said. "I chased after them, but in vain. But that does not matter as we shall find the letter and the effendis themselves in El-Gharak. Is Dinah to go with you?"

"Why not?"

"Perhaps it would be better if she remained. The older gentlemen said nothing about her."

"But they announced on leaving that Dinah was always to accompany the little lady. So she shall ride now."

Chamis bowed, placing his hand on his heart and said:

"Let us hasten, sir, for otherwise the katr (train) will set off."

The baggage was ready, so they were at the station on time. The distance between Medinet and Gharak is not more than nineteen miles, but the trains on the branch line which connects those localities move slowly and the stops were uncommonly frequent. If Stas had been alone he undoubtedly would have preferred to ride camel-back as he calculated that Idris and Gebhr, having started two hours before the train, would be earlier in El-Gharak. But for Nell such a ride would be too long; and the little guardian, who took very much to heart the warnings of both parents, did not want to expose the little girl to fatigue. After all the time passed for both so quickly that they scarcely noticed when they stopped in Gharak.

The little station, from which Englishmen usually make excursions to Wâdi Rayân, was almost entirely deserted. They found only a few veiled women, with baskets of mandarin oranges, two unknown Bedouin camel drivers, together with Idris and Gebhr, with seven camels, one of which was heavily packed. Of Pan Tarkowski and Mr. Rawlinson there was no trace.

But Idris in this manner explained their absence.

"The older gentlemen went into the desert to pitch the tents which they brought with them from Etsah, and ordered us to follow them."

"And how shall we find them among the sand-hills?" asked Stas.

"They sent guides who will lead us to them."

Saying this he pointed to the Bedouins. The older of them bowed, rubbed with his finger the one eye which he possessed, and said:

"Our camels are not so fat but are not less speedy than yours. After an hour we shall be there."

Stas was glad that he would pass the night on the desert, but Nell felt a certain disappointment, for she had been certain that she would meet her papa in Gharak.

In the meantime the station-master, a sleepy Egyptian with a red fez and dark spectacles, approached them, and, not having anything else to do, began to stare at the European children.

"These are the children of those Englishmen who rode this morning with rifles to the desert," said Idris, placing Nell on the saddle.

Stas, handing his short rifle to Chamis, sat beside her, for the saddle was wide and had the shape of a palanquin without a roof. Dinah sat behind Chamis, the others took separate camels, and the party started.

If the station-master had stared at them longer he might perhaps have wondered that those Englishmen, of whom Idris spoke, rode directly to the ruins on the south, while this party at once directed its movements towards Talei, in a different direction. But the station-master before that time had returned home as no other train arrived that day at Gharak.

The hour was five in the afternoon. The weather was splendid. The sun had already passed on that side of the Nile and declined over the desert, sinking into the golden and purple twilight glowing on the western side of the sky. The atmosphere was so permeated with the roseate luster that the eyes blinked from its superfluity. The fields assumed a lily tint, while the distant sand-hills, strongly relieved against the background of the twilight, had a hue of pure amethyst. The world lost the traits of reality and appeared to be one play of supernal lights.

While they rode over a verdant and cultivated region, the guide, a Bedouin, conducted the caravan with a moderate pace. But with the moment that the hard sand creaked under the feet of the camels, everything changed.

"Yalla! Yalla!" suddenly yelled wild voices.

And simultaneously could be heard the swish of whips and the camels, having changed from an ambling pace into a full gallop, began to speed like the whirlwind, throwing up with their feet the sand and gravel of the desert.

"Yalla! Yalla!"

The ambling pace of a camel jolts more, while the gallop with which this animal seldom runs, swings more; so the children enjoyed this mad ride. But it is known that even in a swing, too much rapid movement causes dizziness. Accordingly, after a certain time, when the speed did not cease, Nell began to get dizzy and her eyes grew dim.

"Stas, why are we flying so?" she exclaimed, turning to her companion.

"I think that they allowed them to get into too much of a gallop and now cannot check them," answered Stas.

But observing that the little girl's face was becoming pale, he shouted at the Bedouins, running ahead, to slacken their pace. His calls, however, had only this result: that again resounded the cries of "Yalla," and the animals increased their speed.

The boy thought at first that the Bedouins did not hear him, but when on his repeated orders there was no response and when Gebhr, who was riding behind him, did not cease lashing the camel on which he sat with Nell, he thought it was not the camels that were so spirited but that the men for some reason unknown to him were in a great hurry.

It occurred to him that they might have taken the wrong road and that, desiring to make up for lost time, they now were speeding from fear that the older gentlemen might scold them because of a late arrival. But after a while he understood that such could not be the case, as Mr. Rawlinson would have been more angered for unnecessarily fatiguing Nell. Then what did it mean? And why did they not obey his commands? In the heart of the boy anger and fear for Nell began to rise.

"Stop!" he shouted with his whole strength, addressing Gebhr.

"Ouskout! (be silent)!" the Sudânese yelled in reply; and they sped on.

In Egypt night falls about six o'clock, so the twilight soon became extinct and after a certain time the great moon, ruddy from the reflection of the twilight, rolled on and illuminated the desert with a gentle light.

In the silence could be heard only the heavy breathing of the camels, the rapid hoof-beats on the sand, and at times the swish of whips. Nell was so tired that Stas had to hold her on the saddle. Every little while she asked how soon they would reach their destination, and evidently was buoyed up only by the hope of an early meeting with her father. But in vain both children gazed around. One hour passed, then another; neither tents nor campfires could be seen.

Then the hair rose on Stas' head, for he realized that they were kidnapped.

VI

MESSRS. RAWLINSON and Tarkowski actually expected the children, not amidst the sand-hills of Wâdi Rayân, where they had no need or desire to ride, but in an entirely different direction, in the city of El-Fachn on a canal of the same name at which they were examining the work finished before the end of the year. The distance between El-Fachn and Medinet in a straight line is almost twenty-eight miles. As, however, there is no direct connection and it is necessary to ride to El-Wasta, which doubles the distance, Mr. Rawlinson, after looking over the railway guide, made the following calculations.

"Chamis left the night before last," he said to Pan Tarkowski, "and in El-Wasta he caught the train from Cairo; he was therefore in Medinet yesterday. It would take an hour to pack up. Leaving at noon they would have to wait for the night train running along the Nile, and as I do not permit Nell to ride at night, they would leave this morning and will be here immediately after sunset."

"Yes," said Pan Tarkowski, "Chamis must rest a little, and though Stas is indeed impulsive, nevertheless, where Nell is concerned you may always depend upon him. Moreover, I sent him a postal card not to ride during the night."

"A brave lad, and I trust him," answered Mr. Rawlinson.

"To tell the truth, so do I. Stas with his various faults has an upright character and never lies, for he is brave, and only a coward lies. He also does not lack energy and if in time he acquires a calm judgment, I think he will be able to take care of himself in this world."

"Certainly. As to judgment, were you judicious at his age?"

"I must confess that I was not," replied Pan Tarkowski, laughing, "but I was not so self-confident as he."

"That will pass. Meanwhile, be happy that you have such a boy."

"And you that you have such a sweet and dear creature as Nell."

"May God bless her!" answered Mr. Rawlinson with emotion.

The two friends warmly shook hands, after which they sat down to examine the plans and the report of expenditures connected with the work. At this occupation the time passed until evening.

About six o'clock, when night fell, they were at the station, strolling along the walk, and resumed their conversation about the children.

"Superb weather, but cool," said Mr. Rawlinson. "I wonder if Nell took some warm clothing with her."

"Stas will think of that, and Dinah also."

"I regret, nevertheless, that instead of bringing them here, we did not go to Medinet."

"You will recollect that that is just what I advised."

"I know, and if it were not that we are to go from here farther south, I would have agreed. I calculated, however, that the trip would take too much time and on the whole it would be best to have the children here. Finally, I will confess to you that Chamis suggested the idea to me. He announced that he prodigiously yearned for them and would be happy if I sent for both. I am not surprised that he should be so attached to them."

Further conversation was interrupted by signals announcing the approach of the train. After an interval the fiery eyes of the locomotive appeared in the darkness, and at the same time could be heard its puffs and whistle.

A row of lighted coaches drew alongside the platform, quivered, and stood still.

"I did not see them in any window," said Mr. Rawlinson.

"Perhaps they are seated further inside and surely will come out immediately."

The passengers began to alight, but they were mainly Arabs, as El-Fachn has nothing interesting to see except beautiful groves of palms and acacias. The children did not arrive.

"Chamis either did not make connections in El-Wasta," declared Pan Tarkowski, with a shade of ill-humor, "or after a night of travel overslept himself, and they will not arrive until to-morrow."

"That may be," answered Mr. Rawlinson, with uneasiness, "but it also may be possible that one of them is sick."

"In that case Stas would have telegraphed."

"Who knows but that we may find a despatch in the hotel?"

"Let us go."

But in the hotel no news awaited them. Mr. Rawlinson became more and more uneasy.

"What do you think could have happened?" said Pan Tarkowski. "If Chamis overslept himself, he would not admit it to the children and would come to them to-day and tell them that they are to leave to-morrow.

To us he will excuse himself by claiming that he misunderstood our orders. In any event, I shall telegraph to Stas."

"And I to the Mudir of Fayûm."

After a while the despatches were sent. There was indeed no cause for uneasiness; nevertheless, in waiting for an answer the engineers passed a bad night, and early morning found them on their feet.

The answer from the Mudir came about ten o'clock and was as follows:

"Verified at station. Children left yesterday for Gharak el-Sultani."

It can easily be understood what amazement and anger possessed the parents at this unexpected intelligence. For some time they gazed at each other, as if they did not understand the words of the despatch; after which Pan Tarkowski, who was an impulsive person, struck the table with his hand and said:

"That was Stas' whim, but I will cure him of such whims."

"I did not expect that of him," answered Nell's father.

But after a moment he asked:

"But what of Chamis?"

"He either did not find them and does not know what to do or else rode after them."

"Yes, I think so."

An hour later they started for Medinet. In camp they ascertained that the camels were gone, and at the station it was confirmed that Chamis left with the children for El-Gharak. The affair became darker and darker and it could be cleared up only in El-Gharak.

In fact, only at that station did the dreadful truth begin to dawn.

The station-master, the same sleepy one with dark

spectacles and red fez, told them that he saw a boy about fourteen years old and an eight-year-old girl with an old negress, who rode towards the desert. He did not remember whether there were eight or nine camels altogether, but observed that one was heavily packed as if for a long journey, and the two Bedouins also had big pack-saddles. He recollected also that when he stared at the caravan one of the camel drivers, a Sudânese, said to him that those were the children of the Englishmen who before that had gone to Wâdi Rayân.

"Did those Englishmen return?" asked Pan Tarkowski.

"Yes. They returned yesterday with two slain wolves," answered the station-master; "and I was astonished that they did not return with the children. But I did not ask the reason as that was not my affair."

Saying this he left to attend to his duties.

During this narrative Mr. Rawlinson's face became white as paper. Gazing at his friend with a wild look, he took off his hat, pressed his hand to his forehead, covered with perspiration, and staggered as if he were about to fall.

"Be a man, Rawlinson!" exclaimed Pan Tarkowski. "Our children are kidnapped. It is necessary to rescue them."

"Nell! Nell!" repeated the unhappy Englishman.

"Nell and Stas! It was not Stas' fault. Both were enticed by trickery and kidnapped. Who knows why? Perhaps for a ransom. Chamis undoubtedly is in the plot, and Idris and Gebhr also."

Here he recalled what Fatma had said about both Sudânese belonging to the Dongolese tribe, in which the Mahdi was born, and that Chadigi, the father of Chamis, came from the same tribe. At this recollection his heart for a moment became inert in his breast for he understood that the children were abducted not for a ransom but as an exchange for Smain's family.

"But what will the tribesmen of the ill-omened prophet do with them? They cannot hide them on the desert or anywhere on the banks of the Nile, for they all would die of hunger and thirst on the desert, and they certainly would be apprehended on the Nile. Perhaps they will try to join the Mahdi."

And this thought filled Pan Tarkowski with dismay, but the energetic ex-soldier soon recovered and began in his mind to review all that happened and at the same time seek means of rescue.

"Fatma," he reasoned, "had no cause to revenge herself either upon us or our children. If they have been kidnapped it was evidently for the purpose of placing them in the hands of Smain. In no case does death threaten them. And this is a fortune in misfortune; still a terrible journey awaits them which might be disastrous for them."

And at once he shared these thoughts with his friend, after which he spoke thus:

"Idris and Gebhr, like savage and foolish men, imagine that followers of the Mahdi are not far, while Khartûm, which the Mahdi reached, is about one thousand two hundred and forty miles from here. This journey they must make along the Nile and not keep at a distance from it as otherwise the camels and people would perish from thirst. Ride at once to Cairo and demand of the Khedive that despatches be sent to all the military outposts and that a pursuit be organized right and left along the river. Offer a large reward to the sheiks near the banks for the capture of the fugitives. In the villages let all be detained who approach for water. In this manner

Idris and Gebhr must fall into the hands of the authorities and we shall recover the children."

Mr. Rawlinson had already recovered his composure.

"I shall go," he said. "Those miscreants forgot that Wolseley's English army, hurrying to Gordon's relief, is already on the way and will cut them off from the Mahdi. They will not escape. They cannot escape. I shall send a despatch to our minister in a moment, and afterwards go myself. What do you intend to do?"

"I shall telegraph for a furlough, and not waiting for an answer, shall follow their trail by way of the Nile to Nubia, to attend to the pursuit."

"Then we shall meet, as from Cairo I shall do the same."

"Good! And now to work!"

"With God's help!" answered Mr. Rawlinson.

VII

In the meantime the camels swept like a hurricane over
the sands glistening in the moonlight. A deep night
fell. The moon, at the beginning as big as a wheel and
ruddy, became pale and rolled on high. The distant
desert hills were enveloped with silvery vapors like muslin
which, not veiling their view, transformed them as if into
luminous phenomena. From time to time from beyond
the rocks scattered here and there came the piteous
whining of jackals.

Another hour passed. Stas held Nell in his arms and
supported her, endeavoring in this way to allay the
fatiguing jolts of the mad ride. The little girl began
more and more frequently to ask him why they were
speeding so and why they did not see the tents and their
papas. Stas finally determined to tell her the truth, which
sooner or later he would have to disclose.

"Nell," he said, "pull off a glove and drop it, unob-
served, on the ground."

"Why, Stas?"

And he pressed her to himself and answered with a
kind of tenderness unusual to him:

"Do what I tell you."

Nell held Stas with one hand and feared to let him go,
but she overcame the difficulty in this manner: she began
to pull the glove with her teeth, each finger separately,
and, finally taking it off entirely, she dropped it on the
ground.

"After a time, throw the other," again spoke Stas. "I already have dropped mine, but yours will be easier to observe for they are bright."

And observing that the little girl gazed at him with an inquiring look, he continued:

"Don't get frightened, Nell. It may be that we will not meet your or my father at all — and that these foul people have kidnapped us. But don't fear — for if it is so, then pursuers will follow them. They will overtake them and surely rescue us. I told you to drop the gloves so that the pursuers may find clews. In the meanwhile we can do nothing, but later I shall contrive something — Surely, I shall contrive something; only do not fear, and trust me."

But Nell, learning that she should not see her papa and that they are flying somewhere, far in the desert, began to tremble from fright and cry, clinging at the same time close to Stas and asking him amid her sobs why they kidnapped them and where they were taking them. He comforted her as well as he could — almost in the same words with which his father comforted Mr. Rawlinson. He said that their parents themselves would follow in pursuit and would notify all the garrisons along the Nile. In the end he assured her that whatever might happen, he would never abandon her and would always defend her.

But her grief and longing for her father were stronger even than fear; so for a long time she did not cease to weep — and thus they flew, both sad, on a bright night, over the pale sands of the desert.

Sorrow and fear not only oppressed Stas' heart, but also shame. He was not indeed to blame for what had happened, yet he recalled the former boastfulness for which his father so often had rebuked him. Formerly

he was convinced that there was no situation to which
he was not equal; he considered himself a kind of un-
vanquished swashbuckler, and was ready to challenge
the whole world. Now he understood that he was a small
boy, with whom everybody could do as he pleased, and
that he was speeding in spite of his will on a camel merely
because that camel was driven from behind by a half-
savage Sudânese. He felt terribly humiliated and did
not see any way of resisting. He had to admit to himself that he plainly feared those men and the desert,
and what he and Nell might meet.

He promised sincerely not only to her but to himself
that he would watch over and defend her even at the
cost of his own life.

Nell, weary with weeping and the mad ride, which
had lasted already six hours, finally began to doze, and
at times fell asleep. Stas, knowing that whoever fell
from a galloping camel might be killed on the spot, tied
her to himself with a rope which he found on the saddle.
But after some time it seemed to him that the speed of
the camels became less rapid, though now they flew over
smooth and soft sands. In the distance could be seen
only the shifting hills, while on the plain began the nocturnal illusions common to the desert. The moon shone
in the heaven more and more palely and in the meantime there appeared before them, creeping low, strange
rosy clouds, entirely transparent, woven only from light.
They formed mysteriously and moved ahead as if pushed
by the light breeze. Stas saw how the burnooses of the
Bedouins and the camels became roseate when they
rode into that illuminated space, and afterwards the
whole caravan was enveloped in a delicate, rosy luster.
At times the clouds assumed an azure hue and thus it
continued until the hills were reached.

Near the hills the speed of the camels slackened yet
more. All about could be seen rocks protruding from
sandy knolls or strewn in wild disorder amidst the sand
dunes. The ground became stony. They crossed a few
hollows, sown with stone and resembling the dried-up beds
of rivers. At times their road was barred by ravines about
which they had to make a detour. The animals began
to step carefully, moving their legs with precision as if in
a dance, among the dry and hard bushes formed by roses
of Jericho with which the dunes and rocks were abundantly
covered. Time and again some of the camels would
stumble and it was apparent that it was due to them to
give them rest.

Accordingly the Bedouins stopped in a sunken pass,
and dismounting from the saddles, proceeded to untie
the packs. Idris and Gebhr followed their example.
They began to attend to the camels, to loosen the saddle-
girths, remove the supplies of provisions, and seek flat
stones on which to build a fire. There was no wood or
dried dung, which Arabs use, but Chamis, son of Chadigi,
plucked roses of Jericho and built of them a big pile to
which he set fire. For some time, while the Sudânese
were engaged with the camels, Stas and Nell and her
nurse, old Dinah, found themselves together, somewhat
apart. But Dinah was more frightened than the children
and could not say a word. She only wrapped Nell in a
warm plaid and sitting close to her began with a moan
to kiss her little hands. Stas at once asked Chamis the
meaning of what had happened, but he, laughing, only
displayed his white teeth, and went to gather more roses
of Jericho. Idris, questioned afterwards, answered with
these words: "You will see!" and threatened him with
his finger. When the fire of roses, which smoldered more
than blazed, finally glowed they all surrounded it in a circle,

except Gebhr who remained with the camels, and they began to eat cakes of maize, and dried mutton and goats' meat. The children, famished by the long journey, also ate, though at the same time Nell's eyes were closed by sleepiness. But in the meantime, in the faint light of the fire, appeared dark-skinned Gebhr and with glittering eyes he held up two bright little gloves and asked:

"Whose are these?"

"Mine," answered Nell with a sleepy and tired voice.

"Yours, little viper?" the Sudânese hissed through set teeth. "Then you mark the road so that your father can know where to pursue us."

Saying this, he struck her with a courbash, a terrible Arabian whip, which cuts even the hide of a camel. Nell, though she was wrapped in a thick plaid, shrieked from pain and fright, but Gebhr was unable to strike her a second time, for at that moment Stas leaped like a wildcat, butted Gebhr's breast with his head, and afterwards clutched him by the throat.

It happened so unexpectedly that the Sudânese fell upon his back and Stas on top of him, and both began to roll on the ground. The boy was exceptionally strong for his age, nevertheless Gebhr soon overcame him. He first pulled his hands from his throat, after which he turned him over with face to the ground and, pressing heavily on his neck with his fist, he began to lash his back with the courbash.

The shrieks and tears of Nell, who seizing the hand of the savage at the same time begged him "to forgive" Stas, would not have availed if Idris had not unexpectedly come to the boy's assistance. He was older than Gebhr and from the beginning of the flight from Gharak el-Sultani all complied with his orders. Now he snatched the courbash from his brother's hand and, pushing him away, exclaimed:

"Away, you fool!"

"I 'll flog that scorpion!" answered Gebhr, gnashing his teeth.

But at this, Idris seized his cloak at the breast and gazing into his eyes began to say in a threatening though quiet voice:

"The noble [1] Fatma forbade us to do any harm to those children, for they interceded for her —"

"I 'll flog him!" iterated Gebhr.

"And I tell you that you shall not raise the courbash at either of them. If you do, for every blow, I shall give you ten."

And he began to shake him like a bough of a palm, after which he thus continued:

"Those children are the property of Smain and if either of them does not reach him alive, the Mahdi himself (May God prolong his days infinitely!) would command you to be hung. Do you understand, you fool?"

The name of the Mahdi created such a great impression upon all his believers that Gebhr drooped his head at once and began to repeat as if with fear:

"Allah akbar! Allah akbar!" [2]

Stas rose, panting and whipped, but felt that if his father could have seen and heard him at that moment he would have been proud of him, for he had not only leaped to save Nell, without thinking, but now, though the blows of the courbash burnt him like fire, he did not think of his own pain but instead began to console and ask the little girl whether the blow had injured her.

[1] All relatives of the Mahdi were termed "noble."
[2] This cry means, "God is great"; but Arabs utter it in moments of fear, summoning aid.

And afterwards he said:

"Whatever I got, I got, but he will never attack you. Oh, if I only had some weapon!"

The little woman entwined his neck with her arms and dampening his cheeks with tears began to assure him that it did not pain her very much and that she was crying not from pain but from sorrow for him. At this Stas put his lips to her ear and whispered:

"Nell, I swear that, not because he whipped me, but because he struck you, I shall not forgive him." With that the incident closed.

After a certain time Gebhr and Idris, becoming reconciled, spread out their cloaks upon the ground and lay upon them, and Chamis soon followed their example. The Bedouins poured out durra for the camels, after which, having mounted two unengaged camels, they rode in the direction of the Nile. Nell, supporting her head on old Dinah's knee, fell asleep. The fire was dying out and soon could be heard only the grinding of the durra in the camels' teeth. On high rolled small clouds which at times veiled the moon, but the night was clear. Beyond the rocks resounded the mournful whining of jackals.

After two hours the Bedouins returned with the camels bearing leather bags filled with water. Having fed the fire, they sat on the sand and commenced to eat. Their arrival awoke Stas, who previously had been dozing, as well as Chamis, son of Chadigi, and the two Sudânese. Then at the camp-fire began the following conversation:

"Can we start?" Idris asked.

"No, because we must rest;—we and our camels."

"Did any one see you?"

"Nobody. We reached the river between two villages. In the distance dogs barked."

"It will be necessary always to go for water at midnight and draw it at deserted places. Only let us get past the first 'challa' (cataract); beyond that the villages are farther apart and they are more friendly to the prophet. A pursuing party will undoubtedly follow us."

At this Chamis turned over, with his back up, and resting his face on his hands said:

"The Mehendes will first wait for the children in El-Fachn during the whole night and until the following train; later they will go to Fayûm and from there to Gharak. Only there will they understand what has happened and then they will have to return to Medinet to send words flying over the copper wire to cities on the Nile and to the camel-corps which will pursue us. All that will take at least three days. Therefore we do not need to tire our camels and can peacefully 'drink smoke' from pipe-stems."

Saying this, he pulled out a sprig of a rose of Jericho and lit his pipe with it, while Idris began, according to the Arabian habit, to smack his lips with satisfaction.

"You arranged it well, son of Chadigi," he said, "but it is necessary for us to take advantage of the time and to drive during those three days and nights as far as possible southward. I shall breathe freely only when we shall cross the desert between the Nile and Kharga (a great oasis west of the Nile). God grant that the camels hold out."

"They will hold out," declared one of the Bedouins.

"People also say," interposed Chamis, "that the army of the Mahdi — may God prolong his life — has already reached Assuan."

Here Stas, who did not lose a word of this conversation and remembered also what Idris had said to Gebhr, rose and said:

"The army of the Mahdi is below Khartûm."

"La! La! (no! no!)" Chamis contradicted.

"Don't pay any attention to his words," Stas replied, "for he not only has a dark skin but also a dark brain. Although you bought fresh camels every three days and rushed as you have done this day, you would not reach Khartûm for a month. And perhaps you do not know that an English, not an Egyptian, army bars the road to you."

These words created a certain impression and Stas, observing this, continued:

"Before you find yourselves between the Nile and the great oasis all the roads on the desert will be picketed by a line of army sentinels. Words over the copper wire speed quicker than camels. How will you be able to slip through?"

"The desert is wide," answered one of the Bedouins.

"But you must keep close to the Nile."

"We can cross over, and when they seek us on this side we shall be on the other."

"Words speeding over the copper wire will reach cities and villages on both banks of the river."

"The Mahdi will send us an angel, who will place a finger on the eyes of the Englishmen and the Turks (Egyptians) and will screen us with his wings."

"Idris," said Stas, "I do not address Chamis whose head is like an empty gourd, nor Gebhr who is a vile jackal, but you. I already know that you want to carry us to the Mahdi and deliver us to Smain. But if you are doing this for money, then know that the father of this little 'bint' (girl) is richer than all the Sudânese put together."

"And what of it?" interrupted Idris.

"What of it? Return voluntarily and the great Mehendi will not spare money for you, nor will my father either."

"But they will give us up to the Government, which will order us to be hung."

"No, Idris. You undoubtedly will hang, but only in case they capture you in the flight; and that surely will happen. But if you return, no punishment will be meted out to you, and besides you will be wealthy to the end of your life. You know that the white people of Europe always keep their word. Now I give you the word for both Mehendes that it will be as I say."

And Stas in reality was confident that his father and Mr. Rawlinson would prefer to fulfil the promise made by him than expose both of them, and especially Nell, to the terrible journey and yet more terrible life among the savage and maddened hordes of the Mahdi.

So with palpitating heart, he waited for the reply of Idris who was plunged in silence and only after a long interval said:

"You say that the father of the little 'bint' and yours will give us a great deal of money?"

"Yes."

"But can all their money open for us the gates of paradise which only the blessing of the Mahdi can do?"

"Bismillah!" shouted both Bedouins together with Chamis and Gebhr.

Stas at once lost all hope, for he knew that howsoever much the people in the East are greedy and venal, nevertheless when a true Mohammedan views any matter from the standpoint of faith, there are not any treasures in the world with which he can be tempted.

Idris, encouraged by the shouts, continued, and evidently not for the purpose of replying to Stas, but with a view of gaining greater esteem and praise from his companions.

"We have the good fortune not only to belong to that tribe which gave the holy prophet, but the noble Fatma and her children are his relatives and the great Mahdi loves them. If we deliver you and the little 'bint' to him, he will exchange you for Fatma and her sons and will bless us. Know that even the water, in which every morning according to the precepts of the Koran he makes his ablutions, heals the sick and eliminates sins; and think what his blessing can accomplish!"

"Bismillah!" reiterated the Sudânese and Bedouins.

But Stas, clutching at the last plank for help, said:

"Then take me and let the Bedouins return with the little 'bint.' For me they will surrender Fatma and her sons."

"It is yet more certain that they will surrender her for you two."

At this the boy addressed Chamis:

"Your father shall answer for your conduct."

"My father is already in the desert, on his way to the prophet," retorted Chamis.

"Then they will capture and hang him."

Here, however, Idris deemed it proper to give encouragement to his companions.

"Those vultures," he said, "which will pick the flesh from our bones may not yet be hatched. We know what threatens us, but we are not children, and we know the desert of old. These men (here he pointed at the Bedouins) were many times in Berber and are acquainted with roads over which only gazelles roam. There nobody will find us and nobody will seek us. We must indeed turn for water to the Bahr Yûsuf and later to the Nile, but will do that in the night. Besides, do you think that on the river there are no secret friends of the Mahdi? And I tell you that the farther south we go the more of them we will find. There, tribes and their sheiks are only waiting for the favorable moment to seize the sword in defense of the true faith. These alone will supply water, food, and camels, and lead astray the pursuit. In truth, we know that it is far to the Mahdi, but we know also that every day brings us nearer to the sheep's hide on which the holy prophet kneels to pray."

"Bismillah!" shouted his companions for the third time.

It was apparent that Idris' importance grew among them considerably. Stas understood that all was lost; so, desiring at least to protect Nell from the malice of the Sudânese, he said:

"After six hours the little lady reached here barely alive. How can you think that she can endure such a journey? If she should die, I also will die, and then with what will you come to the Mahdi?"

Now Idris could not find an answer. Stas, perceiving this, continued thus:

"And how will the Mahdi and Smain receive you when they learn that for your folly Fatma and her children must pay with their lives?"

But the Sudânese had recovered himself and replied:

"I saw how you grasped Gebhr's throat. By Allah! you are a lion's whelp and will not die and she —"

Here he gazed at the little head of the sleeping girl resting on the knees of old Dinah and finished in a kind of strangely gentle voice:

"For her we will weave on the camel's hump a nest, as for a bird, that she may not at all feel fatigue and that she may sleep on the road as peacefully as she is sleeping now."

Saying this he walked towards the camels and with the Bedouins began to make a seat for the little girl on the back of the best dromedary. At this they chattered a great deal and quarrelled among themselves but finally, with the aid of ropes, shaggy coverlets, and short bamboo poles they made something in the shape of a deep, immovable basket in which Nell could sit or lie down, but from which she could not fall. Above this seat, so broad that Dinah also could be accommodated in it, they stretched a linen awning.

"You see," said Idris to Stas, "quail's eggs could not crack in those housings. The old woman will ride with the little lady to serve her day and night. — You will sit with me, but can ride near her and watch over her."

Stas was glad that he had secured even this much. Pondering over the situation, he came to the conclusion that in all probability they would be captured before they reached the first cataract, and this thought gave him hope. In the meantime he wanted above all things to sleep; so he promised himself that he would tie himself with some kind of rope to the saddle, and, as he would not have to hold Nell, he could take a nap for a few hours.

The night already became paler and the jackals ceased their whining amid the passes. The caravan was to start immediately, but the Sudânese, observing the dawn, went to a rock, a few paces away, and there, conformably with the precepts of the Koran, began their morning ablutions, using, however, sand instead of water, which they desired to save. Afterwards resounded voices, saying the "soubhg," or morning prayer. Amidst the deep silence plainly could be heard their words: "In the name of the compassionate and merciful God. Glory to the Lord, the sovereign of the world, compassionate and merciful on the day of judgment. Thee we worship and profess. Thee we implore for aid. Lead us over the road of those to whom thou dost not spare benefactions and grace and not over the paths of sinners who have incurred Thy wrath and who err. Amen."

And Stas, hearing these voices, raised his eyes upwards and in that distant region, amidst tawny, gloomy sands, began the prayer:

"We fly to Thy patronage, O Holy Mother of God."

VIII

THE night faded The men already had the saddles on the camels, when suddenly they observed a desert wolf, which, with tail curled beneath it, rushed across the pass, about a hundred paces from the caravan, and reaching the opposite table-land, dashed ahead showing signs of fright as if it fled before some enemy. On the Egyptian deserts there are no wild animals before which wolves could feel any fear and for that reason this sight greatly alarmed the Sudânese Arabs. What could this be? Was the pursuing party already approaching? One of the Bedouins quickly climbed on a rock, but he had barely glanced when he slipped down yet more quickly.

"By the prophet!" he exclaimed, confused and frightened, "a lion is rushing towards us and is already close by!"

And then from beyond the rocks came a bass "wow" after which Stas and Nell shouted together:

"Saba! Saba!"

As in the Arabian language this means a lion, the Bedouins became frightened yet more, but Chamis burst out laughing and said:

"I know that lion."

Saying this he whistled drawlingly and in a moment the gigantic mastiff dashed among the camels. Seeing the children he leaped towards them. From joy he overturned Nell who extended her hands to him; he reared himself on Stas; afterwards whining and barking he ran round both a few times, again overturned Nell, again reared himself on Stas, and finally lying down at their feet began to pant.

His sides were sunken, from his lolling tongue fell clots of froth; nevertheless he wagged his tail and raised his eyes full of love at Nell as if he wanted to say: "Your father ordered me to watch over you, so here I am."

The children sat close to him, one on each side, and began to pat him. The two Bedouins, who never before saw a creature like this, gazed at him with astonishment, repeating: "On Allah! o kelb kebir!" ("By God! that is a big dog!") while he for some time lay quietly. Afterwards he raised his head, inhaled the air through his black nose resembling a big truffle, scented, and jumped towards the extinct camp-fire, near which lay the remnants of food.

In the same moment goat's and lamb's bones began to crack and crumble as straw in his powerful teeth. After eight people, counting old Dinah and Nell, there was enough for such "kelb kebir."

But the Sudânese were worried by his arrival and the two camel drivers, calling Chamis to one side, began to speak to him with uneasiness and even with indignation.

"Iblis [1] brought that dog here," exclaimed Gebhr, "but in what manner did he find the children, since they came to Gharak by rail?"

"Surely by the camel tracks," answered Chamis.

"It happened badly. Everybody who sees him with us will remember our caravan and will point out where we went. We positively must get rid of him."

"But how?" asked Chamis.

[1] Iblis, one of the names of the devil in the Koran. — *Translator's note.*

"We have a rifle, so take it and shoot him in the head."

In a case of urgency, Chamis might be able, for Stas had several times opened and closed his weapon before him, but he was sorry for the dog of whom he was fond, having taken care of him before the arrival of the children at Medinet. He knew perfectly that the Sudânese had no idea how to handle a weapon of the latest model and would be at a loss what to do with it.

"If you don't know how," he said, with a crafty smile, "that little 'nouzrani' (Christian) could kill the dog, but that rifle can fire several times in succession; so I do not advise you to put it in his hands."

"God forbid!" replied Idris; "he would shoot us like quails."

"We have knives," observed Gebhr.

"Try it, but remember that you have a throat which the dog will pull to pieces before you stab him."

"Then what is to be done?"

Chamis shrugged his shoulder.

"Why do you want to kill the dog? If you should afterwards bury him in the sand, the hyenas will dig him out; the pursuers will find his bones and will know that we did not cross the Nile but made off in this direction. Let him follow us. As often as the Bedouins go for water and we hide in the passes, you may be sure that the dog will stay with the children. Allah! It is better that he came now, for otherwise he would lead the pursuing party on our tracks as far as Berber. You do not need to feed him, for if our leavings are not sufficient it will not be difficult for him to get a hyena or jackal. Leave him in peace, I tell you, and do not lose any time in idle talk."

"Perhaps you are right," said Idris.

"If I am right, then I will give him water, so that he shall not run to the Nile and show himself in the villages."

In this manner was decided the fate of Saba who, having somewhat rested himself and eaten his fill, in the twinkling of an eye lapped up a bowl of water and started with renewed strength after the caravan.

They now rode on high, level ground, on which the wind wrinkled the sand and from which could be seen on both sides the immense expanse of the desert. Heaven assumed the tint of a pearl shell. Light little · clouds gathered in the east and changed like opals, after which they suddenly became dyed with gold. One ray darted, afterwards another, and the sun — as is usual in southern countries, in which there are scarcely any twilight and dawn — did not ascend, but burst from behind the clouds like a pillar of fire and flooded the horizon with a bright light. It enlivened heaven, it enlivened the earth, and the immeasurable sandy expanse was unveiled to the eyes of men.

"We must hasten," said Idris, "for here we can be seen from a distance."

Accordingly the rested and satiated camels sped on with the celerity of gazelles. Saba remained behind, but there was no fear that he would get lost and not appear at the first short halt for refreshments. The dromedary on which Idris rode with Stas ran close to the one on which Nell was mounted, so that the children could easily converse with each other. The seat which the Sudânese had made appeared splendid and the little girl really looked like a bird in a nest. She could not fall, even sleeping, and the ride fatigued her far less than during the night. The bright daylight gave courage to both children. In Stas' heart the hope entered that since Saba had overtaken them, the pursuers might do the same. This hope he at once shared with Nell, who smiled at him for the first time since their abduction.

"When will they overtake us?" she asked in French in order that Idris should not understand them.

"I do not know. It may be to-day; perhaps to-morrow; perhaps after two or three days."

"But we will not ride back on camels?"

"No. We will ride only as far as the Nile, and afterwards go by way of the Nile to El-Wasta."

"That is good! oh, good!"

Poor Nell, who had previously loved these rides, had evidently now had enough of them.

"By way of the Nile — to El-Wasta and to papa!" she began to repeat in a sleepy voice.

As at the previous stop she did not enjoy a full sound sleep, she now fell into that deep sleep which after fatigue comes towards morning. In the meantime the Bedouins drove the camels without a rest and Stas observed that they were making their way towards the interior of the desert.

So, desiring to shake Idris' confidence that he would be able to elude the pursuit, and at the same time to show him that he himself relied upon it as a dead certainty, he said:

"You are driving away from the Nile and from Bahr Yûsuf, but that won't help you, for of course they will not seek you on the banks where villages lie side by side, but in the interior of the desert."

And Idris asked:

"How do you know that we are driving away from the Nile, since the banks cannot be seen from here?"

"Because the sun, which is in the eastern part of heaven, is warming our backs; that means we have turned to the west."

"You are a wise boy," said Idris with esteem.

After a while he added:

"But the pursuing party will not overtake us nor will you escape."

"No," answered Stas, "I shall not escape — unless with her."

And he pointed to the sleeping girl.

Until noon they sped almost without pausing for breath, but when the sun rose high in the sky and began to scorch, the camels, which by nature perspire but little, were covered with sweat, and their pace slackened considerably. The caravan again was surrounded by rocks and dunes. The ravines, which during the rainy season are changed into channels of streams, or so-called "khors," came to view more and more frequently. The Bedouins finally halted in one of them which was entirely concealed amid the rocks. But they had barely dismounted from the camels when they raised a cry and dashed ahead, bending over every little while and throwing stones ahead of them. Stas, who had not yet alighted from the saddle, beheld a strange sight. From among the dry bushes overgrowing the bed of the "khor," a big snake emerged and, gliding sinuously with the rapidity of lightning among the fragments of rocks, escaped to some hiding-place known to itself. The Bedouins chased it furiously and Gebhr rushed to their aid with a knife. But owing to the unevenness of the ground it was difficult either to hit the snake with a stone or to pin it with a knife. Soon all three returned with terror visible on their faces.

And the cries, customary with Arabs, resounded:

"Allah!"

"Bismillah!"

"Mashallah!"

Afterwards both Sudânese began to look with a kind

of strange and, at the same time, searching and inquiring
gaze at Stas who could not understand what was the
matter.

In the meantime Nell also dismounted from her camel,
and though she was less tired than during the night,
Stas spread for her a saddle-cloth in the shade on a level
spot and told her to lie down, in order, as he said, that
she might straighten out her little feet. The Arabs prepared their noon meal, which consisted of biscuits and
dates, together with a gulp of water. The camels were
not watered for they had drank during the night. The
faces of Idris, Gebhr and the Bedouins were still dejected,
and the stop was made in silence. Finally Idris called
Stas aside, and began to question him with a countenance
at once mysterious and perturbed.

"Did you see the snake?"

"I did."

"Did you conjure it to appear before us?"

"No."

"Some ill-luck awaits us as those fools did not succeed
in killing it."

"The gallows awaits you."

"Be silent! Is your father a sorcerer?"

"He is," answered Stas without any hesitation, for
he understood in a moment that those savage and superstitious men regarded the appearance of a reptile as an
evil omen and an announcement that the flight would
not succeed.

"So then your father sent it to us," answered Idris,
"but he ought to understand that we can avenge ourselves for his charms upon you."

"You will not do anything to me as the sons of Fatma
would have to suffer for any injury to me."

"And you already understand this? But remember

that if it was not for me, your blood would have flowed under Gebhr's courbash — yours and that little 'bint's' also."

"I therefore shall intercede for you only; but Gebhr shall swing on the rope."

At this Idris gazed at him for a while as if with astonishment and said:

"Our lives are not yet in your hands and you already talk to us as our lord —"

After a while he added:

"You are a strange 'uled' (boy), and such a one I have not yet seen. Thus far I have been kind to you, but take heed and do not threaten."

"God punishes treachery," answered Stas.

It was apparent, however, that the assurance with which the boy spoke in connection with the evil omen in the form of a snake which succeeded in escaping, disquieted Idris in a high degree. Having already mounted the camel he repeated several times: "Yes, I was kind to you," as if in any event he wished to impress this upon Stas' memory, and afterwards he began to finger the beads of a rosary made of the shells of "dum" nuts, and pray.

About two o'clock, though it was in the winter season, the heat became unusual. In the sky there was not a cloudlet, but the horizon's border was disfigured.

Above the caravan hovered a few vultures whose widely outstretched wings cast moving, black shadows on the tawny sands. In the heated air could be smelt an odor like the gas exhaled from burning charcoal. The camels, not ceasing to run, began to grunt strangely. One of the Bedouins approached Idris.

"Some evil is brewing?"

"What, do you think?" asked the Sudânese.

"Wicked spirits awoke the wind slumbering on the

western desert, and he rose from the sands and is rushing upon us."

Idris raised himself on the saddle, gazed into the distance, and replied:

"That is so. He is coming from the west and south but is not as furious as a Khamsin."[1]

"Three years ago near Abu-Hamed he buried a whole caravan and did not sweep the sand away until last winter. Ualla! He may have enough strength to stuff the nostrils of the camels and dry up the water in the bags."

"It is necessary that we speed so that he strike us only with a wing."

"We are flying in his eyes and are not able to avoid him."

"The quicker he comes, the quicker he will pass away."

Saying this, Idris struck his camel with a courbash and his example was followed by the others. For some time could be heard the dull blows of the thick whips, resembling the clapping of hands, and the cries of "Yalla." On the southwest the horizon, previously whitish, darkened. The heat continued and the sun scorched the heads of the riders. The vultures soared very high evidently, for their shadows grew smaller and smaller, and they finally vanished entirely.

It became sultry.

The Arabs yelled at the camels until their throats became parched, after which they were silent and a funereal quiet ensued, interrupted only by the groaning of the animals.

Two very small foxes[2] with big ears stole by the caravan, running in an opposite direction.

[1] A southwest wind which blows in the spring.
[2] An animal smaller than our foxes, called "fennec."

The same Bedouin, who had previously conversed with Idris, spoke out again in a strange and as if not his own voice:

"This will not be a usual wind. Evil charms are pursuing us. The snake is to blame for all —"

"I know," answered Idris.

"Look! the air quivers. That does not happen in winter."

In fact the heated air began to quiver, and in consequence of an illusion of the eyes it seemed to the riders that the sands quivered. The Bedouin took his sweaty cowl from his head and said:

"The heart of the desert beats with terror."

And at this the other Bedouin, riding in the lead as a guide of the camels, turned around and began to shout:

"He is already coming! — He is coming!"

And in truth the wind came up. In the distance appeared as it were dark clouds which in their eyes grew higher and higher and approached the caravan. The nearest waves of air all around became agitated and sudden gusts of wind began to spin the sand. Here and there funnels were formed as if someone had drilled the surface of the desert with a cane. At places rose swift whirlpools resembling pillars, thin at the bottom and outspread on top like plumes of feathers. All this lasted but the twinkling of an eye. The cloud which the camel-guide first espied came flying towards them with an inconceivable velocity. It struck the people and beasts like the wing of a gigantic bird. In one moment the eyes and mouths of the riders were filled with sand. Clouds of dust hid the sky, hid the sun, and the earth became dusky. The men began to lose sight of one another and even the nearest camel appeared indistinctly as if in a fog. Not the rustle — for on the desert there

are no trees — but the roar of the whirlwind drowned
the calls of the guide and the bellowing of the animals.
In the atmosphere could be smelt an odor such as coal
smoke gives. The camels stood still and, turning away
from the wind, they stretched their long necks downward
so that their nostrils almost touched the sand.

The Sudânese, however, did not wish to allow a stop,
as caravans which halt during a hurricane are often buried
in sand. At such times it is best to speed with the whirlwind, but Idris and Gehbr could not do this, for in thus
doing they would return to Fayûm from where they
expected a pursuit. So when the first gale passed they
again drove the camels.

A momentary stillness ensued but the ruddy dusk
dissipated very slowly for the sun could not pierce through
the clouds of dust suspended in the air. The thicker
and heavier particles of sand began to fall. Sand filled all
the cracks and punctures in the saddles and clung to the
folds of the clothes. The people with each breath inhaled dust which irritated their lungs and grated their
teeth.

Besides, the whirlwind might break out again and hide
the whole world. It occurred to Stas that if at the time
of such darkness he was with Nell on the same camel,
he might turn around and escape with the wind northward. Who knows whether they would be observed
amidst the dusk and confusion of the elements, and, if
they succeeded in reaching any village on Bahr Yûsuf
near the Nile, Idris and Gebhr would not dare to pursue
them for they would at once fall into the hands of the
local "police."

Stas, weighing all this, jostled Idris' shoulder and said:
"Give me the gourd with water."

Idris did not refuse for howsoever much that morning

they had turned into the interior of the desert and quite far from the river, they had enough of water, and the camels drank copiously during the time of their night stop. Besides this, as a man acquainted with the desert, he knew that after a hurricane, rain usually follows and the dried-up "khors" change temporarily into streams.

Stas in reality was thirsty, so he took a good drink, after which, not returning the gourd, he again jostled Idris' arm.

"Halt the caravan."

"Why?" asked the Sudânese.

"Because I want to sit on the camel with the little 'bint' and give her water."

"Dinah has a bigger gourd than mine."

"But she is greedy and surely has emptied it. A great deal of sand must have fallen into her saddle which you made like a basket. Dinah will be helpless."

"The wind will break out after a while and will refill it."

"That is the more reason why she will require help."

Idris lashed the camel with his whip and for a while they rode in silence.

"Why don't you answer?" Stas asked.

"Because I am considering whether it would be better to tie you to the saddle or tie your hands behind."

"You have become insane."

"No. I have guessed what you intended to do."

"The pursuers will overtake us anyway; so I would not have to do it."

"The desert is in the hands of God."

They became silent again. The thicker sand fell entirely; there remained in the air a subtile red dust, something of the nature of pollen, through which the sun shone like a copper plate. But already they could see ahead. Before the caravan stretched level ground at the borders of which the keen eyes of the Arabs again espied a cloud. It was higher than the previous one and, besides this, there shot from it what seemed like pillars, or gigantic chimneys expanding at the top. At this sight the hearts of the Arabs and Bedouins quailed for they recognized the great sandy whirlpools. Idris raised his hands and drawing his palms towards his ears began to prostrate himself to the approaching whirlwind. His faith in one God evidently did not prevent his worship and fear of others for Stas distinctly heard him say:

"Lord! We are thy children; therefore do not devour us."

But the "lord" just dashed at them and assailed the camels with a force so terrible that they almost fell to the ground. The animals now formed a compact pack with heads turned to the center towards each other. Whole masses of sand were stirred. The caravan was enveloped by a dusk deeper than before and in that dusk there flew beside the riders dark and indistinct objects, as though gigantic birds or camels were dispersed with the hurricane. Fear seized the Arabs, to whom it seemed that these were the spirits of animals and men who had perished under the sands. Amid the roar and howling could be heard strange voices similar to sobs, to laughter, to cries for help. But these were delusions. The caravan was threatened by real danger, a hundred-fold greater. The Sudânese well knew that if any one of the great whirlpools, forming incessantly in the bosom of the hurricane, should catch them in its whirls, it would hurl the riders to the ground and disperse the camels, and if it should break and fall upon them then in the twinkling of an eye an immense sandy mound would cover them in which they would remain until the next hurricane, blowing away the sand, should reveal their skeletons.

Stas' head swam, his lungs seemed choked, and the sand blinded him. But at times it seemed to him that he heard Nell crying and calling; so he thought only of her. Taking advantage of the fact that the camels stood in a close pack and that Idris might not observe him, he determined to creep over quietly to the girl's camel, not for the purpose of escaping, but to give her assistance and encouragement. But he had barely extended his limbs from under him and stretched out his hands to grasp the edge of Nell's saddle, when the giant hand of Idris grabbed him. The Sudânese snatched him like a feather, laid him before him and began to tie him with a palm rope, and after binding his hands, placed him across the saddle. Stas pressed his teeth and resisted as well as he could, but in vain. Having a parched throat and a mouth filled with sand he could not convince Idris that he desired only to go to the girl's assistance and did not want to escape.

After a while, however, feeling that he was suffocating, he began to shout in a stifled voice:

"Save the little ' bint '! Save the little ' bint '!"

But the Arabs preferred to think of their own lives. The blasts became so terrible that they could not sit on the camels nor could the camels stand in their places. The two Bedouins with Chamis and Gebhr leaped to the ground, in order to hold the animals by cords attached to the mouthpieces under their lower jaws. Idris, shoving Stas to the rear of the saddle, did the same. The animals spread out their legs as widely as possible in order to resist the furious whirlwind, but they lacked strength, and the caravan, scourged by gravel which cut like hundreds of whips and the sand which pricked like pins, began now slowly, then hurriedly, to turn about and retreat under the pressure. At times the whirlwind tore holes under their feet, then again the sand and gravel bounding from the sides of the camels would form, in the twinkling of an eye, mounds reaching to their knees and higher. In this manner hour passed after hour. The danger became more and more terrible. Idris finally understood that the only salvation was to remount the camels and fly with the whirlwind. But this would be returning in the direction of Fayûm, where Egyptian Courts and the gallows were waiting for them.

"Ha! it cannot be helped," thought Idris. "The hurricane will also stop the pursuit and when it ceases, we will again proceed southward."

And he began to shout that they should resume their seats on the camels.

But at this moment something happened which entirely changed the situation.

Suddenly, the dusky, almost black, clouds of sand were illumined with a livid light. The darkness then became still deeper, but at the same time there arose, slumbering on high and awakened by the whirlwind, thunder; it began to roll between the Arabian and Libyan deserts, — powerful, threatening, one might say, angry. It seemed as if from the heavens, mountains and rocks were tumbling down. The deafening peal intensified, grew, shook the world, began to roam all over the whole horizon; in places it burst with a force as terrible as if the shattered vault of heaven had fallen upon earth and afterwards it again rolled with a hollow, continual rumble; again it burst forth, again broke, it blinded with lightning, and struck with thunderbolts, descended, rose, and pealed continuously.[1]

[1] The author heard in the vicinity of Aden thunder which lasted without intermission for half an hour. See "Letters from Africa."

The wind subsided as if overawed, and when after a long time somewhere in the immeasurable distance the chain-bolt of heaven rattled, a deadly stillness followed the thunder.

But after a while in that silence the voice of the guide resounded.

"God is above the whirlwind and the storm. We are saved."

They started. But they were enveloped by a night so impenetrable that though the camels ran close together, the men could not see each other and had to shout aloud every little while in order not to lose one another. From time to time glaring lightning, livid or red, illuminated the sandy expanse, but afterwards fell a darkness so thick as to be almost palpable. Notwithstanding the hope, which the voice of the guide poured into the hearts of the Sudânese, uneasiness did not yet leave them, because they moved blindly, not knowing in truth in which direction they were going; — whether they were moving around in a circle or were returning northward. The animals stumbled against each other every little while and could not run swiftly, and besides they panted strangely, and so loudly that it seemed to the riders that the whole desert panted from fear. Finally fell the first drops of rain, which almost always follows a hurricane, and at the same time the voice of the guide broke out amidst the darkness:

"Khor!"

They were above a ravine. The camels paused at the brink; after which they began to step carefully towards the bottom.

IX

THE khor was wide, covered on the bottom with stones
among which grew dwarfish, thorny shrubs. A high
rock full of crevices and fissures formed its southern
wall. The Arabs discerned all this by the light of quiet
but more and more frequent lightning flashes. Soon
they also discovered in the rocky wall a kind of shallow
cave or, rather, a broad niche, in which people could easily
be harbored and, in case of a great downpour, could
find shelter. The camels also could be comfortably
lodged upon a slight elevation close by the niche. The
Bedouins and two Sudânese removed from them their
burdens and saddles, so that they might rest well, and
Chamis, son of Chadigi, occupied himself in the meantime
with pulling thorny shrubs for a fire. Big single drops
fell continually but the downpour began only when the
party lay down to sleep. At first it was like strings of
water, afterwards ropes, and in the end it seemed as if
whole rivers were flowing from invisible clouds. Such
rains, which occur only once in several years, swell, even
in winter time, the water of the canals and the Nile, and
in Aden fill immense cisterns, without which the city
could not exist at all. Stas never in his life had seen
anything like it. At the bottom of the khor the stream
began to rumble; the entrance to the niche was veiled
as if by a curtain of water; around could be heard only
splashing and spluttering.

The camels stood on an elevation and the downpour at most would give them a bath; nevertheless the Arabs peered out every little while to see if any danger threatened the animals. To the others it was agreeable to sit in the cave, safe from danger, by the bright fire of brushwood, which was not yet soaked. On their faces joy was depicted. Idris, who immediately after their arrival had untied Stas' hands so that he could eat, now turned to him and smiling contemptuously said:

"The Mahdi is greater than all white sorcerers. He subdued the hurricane and sent rain."

Stas did not reply for he was occupied with Nell, who was barely alive. First he shook the sand from her hair, afterwards directed old Dinah to unpack the things which she, in the belief that the children were going to their parents, brought with her from Fayûm. He took a towel, wet it, and wiped the little girl's eyes and face with it. Dinah could not do this as seeing but poorly with one eye only, she lost her sight almost entirely during the hurricane and washing her heated eyelids did not bring her any relief. Nell submitted passively to all of Stas' efforts; she only gazed at him like an exhausted bird, and only when he removed her shoes to spill out the sand and afterwards when he smoothed out the saddle-cloths did she throw her arms around his neck.

His heart overflowed with great pity. He felt that he was a guardian, an older brother, and at that time Nell's only protector, and he felt at the same time that he loved this little sister immensely, far more than ever before. He loved her indeed in Port Said, but he regarded her as a "baby"; so, for instance, it never even occurred to him to kiss her hand in bidding her good night. If any one had suggested such an idea to him he would have thought that a bachelor, who had finished his thirteenth year, could not without derogation to his dignity and age do anything like that. But, at present, a common distress awoke in him dormant tenderness; so he kissed not one but both hands of the little girl.

Lying down, he continued to think of her and determined to perform some extraordinary deed to snatch her from captivity. He was prepared for everything, even for wounds and death; only with this little reservation secreted in his heart, that the wounds should not be too painful, and that the death should not be an inevitable and real death, as in such case he could not witness the happiness of Nell when liberated. Afterwards he began to ponder upon the most heroic manner of saving her, but his thoughts became confused. For a while it seemed to him that whole clouds of sand were burying him; afterwards that all the camels were piling on his head, — and he fell asleep.

The Arabs, exhausted by the battle with the hurricane, after attending to the camels, also fell into a sound sleep. The fire became extinct and a dusk prevailed in the niche. Soon the snores of the men resounded, and from outside came the splash of the downpour and the roar of the waters dashing over the stones on the bottom of the khor. In this manner the night passed.

But before dawn Stas was awakened from a heavy sleep by a feeling of cold. It appeared that water which accumulated in the fissures on the top of the rock slowly passed through some cleft in the vault of the cave and began finally to trickle onto his head. The boy sat up on the saddle-cloth and for some time struggled with sleep; he did not realize where he was and what had happened to him.

After a while, however, consciousness returned to him.

"Aha!" he thought, "yesterday there was a hurricane and we are kidnapped, and this is a cave in which we sought shelter from the rain."

And he began to gaze around. At first he observed with astonishment that the rain had passed away and that it was not at all dark in the cave, as it was illuminated by the moon which was about to set. In its pale beams could be seen the whole interior of that wide but shallow niche. Stas saw distinctly the Arabs lying beside each other, and under the other wall of the cave the white dress of Nell who was sleeping close to Dinah.

And again great tenderness possessed his heart.

"Sleep, Nell — sleep," he said to himself; "but I do not sleep, and must save her."

After this, glancing at the Arabs, he added in his soul:

"Ah! I do want to have all these rogues — "

Suddenly he trembled.

His gaze fell upon the leather case containing the short rifle presented to him as a Christmas gift, and the cartridge boxes lying between him and Chamis, so near that it would suffice for him to stretch out his hand.

And his heart began to beat like a hammer. If he could secure the rifle and boxes he would certainly be the master of the situation. It would be enough in that case to slip noiselessly out of the niche, hide about fifty paces away, among the rocks, and from there watch the exit of the Sudânese and Bedouins. He thought that if they awakened and observed his absence they would rush out of the cave together but at that time he could with two bullets shoot down the first two and, before the others could reach him, the rifle could be reloaded. Chamis would remain but he could take care of him.

Here he pictured to himself four corpses lying in a pool

of blood, and fright and horror seized his breast. To kill four men! Indeed they were knaves, but even so it was a horrifying affair. He recollected that at one time he saw a laborer — a fellah — killed by the crank of a steam dredge, and what a horrible impression his mortal remains, quivering in a red puddle, made upon him! He shuddered at the recollection. And now four would be necessary! four! The sin and the horror! No, no, he was incapable of that.

He began to struggle with his thoughts. For himself, he would not do that — No! But Nell was concerned; her protection, her salvation, and her life were involved, for she could not endure all this, and certainly would die either on the road or among the wild and brutalized hordes of dervishes. What meant the blood of such wretches beside the life of Nell, and could any one in such a situation hesitate?

"For Nell! For Nell!"

But suddenly a thought flew like a whirlwind through Stas' mind and caused the hair to rise on his head. What would happen if any one of the outlaws placed a knife at Nell's breast, and announced that he would murder her if he — Stas — did not surrender and return the rifle to them.

"Then," answered the boy to himself, "I should surrender at once."

And with a realization of his helplessness he again flung himself impotently upon the saddle-cloth.

The moon now peered obliquely through the opening of the cave and it became less dark. The Arabs snored continually. Some time passed and a new idea began to dawn in Stas' head.

If, slipping out with the weapon and hiding among the rocks, he should kill not the men but shoot the camels?

It would be too bad and a sad ending for the innocent
animals; — that is true, but what was to be done? Why,
people kill animals not only to save life but for broth and
roast meat. Now it was a certainty that if he succeeded
in killing four, and better still five camels, further travel
would be impossible. No one in the caravan would dare
to go to the villages near the banks to purchase new
camels. And in such a case Stas, in the name of his
father, would promise the men immunity from punishment and even a pecuniary reward and — nothing else
would remain to do but to return.

Yes, but if they should not give him time to make
such a promise and should kill him in the first transports
of rage?

They must give him time and hear him for he would
hold the rifle in his hand; he would be able to hold them
at bay until he stated everything. When he had done,
they would understand that their only salvation would
be to surrender. Then he would be in command of the
caravan and lead it directly to Bahr Yûsuf and the Nile.
To be sure, at present they are quite a distance from it,
perhaps one or two days' journey, as the Arabs through
caution had turned considerably into the interior of the
desert. But that did not matter; there would remain,
of course, a few camels and on one of them Nell would
ride.

Stas began to gaze attentively at the Arabs. They
slept soundly, as people exceedingly tired do, but as the
night was waning, they might soon awaken. It was
necessary to act at once. The taking of the cartridge
boxes did not present any difficulties as they lay close
by. A more difficult matter was to get the rifle, which
Chamis had placed at his further side. Stas hoped that he
would succeed in purloining it, but he decided to draw it

out of the case and put the stock and the barrels together when he should be about fifty paces from the cave, as he feared that the clank of the iron against iron would wake the sleepers.

The moment arrived. The boy bent like an arch over Chamis and, seizing the case by the handle, began to transfer it to his side. His heart and pulse beat heavily, his eyes grew dim, his breathing became rapid, but he shut his teeth and tried to control his emotions. Nevertheless when the straps of the case creaked lightly, drops of cold perspiration stood on his forehead. That second seemed to him an age. But Chamis did not even stir. The case described an arch over him and rested silently beside the box with cartridges.

Stas breathed freely. One-half of the work was done. Now it was necessary to slip out of the cave noiselessly and run about fifty paces; afterwards to hide in a fissure, open the case, put the rifle together, load it, and fill his pockets with cartridges. The caravan then would be actually at his mercy.

Stas' black silhouette was outlined on the brighter background of the cave's entrance. A second more and he would be on the outside, and would hide in the rocky fissure. And then, even though one of the outlaws should wake, before he realized what had happened and before he aroused the others — it would be too late. The boy, from fear of knocking down some stone, of which a large number lay at the threshold of the niche, shoved out one foot and began to seek firm ground with his step.

And already his head leaned out of the opening and he was about to slip out wholly when suddenly something happened which turned the blood in his veins to ice.

Amid the profound stillness pealed like a thunder-bolt the joyous bark of Saba; it filled the whole ravine and awoke the echoes reposing in it. The Arabs as one man were startled from their sleep, and the first object which struck their eyes was the sight of Stas with the case in one hand and the cartridge box in the other.

Ah, Saba! what have you done?

X

WITH cries of horror, all in a moment rushed at Stas; in the twinkling of an eye they wrested the rifle and cartridges from him and threw him on the ground, tied his hands and feet, striking and kicking him all the time, until finally Idris, from fear of the boy's life, drove them off. Afterwards they began to converse in disjointed words, as people do over whom had impended a terrible danger and whom only an accident had saved.

"That is Satan incarnate," exclaimed Idris, with face pallid with fright and emotion.

"He would have shot us like wild geese for food," added Gebhr.

"Ah, if it was not for that dog."

"God sent him."

"And you wanted to kill him?" said Chamis.

"From this time no one shall touch him."

"He shall always have bones and water."

"Allah! Allah!" repeated Idris, not being able to compose himself. "Death was upon us. Ugh!"

And they began to stare at Stas lying there, with hatred but with a certain wonder that one small boy might have been the cause of their calamity and destruction.

"By the prophet!" spoke out one of the Bedouins, "it is necessary to prevent this son of Iblis from twisting our necks. We are taking a viper to the Mahdi. What do you intend to do with him?"

"We must cut off his right hand!" exclaimed Gebhr.

The Bedouins did not answer, but Idris would not consent to this proposition. It occurred to him that if the pursuers should capture them, a more terrible punishment would be meted to them for the mutilation of the boy. Finally, who could guarantee that Stas would not die after such an operation? In such a case for the exchange of Fatma and her children only Nell would remain. So when Gebhr pulled out his knife with the intention of executing his threat, Idris seized him by the wrist and held it.

"No!" he said. "It would be a disgrace for five of the Mahdi's warriors to fear one Christian whelp so much as to cut off his fist; we will bind him for the night, and for that which he wanted to do, he shall receive ten lashes of the courbash."

Gebhr was ready to execute the sentence at once but Idris again pushed him away and ordered the flogging to be done by one of the Bedouins, to whom he whispered not to hit very hard. As Chamis, perhaps out of regard for his former service with the engineers or perhaps from some other reason, did not want to mix in the matter, the other Bedouin turned Stas over with his back up and the punishment was about to take place, when at that moment an unexpected obstacle came.

At the opening of the niche Nell appeared with Saba.

Occupied with her pet, who, dashing into the cave, threw himself at once at her little feet, she had heard the shouts of the Arabs, but, as in Egypt Arabs as well as Bedouins yell on every occasion as if they are about to annihilate each other, she did not pay any attention to them. Not until she called Stas and received no reply from him, did she go out to see whether he was not already seated on the camels. With terror she saw in the first luster of the morning Stas lying on the ground and above him a Bedouin with a courbash in his hand. At the sight of this she screamed with all her strength and stamped with her little feet, and when the Bedouin, not paying any attention to this, aimed the first blow, she flung herself forward and covered the boy with her body.

The Bedouin hesitated, as he did not have an order to strike the little girl, and in the meantime her voice resounded full of despair and horror:

"Saba! Saba!"

And Saba understood what was the matter and in one leap was in the niche. The hair bristled on his neck and back, his eyes flamed redly, in his breast and powerful throat there was a rumble as if of thunder.

And afterwards, the lips of his wrinkled jaws rose slowly upward and the teeth as well as the white fangs, an inch long, appeared as far as the bloody gums. The giant mastiff now began to turn his head to the right and to the left as if he wanted to display well his terrible equipment to the Sudânese and Bedouins and tell them:

"Look! here is something with which I shall defend the children!"

They, on the other hand, retreated hurriedly for they knew in the first place that Saba had saved their lives and again that it was a clear thing that whoever approached Nell at that moment would have the fangs of the infuriated mastiff sunk at once in his throat. So they stood irresolute, staring with an uncertain gaze and as if asking one another what in the present situation had better be done.

Their hesitation continued so long that Nell had sufficient time to summon old Dinah and order her to cut Stas' bonds. Then the boy, placing his hand on Saba's head, turned to his assailants:

"I did not want to kill you — only the camels," he said through his set teeth.

But this information so startled the Arabs that they undoubtedly would have again rushed at Stas were it not for Saba's flaming eyes and bristling hair. Gebhr even started to dash towards him, but one hollow growl riveted him to the spot.

A moment of silence followed, after which Idris' loud voice resounded:

"To the road! To the road!"

XI

A DAY passed, a night, and yet another day and they
drove constantly southward, halting only for a brief
time in the khors in order not to fatigue the camels too
much, to water and feed them, and also to divide their
provisions and water. From fear of the pursuit they
turned yet farther to the west, for they did not have to
concern themselves about water for some time. The
downpour had lasted indeed not more than seven hours,
but it was as tremendous as if a cloud-burst had occurred
on the desert. Idris and Gebhr as well as the Bedouins
knew that on the beds of the khors and in those places
where the rocks formed natural cavities and wells they
would, for a few days, find enough water to suffice not
only for their and the camels' immediate wants but even
for replenishing their supplies. After the great rain, as
usual, splendid weather followed. The sky was cloudless, and the air so transparent that the view reached
over an immeasurable distance. At night the heaven,
studded with stars, twinkled and sparkled as if with
thousands of diamonds. From the desert sands came
a refreshing coolness.

The camel-humps already grew smaller but the animals, being well-fed, were, according to the Arabian expression, "harde," that is, they were unimpaired in strength
and ran so willingly that the caravan advanced but little
slower than on the first day after their departure from

Gharak el-Sultani. Stas with astonishment observed
that in some of the khors, in rocky fissures protected
from rain, were supplies of durra and dates. He in-
ferred from this that, before their abduction, certain
preparations were made and everything was pre-arranged
between Fatma, Idris, and Gebhr on one side and the
Bedouins on the other. It was also easy to surmise that
both the Bedouins were Mahdist adherents and believers,
who wanted to join their leader, and for that reason were
easily drawn into the plot by the Sudânese. In the neighborhood of Fayûm and around Gharak el-Sultani there
were quite a number of Bedouins who with their children
and camels led a migratory life on the desert and came to
Medinet and the railway stations for gain.

Stas, however, had never seen these two before, and
they also could not have been in Medinet, for it appeared
they did not know Saba.

The idea of attempting to bribe them occurred to the
boy, but recollecting their shouts, full of fervor, whenever
the name of the Mahdi was mentioned by them, he deemed
this an impossibility. Nevertheless, he did not submit
passively to the events, for in that boyish soul there was
imbedded a really astonishing energy, which was inflamed
by the past failures.

"Everything which I have undertaken," he soliloquized, "ended in my getting a whipping. But even
if they flog me with that courbash every day and even
kill me, I will not stop thinking of rescuing Nell and
myself from the hands of these villains. If the pursuers
capture them, so much the better. I, however, will act
as if I did not expect them." And at the recollection
of what he had met at the thought of those treacherous
and cruel people who, after snatching away the rifle,
had belabored him with fists and kicked him, his heart

rebelled and rancor grew. He felt not only vanquished but humiliated by them in his pride as a white man. Above all, however, he felt Nell's wrong and this feeling, with the bitterness which intensified within him after the last failure, changed into an inexorable hatred of both Sudânese. He had often heard, indeed, from his father that hatred blinds, and that only such souls yield to it as are incapable of anything better; but for the time being he could not subdue it within him, and did not know how to conceal it.

He did not know to what extent Idris had observed it and had begun to get uneasy, understanding that, in case the pursuing party should capture them, he could not depend upon the boy's intercession. Idris was always ready for the most audacious deed, but as a man not deprived of reason, he thought that it was necessary to provide for everything and in case of misfortune to leave some gate of salvation open. For this reason, after the last occurrence he wanted in some manner to conciliate Stas and, with this object, at the first stop, he began the following conversation with him.

"After what you wanted to do," he said, "I had to punish you as otherwise they would have killed you, but I ordered the Bedouin not to strike you hard."

And when he received no reply, he, after a while, continued thus:

"Listen! you yourself have said that the white people always keep their oath. So if you will swear by your God and by the head of that little 'bint' that you will do nothing against us, then I will not order you to be bound for the night."

Stas did not answer a single word to this and only from the glitter of his eyes did Idris perceive that he spoke in vain.

Nevertheless, notwithstanding the urging of Gebhr and the Bedouins, he did not order him to be bound for the night, and when Gebhr did not cease his importunities, he replied with anger:

"Instead of going to sleep, you will to-night stand on guard. I have decided that from this time one of us shall watch during the sleep of the others."

And in reality a change of guards was introduced permanently from that day. This rendered more difficult and completely frustrated all plans of Stas to whom every sentinel paid watchful attention.

But on the other hand the children were left in greater freedom so that they could approach each other and converse without hindrance. Immediately after the first stop Stas sat close to Nell for he was anxious to thank her for her aid.

But though he felt great gratitude to her he did not know how to express himself, either in a lofty style or tenderly; so he merely began to shake both of her little hands.

"Nell!" he said, "you are very good and I thank you; and besides this I frankly say that you acted like a person of at least thirteen years."

On Stas' lips words like these were the highest praise; so the heart of the little woman was consumed with joy and pride. It seemed to her at that moment that nothing was impossible. "Wait till I grow up, then they will see!" she replied, throwing a belligerent glance in the direction of the Sudânese.

But as she did not understand the cause of the trouble and why all the Arabs rushed at Stas, the boy told her how he had determined to purloin the rifle, kill the camels, and force all to return to the river.

"If I had succeeded," he said, "we would now be free."

"But they awoke?" asked the little girl with palpitating heart.

"They did. That was caused by Saba, who came running toward me, barking loud enough to awaken the dead."

Then her indignation was directed against Saba.

"Nasty Saba! nasty! For this when he comes running up to me I won't speak a word to him and will tell him that he is horrid."

At this Stas, though he was not in a laughing mood, laughed and asked:

"How will you be able not to say a word to him and at the same time tell him he is horrid?"

Nell's eyebrows rose and her countenance reflected embarrassment, after which she said:

"He will know that from my looks."

"Perhaps. But he is not to blame, for he could not know what was happening. Remember also that afterwards he came to our rescue."

This recollection placated Nell's anger a little. She did not, however, want to grant pardon to the culprit at once.

"That is very well," she said, "but a real gentleman ought not to bark on greeting."

Stas burst out laughing again.

"Neither does a real gentleman bark on leave-taking unless he is a dog, and Saba is one."

But after a while sorrow dimmed the boy's eyes; he sighed once, then again; after which he rose from the stone on which they sat and said:

"The worst is that I could not free you."

And Nell raised herself on her little toes and threw her arms around his neck. She wanted to cheer him; she wanted, with her little nose close to his face, to whisper her gratitude, but, as she could not find appropriate words,

she only squeezed his neck yet more tightly and kissed
his ear. In the meantime Saba, always late — not so
much because he was unable to keep pace with the camels,
but because he hunted for jackals on the way, or drove
away vultures perched on the crests of rocks with his
barking — came rushing up, making his customary noise.
The children at the sight of him forgot about everything,
and notwithstanding their hard situation began their
usual caresses and play until they were interrupted by
the Arabs. Chamis gave the dog food and water, after
which all mounted the camels and started with the
greatest speed southward.

XII

IT was their longest journey, for they rode with small interruption for eighteen hours. Only real saddle-camels, having a good supply of water in their stomachs, could endure such a drive. Idris did not spare them, for he really feared the pursuit. He understood that it must have started long ago, and he assumed that both engineers would be at its head and would not lose any time. Danger threatened from the direction of the river, for it was certain that immediately after the abduction telegraphic orders were despatched to all settlements on the banks directing the sheiks to start expeditions into the interior of the desert on both sides of the Nile, and to detain all parties riding southward. Chamis assured the others that the Government and engineers must have offered a large reward for their capture and that in consequence of this the desert was undoubtedly swarming with searching parties. The only course to pursue would be to turn as far as possible to the west; but on the west lay the great oasis of Kharga, to which despatches also could reach, and besides, if they rode too far west they would lack water after a few days, and death from thirst would await them.

And the question of food became a vital one. The Bedouins in the course of the two weeks preceding the abduction of the children had placed in hiding-places, supplies of durra, biscuits, and dates, but only for a distance of four days' journey from Medinet. Idris, with fear, thought that when provisions should be lacking it would be imperatively necessary to send men to purchase supplies at the villages on the river banks, and then these men, in view of the aroused vigilance and reward offered for the capture of the fugitives, might easily fall into the hands of the local sheiks, — and betray the whole caravan. The situation was indeed difficult, almost desperate, and Idris each day perceived more plainly upon what an insane undertaking he had ventured.

"If we could only pass Assuan! If we could only pass Assuan!" he said to himself with alarm and despair in his soul. He did not indeed believe Chamis who claimed that the Mahdi's warriors had already reached Assuan, as Stas denied this.

Idris long since perceived that the white "uled" knew more than all of them. But he supposed that beyond the first cataract, where the people were wilder and less susceptible to the influences of Englishmen and the Egyptian Government, he would find more adherents of the prophet, who in a case of emergency would give them succor, and would furnish food and camels. But it was, as the Bedouins reckoned, about five days' journey to Assuan over a road which became more and more desolate, and every stop visibly diminished their supplies for man and beast.

Fortunately they could urge the camels and drive with the greatest speed, for the heat did not exhaust their strength. During daytime, at the noon hour, the sun, indeed, scorched strongly but the air was continually invigorating and the nights so cool that Stas, with the consent of Idris, changed his seat to Nell's camel, desiring to watch over her and protect her from catching cold.

But his fears were vain, as Dinah, whose eyes, or rather,

eye, improved considerably, watched with great solicitude over her little lady. The boy was even surprised that the little one's health thus far did not suffer any impairment and that she bore the journey, with ever-decreasing stops, as well as himself. Grief, fear, and the tears which she shed from longing for her papa evidently did not harm her much. Perhaps her slightly emaciated and bright little countenance was tanned by the wind, but in the later days of the journey she felt far less fatigued than at the beginning. It is true that Idris gave her the easiest carrying camel and had made an excellent saddle so that she could sleep in it lying down; nevertheless the desert air, which she breathed day and night, mainly gave her strength to endure the hardships and irregular hours.

Stas not only watched over her but intentionally surrounded her with a worship which, notwithstanding his immense attachment to his little sister, he did not at all feel for her. He observed, however, that this affected the Arabs and that they involuntarily were fortified in the conviction that they were bearing something of unheard-of value, some exceptionally important female captive, with whom it was necessary to act with the greatest possible care. Idris had been accustomed to this while at Medinet; so now all treated her well. They did not spare water and dates for her. The cruel Gebhr would not now have dared to raise his hand against her. Perhaps the extraordinarily fine stature of the little girl contributed to this, and also that there was in her something of the nature of a flower and of a bird, and this charm even the savage and undeveloped souls of the Arabs could not resist. Often also, when at a resting place she stood by the fire fed by the roses of Jericho or thorns, rosy from the flame and silvery in the moonlight, the Sudânese as well as the

Bedouins could not tear their eyes from her, smacking
their lips from admiration, according to their habit, and
murmuring:

"Allah! Mashallah! Bismillah!"

The second day at noon after that long rest, Stas and
Nell who rode this time on the same camel, had a moment
of joyful emotion. Immediately after sunrise a light and
transparent mist rose over the desert, but it soon fell.
Afterwards when the sun ascended higher, the heat became greater than during the previous days. At moments when the camels halted there could not be felt the
slightest breeze, so that the air as well as the sands seemed
to slumber in the warmth, in the light, and in the stillness. The caravan had just ridden upon a great monotonous level ground, unbroken by khors, when suddenly
a wonderful spectacle presented itself to the eyes of the
children. Groups of slender palms and pepper trees,
plantations of mandarins, white houses, a small mosque
with projecting minaret, and, lower, walls surrounding
gardens, all these appeared with such distinctness and at
distance so close that one might assume that after the
lapse of half an hour the caravan would be amid the trees
of the oasis.

"What is this?" exclaimed Stas. "Nell, Nell! Look!"

Nell rose, and for a time was silent with astonishment,
but after a while began to cry with joy:

"Medinet! to papa! to papa!"

And Stas turned pale from emotion.

"Truly — Perhaps that is Kharga — But no! That
is Medinet perhaps — I recognize the minaret and even
see the windmills above the wells — "

In fact, in the distance the highly elevated American
windmills resembling great white stars, actually glistened. On the verdant background of the trees they

could be seen so perfectly that Stas' keen sight could distinguish the borders of the vanes painted red.

"That is Medinet! —"

Stas knew from books and narratives that there were on the desert phantasms known as "fata morgana" and that sometimes travelers happen to see oases, cities, tufts of trees and lakes, which are nothing more than an illusion, a play of light, and a reflection of real distant objects. But this time the phenomenon was so distinct, so well-nigh palpable that he could not doubt that he saw the real Medinet. There was the turret upon the Mudir's house, there the circular balcony near the summit of the minaret from which the muezzin called to prayers, there that familiar group of trees, and particularly those windmills. No, — that must be the reality. It occurred to the boy that the Sudânese, reflecting upon their situation, had come to the conclusion that they could not escape and, without saying anything to him, had turned back to Fayûm. But their calmness suggested to him the first doubts. If that really was Fayûm, would they gaze upon it so indifferently? They, of course, saw the phenomenon and pointed it out to each other with their fingers, but on their faces could not be seen the least perplexity or emotion. Stas gazed yet once more and perhaps this indifference of the Arabs caused the picture to seem fainter to him. He also thought that, if in truth they were returning, the caravan would be grouped together, and the men, though only from fear, would ride in a body. But, in the meanwhile, the Bedouins, who, by Idris' order, for the past few days drove considerably in advance, could not be seen at all; while Chamis, riding as a rear guard, appeared at a distance not greater than the vulture lying on the ground.

"Fata Morgana," said Stas to himself.

In the meantime Idris approached him and shouted:

"Heigh! Speed your camel! You see Medinet!"

He evidently spoke jokingly and there was so much spite in his voice that the last hope that the real Medinet was before him vanished in the boy's heart.

And with sorrow in his heart he turned to Nell to dispel her delusion, when unexpectedly an incident occurred which drew the attention of all in another direction.

At first a Bedouin appeared, running towards them at full speed and brandishing from afar a long Arabian rifle which no one in the caravan possessed before that time. Reaching Idris, he exchanged a few hurried words with him, after which the caravan turned precipitately into the interior of the desert. But, after a time, the other Bedouin appeared leading by a rope a fat she-camel, with a saddle on its hump and leather bags hanging on its sides. A short conversation commenced, of which Stas could not catch a word. The caravan in full speed made for the west. It halted only when they chanced upon a narrow khor full of rocks scattered in wild disorder, and of fissures and caverns. One of these was so spacious that the Sudânese hid the people and camels in it. Stas, although he conjectured more or less what had happened, lay beside Idris and pretended to sleep, hoping that the Arabs, who thus far had exchanged but a few words about the occurrence, would now begin to speak about it. In fact, his hope was not disappointed, for immediately after pouring out fodder for the camels, the Bedouins and the Sudânese with Chamis sat down for a consultation.

"Henceforth we can ride only in the night; in the daytime we will have to hide!" spoke out the one-eyed Bedouin. "There will be many khors now and in each one of them we will find a safe hiding-place."

"Are you sure that he was a sentinel?" asked Idris.

"Allah! We spoke with him. Luckily there was only one. He stood hidden by a rock, so that we could not see him, but we heard from a distance the cry of his camel. Then we slackened our speed and rode up so quietly that he saw us only when we were a few paces away. He became very frightened and wanted to aim his rifle at us. If he had fired, though he might not have killed any of us, the other sentinels would have heard the shot; so, as hurriedly as possible, I yelled to him: 'Halt! we are pursuing men who kidnapped two white children, and soon the whole pursuit will be here.' The boy was young and foolish, so he believed us; only he ordered us to swear on the Koran that such was the case. We got off our camels and swore — "

"The Mahdi will absolve us — "

"And bless you," said Idris. "Speak! what did you do afterwards?"

"Now," continued the Bedouin, "when we swore, I said to the boy: 'But who can vouch that you yourself do not belong to the outlaws who are running away with the white children, and whether they did not leave you here to hold back the pursuit?' And I ordered him also to take an oath. To this he assented and this caused him to believe us all the more. We began to ask him whether any orders had come over the copper wire to the sheiks and whether a pursuit was organized. He replied: 'Yes! and told us that a great reward was offered, and that all khors at a two days' distance from the river were guarded, and that the great 'baburs' (steamers), with Englishmen and troops are continually floating over the river."

"Neither the 'baburs' nor the troops can avail against the might of Allah and the prophet — "

"May it be as you say!"

"Tell us how you finished with the boy?"

The one-eyed Bedouin pointed at his companion.

"Abu-Anga," he said, "asked him whether there was not another sentinel near-by, and the sentinel replied that there was not; then Abu-Anga thrust his knife into the sentinel's throat so suddenly that he did not utter a word. We threw him into a deep cleft and covered him with stones and thorns. In the village they will think that he ran away to the Mahdi, for he told us that this does happen."

"May God bless those who run away as he blessed you," answered Idris.

"Yes! He did bless us," retorted Abu-Anga, "for we now know that we will have to keep at a three days' distance from the river, and besides we captured a rifle which we needed and a milch she-camel."

"The gourds," added the one-eyed, "are filled with water and there is considerable millet in the sacks; but we found but little powder."

"Chamis is carrying a few hundred cartridges for the white boy's rifle, from which we cannot shoot. Powder is always the same and can be used in ours."

Saying this, Idris nevertheless pondered, and heavy anxiety was reflected in his dark face, for he understood that when once a corpse had fallen to the ground, Stas' intercession would not secure immunity for them from trial and punishment, if they should fall into the hands of the Egyptian Government.

Stas listened with palpitating heart and strained attention. In that conversation there were some comforting things, especially that a pursuit was organized, that a reward was offered, and that the sheiks of the tribes on the river banks had received orders to detain caravans going southward. The boy was comforted also by the

intelligence about steamers filled with English troops
plying on the upper river.   The dervishes of the Mahdi
might cope with the Egyptian army and even defeat it,
but it was an entirely different matter with English people,
and Stas did not doubt for a moment that the first battle
would result in the total rout of the savage multitude.
So, with comfort in his soul, he soliloquized thus: "Even
though they wish to bring us to the Mahdi, it may happen
that before we reach his camp there will not be any Mahdi
or his dervishes."   But this solace was embittered by
the thought that in such case there awaited them whole
weeks of travel, which in the end must exhaust Nell's
strength, and during all this time they would be forced
to remain in the company of knaves and murderers.   At
the recollection of that young Arab, whom the Bedouins
had butchered like a lamb, fear and sorrow beset Stas.
He decided not to speak of it to Nell in order not to
frighten her and augment the sorrow she felt after the
disappearance of the illusory picture of the oasis of
Fayûm and the city of Medinet.   He saw before their
arrival at the ravine that tears were involuntarily surging
to her eyes; therefore, when he had learned everything
which he wished to know from the Bedouins' narratives,
he pretended to awake and walked towards her.   She
sat in a corner near Dinah, eating dates, moistened a
little with her tears.   But seeing Stas, she recollected
that not long before he declared that her conduct was
worthy of a person of at least thirteen years; so, not
desiring to appear again as a child, she bit the kernel
of a date with the full strength of her little teeth, so as
to suppress her sobs.

"Nell," said the boy, "Medinet — that was an illusion,
but I know for a certainty that we are being pursued;
so don't grieve, and don't cry."

At this the little girl raised towards him her tearful
pupils and replied in a broken voice·

"No, Stas — I do not want to cry — only my eyes —
perspire so."

But at that moment her chin began to quiver; from
under her closed eyelashes big tears gushed and she wept
in earnest.

However, as she was ashamed of her tears and expected
a rebuke for them from Stas, a little from shame and a
little from fear she hid her head on his bosom, wetting
his clothes copiously.

But he at once consoled her.

"Nell, don't be a fountain. You saw that they took
away from some Arab a rifle and a she-camel. Do you
know what that means? It means that the desert is full
of soldiers. Once these wretches succeeded in trapping
a sentinel, but the next time they themselves will get
caught. A large number of steamboats are plying over
the Nile also — Why, of course, Nell, we will return. We
will return, and in a steamer to boot. Don't be afraid."

And he would have comforted her further in this manner, were not his attention attracted by a strange sound
coming from the outside, from the sand-drifts, which
the hurricane blew onto the bottom of the ravine. It
was something resembling the thin, metallic notes of a
reed pipe. Stas broke off the conversation and began
to listen. After a while these very thin and mournful
sounds came from many sides simultaneously. Through
the boy's mind the thought flashed that these might be
Arabian guards surrounding the ravine and summoning
aid with whistles. His heart began to beat. He glanced
once and again at the Sudânese, hoping that he would
behold consternation on their faces; but no! Idris,
Gebhr and the two Bedouins calmly chewed biscuits, only

Chamis appeared a little surprised. The sounds continued. After a while Idris rose and looked out of the cavern; returning, he stopped near the children, and said:

"The sands are beginning to sing."

Stas' curiosity was so aroused that he forgot that he had determined not to speak to Idris any more and asked:

"Sands? What does it mean?"

"It happens thus, and means that for a long time there will be no rain. But the heat will not distress us, since as far as Assuan we will ride only during the night."

And no more could be learned from him. Stas and Nell listened long to these peculiar sounds which continued until the sun descended in the west, after which night fell and the caravan started on its further journey.

XIII

In the daytime they hid in places concealed and difficult
of access, amid rocks and chasms, and during the night
they hurried, without respite, until they passed the First
Cataract. When finally the Bedouins discerned from
the situation and form of the khors that Assuan was
behind them, a great burden fell off Idris' breast. As
they suffered already from want of water they drew
nearer to the river a half day's distance. There Idris,
concealing the caravan, sent all the camels with the Bedouins to the Nile in order to water them well and for a
longer time. Beyond Assuan the fertile belt along the
river was narrower. In some places the desert reached
the river; the villages lay at a considerable distance
from each other. The Bedouins, therefore, returned
successfully, unseen by any one, with a considerable
supply of water. It was necessary now to think of provisions. As the animals had been fed sparingly during
the past week they grew lean; their necks lengthened,
their humps sank, and their legs became weak. The
durra and the supplies for the people, with the greatest
stint, would suffice for two days more. Idris thought,
however, that they might, if not during daytime then
at night, approach the pastures on the river banks and
perhaps buy biscuits and dates in some village. Saba
already was given nothing at all to eat or drink, and
the children hid leavings of food for him, but he somehow

managed to take care of himself and came running to the
stopping places with bleeding jaws and marks of bites
on his neck and breast. Whether the victim of these
fights was a jackal, or a hyena, or perhaps a desert fox
or a gazelle no one knew; it was enough that there were
no signs of great hunger on him. At times also his black
lips were moist as if he drank. The Bedouins surmised
that he must have dug deep holes at the bottom of the
ravines, and in this manner reached water which he
scented under the ground. In this manner travelers
who get lost dig the bottoms of chasms and, if they do
not often find water, they almost always reach damp
sand and, sucking it, cheat in this way the pangs of thirst.
In Saba, however, considerable changes took place. He
still had a powerful breast and neck, but his sides were
sunken, through which he appeared taller. In his eyes,
about the reddened whites, there was now something
savage and threatening. To Nell and to Stas he was
as attached as previously and permitted them to do with
him whatever they pleased. He still at times wagged
his tail at Chamis, but he growled at the Bedouins and
Sudânese or snapped with his terrible teeth, which at
such times clashed against each other like steel nails.
Idris and Gebhr plainly began to fear and hate him to
the extent that they would have killed him with the
captured rifle, were it not that they desired to bring this
extraordinary animal to Smain, and were it not also that
they had already passed Assuan.

They had passed Assuan! Stas thought of this continually, and doubt that the pursuit would ever overtake
them stole gradually into his soul. He knew, indeed, that
not only Egypt proper, which ends at Wâdi Halfa, that
is, at the Second Cataract, but the whole of Nubia was
up to that time in the hands of the Egyptian Government,

but he also understood that beyond Assuan and particularly Wâdi Halfa the pursuit would be more difficult and the commands of the Government would be executed carelessly. His only hope was that his father with Mr. Rawlinson, after making arrangements for the pursuit from Fayûm, would go to Wâdi Halfa by steamer, and there securing troops of the camel-corps, would endeavor to intercept the caravan from the south. The boy reasoned that if he were in their place he would do just this, and for that reason he assumed that his supposition was very probable.

He did not, however, abandon the thought of a rescue on his own account. The Sudânese wanted to have powder for the captured rifle and with this object decided to disjoin a score of the rifle cartridges, so he told them that he alone was able to do that, and that if any one of them should undertake the task unskilfully, the cartridge would explode in his fingers and tear off his hands. Idris, fearing English inventions and unknown things generally, determined finally to entrust the boy with this undertaking. Stas went at it willingly, hoping in the first place that the powerful English powder at the first shot would burst the old Arabian rifle to pieces, and, again, that he might be able to hide a few cartridges. In fact, he succeeded more easily than he expected. Apparently they watched him at the work, but the Arabs began at once to talk among themselves and soon they were more occupied with their conversation than with their supervision. Finally this loquacity and inbred carelessness permitted Stas to conceal in his bosom seven cartridges. Now all that was necessary was to secure the rifle.

The boy judged that beyond Wâdi Halfa, the Second Cataract, this would not be a very difficult matter as he

foresaw that as they drew nearer to their destination
the Arabs' vigilance would relax.   The thought that he
would have to kill the Sudânese, the Bedouins, and even
Chamis, always caused him to shudder, but after the
murder which the Bedouins had committed, he did not
have any scruples.   He said to himself that the defense,
liberty, and life of Nell were involved, and in view of this
the lives of his adversaries did not deserve any consideration, especially if they did not surrender and it came to
a fight.

But he was anxious about the short rifle.   Stas resolved
to secure it by stratagem, whenever the opportunity presented itself, and not to wait until they reached Wâdi
Halfa, but perform the deed as soon as possible.

Accordingly he did not wait.

Two days had elapsed since they passed Assuan, and
Idris finally at the dawn of the third day was forced to
despatch the Bedouins for provisions, which were totally
lacking.   In view of the diminished number of adversaries
Stas said to himself: "Now or never!" and immediately
turned to the Sudânese with the following question:

"Idris, do you know that the country which begins
not far beyond Wâdi Halfa is really Nubia?"

"I know.   I was fifteen years old and Gebhr eight,
when my father took us from the Sudân to Fayûm, and I
remember that we rode at that time on camels over the
whole of Nubia.   But this country belongs still to the
Turks (Egyptians)."

"Yes.   The Mahdi is only before Khartûm and you
see how foolishly Chamis chattered when he told you
that the army of dervishes reached as far as Assuan.
However, I shall ask you something else.   Now I have
read that in Nubia there are many wild animals and
many brigands who do not serve any one and who attack

alike the Egyptians and the faithful Mahdists. With
what will you defend yourself, if wild animals or brigands
attack you?"

Stas purposely exaggerated in speaking of wild animals,
but, on the other hand, highway robberies in Nubia,
from the time of the war, occurred quite frequently,
particularly in the southern part of the country bordering
upon the Sudân.

Idris pondered for a while over the question, which
surprised him, as heretofore he had not thought of these
new dangers, and replied:

"We have knives and a rifle."

"Such a rifle is good for nothing."

"I know. Yours is better, but we do not know how
to shoot from it, and we will not place it in your hands."

"Even unloaded?"

"Yes, for it may be bewitched."

Stas shrugged his shoulders.

"Idris, if Gebhr said that, I would not be surprised,
but I thought that you had more sense. From an unloaded
rifle even your Mahdi could not fire —"

"Silence!" interrupted Idris sternly. "The Mahdi is
able to fire even from his finger."

"Then you also can fire in that way."

The Sudânese looked keenly into the boy's eyes.

"Why do you want me to give you the rifle?"

"I want to teach you how to fire from it."

"Why should that concern you?"

"A great deal, for if the brigands attack us they might
kill us all. But if you are afraid of the rifle and of me
then it does not matter."

Idris was silent. In reality he was afraid, but did not
want to admit it. He was anxious, however, to get acquainted with the English weapon, for its possession and

skill in its use would increase his importance in the
Mahdists' camp, to say nothing of the fact that it
would be easier for him to defend himself in case of an
attack.

So after a brief consideration he said:

"Good. Let Chamis hand you the rifle-case and you
can take it out."

Chamis indifferently performed the order, which Gebhr
could not oppose, as he was occupied at some distance
with the camels. Stas with quivering hands took out the
stock and afterwards the barrels, and handed them to
Idris.

"You see they are empty."

Idris took the barrels and peered upwards through
them.

"Yes, there is nothing in them,"

"Now observe," said Stas. "This is the way to put a
rifle together" (and saying this he united the barrel and
stock). "This is the way to open it. Do you see? I
will take it apart again and you can put it together."

The Sudânese, who watched Stas' motions with great
attention, tried to imitate him. At first it was not easy
for him, but as Arabians are well known for their skil-
fulness, the rifle, after a while, was put together.

"Open!" commanded Stas.

Idris opened the rifle easily.

"Close."

This was done yet more easily.

"Now give me two empty shells. I will teach you how
to load the cartridges."

The Arabs had kept the empty cartridges as they had
a value for them as brass; so Idris handed two of them
to Stas and the instruction began anew.

The Sudânese at first was frightened a little by the

crack of the caps of the shells, but finally became convinced that no one was able to fire from empty barrels
and empty shells. In addition, his trust in Stas returned
because the boy handed the weapon to him every little
while.

"Yes," said Stas, "you already know how to put a
rifle together, you know how to open, to close, and to
pull the trigger. But now it is necessary for you to learn
to aim. That is the most difficult thing. Take that
empty water gourd and place it at a hundred paces —
on those stones, and afterwards return to me; I will
show you how to aim."

Idris took the gourd and without the slightest hesitation walked to the place by the stones which Stas had
indicated. But before he made the first hundred steps,
Stas extracted the empty shells and substituted loaded
cartridges. Not only his heart but the arteries in his
temples began to throb with such a force that he thought
that his head would burst. The decisive moment arrived
— the moment of freedom for Nell and himself — the
moment of victory — terrible and at the same time
desirable.

Now Idris' life was in his hands. One pull of the trigger and the traitor who had kidnapped Nell would fall
a corpse. But Stas, who had in his veins both Polish
and French blood, suddenly felt that for nothing in the
world could he be capable of shooting a man in the back.
Let him at least turn around and face death in the eye.
And after that, what? After that, Gebhr would come
rushing up, and before he ran ten paces he also would
bite the dust. Chamis would remain. But Chamis would
lose his head, and even though he should not lose it, there
would be time to insert new cartridges in the barrels.
When the Bedouins arrived, they would find three corpses,

and meet a fate they richly deserved. After that he would
only have to guide the camels to the river.

All these thoughts and pictures flew like a whirlwind
through Stas' brain. He felt that what was to happen
after a few minutes was at the same time horrible and imperative. The pride of a conqueror surged in his breast
with a feeling of aversion for the dreadful deed. There
was a moment when he hesitated, but he recalled the
tortures which the white prisoners endured; he recalled
his father, Mr. Rawlinson, Nell, also Gebhr, who struck
the little girl with a courbash, and hatred burst out in
him with renewed force. "It is necessary!" he said through
his set teeth, and inflexible determination was reflected
on his countenance, which became as if carved out of
stone.

In the meantime Idris placed the gourd on a stone
about a hundred paces distant and turned around. Stas
saw his smiling face and his whole tall form upon the
plain. For the last time the thought flashed through his
mind that this living man would fall after a moment upon
the ground, clutching the sand with his fingers in the last
convulsions of the throes of death. But the hesitation
of the boy ended, and when Idris sauntered fifty paces
toward him, he began slowly to raise the weapon to his
eye.

But before he touched the trigger with his finger, from
beyond the dunes, about a few hundred paces distant,
could be heard tumultuous cheers, and in the same minute
about twenty riders on horses and camels debouched on
the plain. Idris became petrified at the sight. Stas was
amazed no less, but at once amazement gave way to insane joy. The expected pursuit at last! Yes! That
could not be anything else. Evidently the Bedouins had
been captured in a village and were showing where the

rest of the caravan was concealed! Idris thought the same. When he collected himself he ran to Stas, with face ashen from terror, and, kneeling at his feet, began to repeat in a voice out of breath:

"Sir, I was kind to you! I was kind to the little 'bint'! Remember that!"

Stas mechanically extracted the cartridges from the barrels and gazed. The riders drove horses and camels at the fullest speed, shouting from joy and flinging upwards their long Arabian rifles, which they caught while in full gallop with extraordinary dexterity. In the bright transparent air they could be seen perfectly. In the middle, at the van, ran the two Bedouins waving their hands and burnooses as if possessed.

After a few minutes the whole band dashed to the caravan. Some of the riders leaped off the horses and camels; some remained on their saddles, yelling at the top of their voices. Amid these shouts only two words could be distinguished.

"Khartûm! Gordon! Gordon! Khartûm!"

Finally one of the Bedouins — the one whom his companion called Abu-Anga — ran up to Idris cringing at Stas' feet, and began to exclaim:

"Khartûm is taken! Gordon is killed! The Mahdi is victorious!"

Idris stood erect but did not yet believe his ears.

"And these men?" he asked with quivering lips.

"These men were to seize us, but now are going together with us to the prophet."

Stas' head swam.

XIV

It was evident that the last hope of escaping during the journey had become extinct. Stas now knew that his schemes would avail nothing; that the pursuit would not overtake them, and that if they endured the hardships of the journey they would reach the Mahdi and would be surrendered to Smain. The only consolation now was the thought that they were kidnapped so that Smain might exchange them for his children. But when would that happen, and what would they encounter before that time? What dreadful misfortune awaited them among the savage hordes intoxicated with blood? Would Nell be able to endure all these fatigues and privations?

This no one could answer. On the other hand, it was known that the Mahdi and his dervishes hated Christians, and Europeans in general; so in the soul of the boy there was bred a fear that the influence of Smain might not be sufficient to shield them from indignities, from rough treatment, from the cruelties and the rage of the Mahdist believers, who even murdered Mohammedans loyal to the Government. For the first time since the abduction deep despair beset the boy, and at the same time some kind of vague notion that an untoward fate was persecuting them. Why, the idea itself of abducting them from Fayûm and conveying them to Khartûm was sheer madness which could be

committed only by such wild and foolish men as Idris
and Gebhr, not understanding that they would have
to traverse thousands of kilometers over a country subject to the Egyptian Government or, more properly,
English people. With proper methods they ought to
have been caught on the second day, and nevertheless
everything combined so that now they were not far from
the Second Cataract and none of the preceding pursuing
parties had overtaken them, and the last one which
could have detained them joined the kidnappers and,
from this time, would aid them. To Stas' despair,
to his fears about little Nell's fate, was linked a feeling
of humiliation that he was unequal to the situation and,
what was more, was unable now to devise anything, for
even if they returned the rifle and cartridges to him,
he could not, of course, shoot all the Arabs composing
the caravan.

And he was gnawed all the more by these thoughts because deliverance had been already so near. If Khartûm
had not fallen, or if it had fallen only a few days later,
these same men, who went over to the side of the Mahdi,
would have seized their captors and delivered them to
the Government. Stas, sitting on the camel behind Idris
and listening to their conversation, became convinced
that this undoubtedly would have happened. For,
immediately after they proceeded upon their further
journey, the leader of the pursuing party began to relate
to Idris what induced them to commit treason to the
Khedive. They knew previously that a great army —
not an Egyptian now but an English one — had started
southward against the dervishes under the command
of General Wolseley. They saw a multitude of steamers,
which carried formidable English soldiers from Assuan
to Wâdi Halfa, from whence a railroad was built for them

to Abu Hâmed. For a long time all the sheiks on the
river banks, — those who remained loyal to the Government as well as those who in the depth of their souls
favored the Mahdi, — were certain that the destruction
of the dervishes and their prophet was inevitable, for
no one had ever vanquished the Englishmen.

"Akbar Allah!" interrupted Idris, raising his hands
upwards. "Nevertheless, they have been vanquished."

"No," replied the leader of the pursuing party. "The
Mahdi sent against them the tribes of Jaalin, Barabra,
and Janghey, nearly thirty thousand in all of his best
warriors, under the command of Musa, the son of Helu.
At Abu Klea a terrible battle took place in which God
awarded the victory to the unbelievers. — Yes, it is so.
Musa, the son of Helu, fell, and of his soldiers only a
handful returned to the Mahdi. The souls of the others
are in Paradise, while their bodies lie upon the sands,
awaiting the day of resurrection. News of this spread
rapidly over the Nile. Then we thought that the English
would go farther south and relieve Khartûm. The people repeated, 'The end! the end!' And in the meantime
God disposed otherwise."

"How? What happened?" asked Idris feverishly.

"What happened?" said the leader with a brightened
countenance. "Why, in the meantime the Mahdi captured
Khartûm, and during the assault Gordon's head was cut
off. And as the Englishmen were concerned only about
Gordon, learning of his death, they returned to the north.
Allah! We again saw the steamers with the stalwart
soldiers floating down the river, but did not understand
what it meant. The English publish good news immediately and suppress bad. Some of our people said that
the Mahdi had already perished. But finally the truth
came to the surface. This region belongs yet to the

Government. In Wâdi Halfa and farther, as far as
the Third and perhaps the Fourth Cataract, the soldiers
of the Khedive can be found; nevertheless, after the
retirement of the English troops, we believe now that the
Mahdi will subdue not only Nubia and Egypt, not only
Mecca and Medina, but the whole world. For that reason
instead of capturing you and delivering you to the hands
of the Government we are going together with you to
the prophet."

"So orders came to capture us?"

"To all the villages, to all the sheiks, to the military
garrisons. Wherever the copper wire, over which fly the
commands of the Khedive, does not reach, there came
the 'zabdis' (gendarmes) with the announcement that
whoever captures you will receive one thousand pounds
reward. Mashallah! — That is great wealth! — Great!"

Idris glanced suspiciously at the speaker.

"But you prefer the blessing of the Mahdi?"

"Yes. He captured such immense booty and so
much money in Khartûm that he measures the Egyptian
pounds in fodder sacks and distributes them among his
faithful — "

"Nevertheless, if the Egyptian troops are yet in Wâdi
Halfa, and further, they may seize us on the way."

"No. It is necessary only to hurry before they recover their wits. Now since the retreat of the Englishmen they have lost their heads entirely — the sheiks,
the loyal to the Government, as well as the soldiers and
'zabdis.' All think that the Mahdi at any moment will
arrive; for that reason those of us who in our souls favored
him are now running to him boldly, and nobody is pursuing us, for in the first moments no one is issuing orders
and no one knows whom to obey."

"Yes," replied Idris, "you say truly that it is necessary

to hurry, before they recover their wits, since Khartûm is yet far — "

For an instant a faint gleam of hope glimmered again for Stas. If the Egyptian soldiers up to that time occupied various localities on the banks in Nubia, then in view of the fact that the English troops had taken all the steamers, they would have to retreat before the Mahdi's hordes by land. In such case it might happen that the caravan would encounter some retreating detachment and might be surrounded. Stas reckoned also that before the news of the capture of Khartûm circulated among the Arabian tribes north of Wâdi Halfa, considerable time would elapse; the more so as the Egyptian Government and the English people suppressed it. He therefore assumed that the panic which must have prevailed among the Egyptians in the first moment must have already passed away. To the inexperienced boy it never occurred that in any event the downfall of Khartûm and the death of Gordon would cause people to forget about everything else, and that the sheiks loyal to the Government as well as the local authorities would now have something else to do than to think of rescuing two white children.

And in fact the Arabs who joined the caravan did not fear the pursuit very much. They rode with great haste and did not spare the camels, but they kept close to the Nile and often during the night turned to the river to water the animals and to fill the leather bags with water. At times they ventured to ride to villages even in daytime. For safety they sent in advance for scouting a few men who, under the pretext of buying provisions, inquired for news of the locality; whether there were any Egyptian troops near-by and whether the inhabitants belonged to "the loyal Turks." If they met residents secretly favoring the Mahdi, then the entire caravan would visit the village, and often it happened that it was increased by a few or even a dozen or more young Arabs who also wanted to fly to the Mahdi.

Idris learned also that almost all the Egyptian detachments were stationed on the side of the Nubian Desert, therefore on the right, the eastern side of the Nile. In order to avoid an encounter with them it was necessary only to keep to the left bank and to pass by the larger cities and settlements. This indeed lengthened their route a great deal, for the river, beginning at Wâdi Halfa, forms a gigantic arch inclining far towards the south and afterwards again curving to the northeast as far as Abu Hâmed, where it takes a direct southern course, but on the other hand this left bank, particularly from the Oasis of Selimeh, was left almost entirely unguarded. The journey passed merrily for the Sudânese in an increased company with an abundance of water and supplies. Passing the Third Cataract, they ceased even to hurry, and rode only at night, hiding during the day among sandy hills and ravines with which the whole desert was intersected. A cloudless sky now extended over them, gray at the horizon's edges, bulging in the center like a gigantic cupola, silent and calm. With each day, however, the heat, in proportion to their southward advance, became more and more terrible, and even in the ravines, in the deep shade, it distressed the people and the beasts. On the other hand, the nights were very cool; they scintillated with twinkling stars which formed, as it were, greater and smaller clusters. Stas observed that they were not the same constellations which shone at night over Port Said. At times he had dreamed of seeing sometime in his life the Southern Cross, and finally beheld it beyond El-Ordeh. But at present its luster pro-

claimed to him his own misfortune. For a few nights
there shone for him the pale, scattered, and sad zodiacal
light, which, after the waning of the evening twilight, silvered until a late hour the western side of the
sky.

XV

In two weeks after starting from the neighborhood of Wâdi Halfa the caravan entered upon the region subdued by the Mahdi. They speedily crossed the hilly Jesira Desert, and near Shendi, where previously the English forces had completely routed Musa, Uled of Helu, they rode into a locality entirely unlike the desert. Neither sands nor dunes could be seen here. As far as the eye could reach stretched a steppe overgrown in part by green grass and in part by a jungle amid which grew clusters of thorny acacias, yielding the well-known Sudânese gum; while here and there stood solitary gigantic nabbuk trees, so expansive that under their boughs a hundred people could find shelter from the sun. From time to time the caravan passed by high, pillar-like hillocks of termites or white ants, with which tropical Africa is strewn. The verdure of the pasture and the acacias agreeably charmed the eyes after the monotonous, tawny-hued sands of the desert.

In the places where the steppe was a meadow, herds of camels pastured, guarded by the armed warriors of the Mahdi. At the sight of the caravan they started up suddenly, like birds of prey; rushed towards it, surrounded it from all sides; and shaking their spears and at the same time yelling at the top of their voices they asked the men from whence they came, why they were going southward, and whither they were bound? At times they assumed such a threatening attitude that Idris was compelled to reply to their questions in the greatest haste in order to avoid attack.

Stas, who had imagined that the inhabitants of the Sudân differed from other Arabs residing in Egypt only in this, that they believed in the Mahdi and did not want to acknowledge the authority of the Khedive, perceived that he was totally mistaken. The greater part of those who every little while stopped the caravan had skins darker than even Idris and Gebhr, and in comparison with the two Bedouins were almost black. The negro blood in them predominated over the Arabian. Their faces and breasts were tattooed and the prickings represented various designs, or inscriptions from the Koran. Some were almost naked; others wore "jubhas" or wrappers of cotton texture sewed out of patches of various colors. A great many had twigs of coral or pieces of ivory in their pierced nostrils, lips and ears. The heads of the leaders were covered with caps of the same texture as the wrappers, and the heads of common warriors were bare, but not shaven like those of the Arabs in Egypt. On the contrary, they were covered with enormous twisted locks, often singed red with lime, with which they rubbed their tufts of hair for protection against vermin. Their weapons were mainly spears, terrible in their hands; but they did not lack Remington carbines which they had captured in their victorious battles with the Egyptian army and after the fall of Khartûm. The sight of them was terrifying and their behavior toward the caravan was hostile, for they suspected that it consisted of Egyptian traders, whom the Mahdi, in the first moments after the victory, prohibited from entering the Sudân.

Having surrounded the caravan, they pointed the spears with tumult and menace at the breasts of the

people, or aimed carbines at them. To this hostile
demonstration Idris answered with a shout that he and
his brother belonged to the Dongolese tribe, the same
as that of the Mahdi, and that they were conveying to the prophet two white children as slaves; this
alone restrained the savages from violence. In Stas,
when he came in contact with this dire reality, the spirit
withered at the thought of what awaited them on the
ensuing days. Idris, also, who previously had lived long
years in a civilized community, had never imagined anything like this. He was pleased when one night they
were surrounded by an armed detachment of the Emir
Nur el-Tadhil and conducted to Khartûm.

Nur el-Tadhil, before he ran away to the Mahdi, was
an Egyptian officer in a negro regiment of the Khedive:
so he was not so savage as the other Mahdists and Idris
could more easily make himself understood. But here
disappointment awaited him. He imagined that his arrival at the Mahdi's camp with the white children would
excite admiration, if only on account of the extraordinary
hardships and dangers of the journey. He expected that
the Mahdists would receive him with ardor, with open
arms, and lead him in triumph to the prophet, who would
lavish gold and praises upon him as a man who had not
hesitated to expose his head in order to serve his relative,
Fatma. In the meantime the Mahdists placed spears at
the breasts of members of the caravan, and Nur el-Tadhil
heard quite indifferently his narrative of the journey,
and finally to the question, whether he knew Smain, the
husband of Fatma, answered:

"No. In Omdurmân and Khartûm there are over one
hundred thousand warriors, so it is easy not to meet one
another, and not all the officers are acquainted with each
other. The domain of the prophet is immense; therefore

many emirs rule in distant cities in Sennâr, in Kordofân, and Darfur, and around Fashoda. It may be that this Smain, of whom you speak, is not at present at the prophet's side."

Idris was nettled by the slighting tone with which Nur spoke of "this Smain," so he replied with a shade of impatience:

"Smain is married to a first cousin of the Mahdi, and therefore Smain's children are relatives of the prophet."

Nur el-Tadhil shrugged his shoulders.

"The Mahdi has many relatives and cannot remember all of them."

For some time they rode in silence; after which Idris again asked:

"How soon shall we arrive at Khartûm?"

"Before midnight," replied el-Tadhil, gazing at the stars which began to appear in the eastern part of the heavens.

"Shall we at that late hour be able to obtain food and fodder? Since our last rest at noon we have not eaten anything."

"You will pass this night with me and I shall feed you in my house, but to-morrow in Omdurmân you will have to seek for food yourself, and I warn you in advance that this will not be an easy matter."

"Why?"

"Because we have a war. The people for the past few years have not tilled the fields and have lived solely upon meat; so when finally cattle were lacking, famine came. There is famine in all the Sudân, and a sack of durra to-day costs more than a slave."

"Allah akbar!" exclaimed Idris with surprise, "I saw nevertheless herds of camels and cattle on the steppes."

"They belong to the prophet, to the 'Noble,'[1] and to

[1] The Noble — brothers and relatives of the Mahdi.

the caliphs. — Yes — The Dongolese, from which tribe the Mahdi came and the Baggara, whose leader is the chief caliph, Abdullahi, have still quite numerous herds, but for other tribes it has become more and more difficult to live in the world."

Here Nur el-Tadhil patted his stomach, and said:

"In the service of the prophet I have a higher rank, more money, and a greater authority, but I had a fuller stomach in the Khedive's service."

But, realizing that he might have said too much, after a while he added:

"But all this will change when the true faith conquers."

Idris, hearing these words, involuntarily thought that nevertheless in Fayûm, in the service of the Englishmen, he had never suffered from hunger, and gains could be more easily secured; so he was cast into a deep gloom.

After which he began to ask further:

"Are you going to transport us to-morrow to Omdurmân?"

"Yes. Khartûm by command of the prophet is to be abandoned and very few reside there. They are razing the large buildings and conveying the bricks with the other booty to Omdurmân. The prophet does not wish to live in a place polluted by unbelievers."

"I shall beat my forehead before him to-morrow, and he will command that I be supplied with provisions and fodder."

"Ha! If in truth you belong to the Dongolese, then perhaps you might be admitted to his presence. But know this, that his house is guarded day and night by a hundred men equipped with courbashes, and these do not spare blows to those who crave to see the Mahdi without permission. Otherwise the swarm would not

give the holy man a moment of rest — Allah! I saw even
Dongolese with bloody welts on their backs — "

Idris with each moment was possessed by greater
disillusionment.

"So the faithful do not see the prophet?" he asked.

"The faithful see him daily at the place of prayer
where, kneeling on the sheep's hide, he raises his hands
to God, or when he instructs the swarm and strengthens
them in the true faith. But it is difficult to reach and
speak with him, and whoever attains that happiness is
envied by all, for upon him flows the divine grace which
wipes away his former sins."

A deep night fell and with it came a piercing chill.
In the ranks resounded the snorting of horses; the sudden
change from the daily heat to cold was so strong that
the hides of the steeds began to reek, and the detachment
rode as if in a mist. Stas, behind Idris, leaned towards
Nell and asked:

"Do you feel cold?"

"No," answered the little girl, "but no one will protect
us now — "

And tears stifled her further words.

This time he did not find any comfort for her, for he
himself was convinced that there was no salvation for
them. Now they rode over a region of wretchedness,
famine, bestial cruelties, and blood. They were like
two poor little leaves in a storm which bore death and
annihilation not only to the heads of individuals, but
to whole towns and entire tribes. What hand could
snatch from it and save two small, defenseless children?

The moon rolled high in the heaven and changed, as
if into silvery feathers, the mimosa and acacia twigs. In
th edense jungles resounded here and there the shrill
and, at the same time. mockingly mirthful laugh of the

hyenas, which in that gory region found far too many corpses. From time to time the detachment conducting the caravan encountered other patrols and exchanged with them the agreed countersign. They came to the hills on the river banks and through a long pass reached the Nile. The people and the camels embarked upon wide and flat "dahabeahs," and soon the heavy oars began with measured movements to break and ruffle the smooth river's depth, strewn with starry diamonds.

After the lapse of half an hour, on the southern side, on which dahabeahs floated upon the water, flashed lights which, as crafts approached them, changed into sheaves of red luster lying on the water. Nur el-Tadhil shook Idris' arm, after which, stretching out his hand before him, he said:

"Khartûm!"

XVI

THEY stopped at the city's limits in a house which
formerly was the property of a rich Italian merchant,
and after his murder during the assault upon the city, had
fallen to Tadhil at the division of the spoils. The wives
of the emir in quite a humane manner took charge of
Nell who was barely alive after the rough treatment, and,
though in all Khartûm could be felt a want of provisions,
they found for the little "jan"[1] a few dried dates and
a little rice with honey; after which they led her upstairs
and put her to bed. Stas, who passed the night among
the camels and horses in the courtyard, had to be content with one biscuit; on the other hand, he did not
lack water, for the fountain in the garden, by a strange
chance, was not wrecked. Notwithstanding great weari-
ness, he could not sleep; first on account of scorpions
creeping incessantly over the saddle-cloth on which he
lay, and again on account of a mortal dread that they
would separate him from Nell, and that he would not
be able to watch over her personally. This uneasiness was
evidently shared by Saba, who scented about and from time
to time howled, all of which enraged the soldiers. Stas
quieted him as well as he could from fear that some injury might be done to him. Fortunately the giant mastiff
aroused such admiration in the emir himself and in all
the dervishes that no one lifted a hand against him.

[1] "Jan," an expression of endearment, like "little lamb."

Idris also did not sleep. From the previous day he had felt unwell and, besides, after the conversation with Nur el-Tadhil he lost many of his delusions, and gazed at the future as though through a thick veil. He was glad that on the morrow they would be transported to Omdurmân, which was separated from Khartûm only by the width of the White Nile; he had a hope that he would find Smain there, but what further? During the journey everything had presented itself to him somewhat more distinctly and far more splendidly. He sincerely believed in the prophet and his heart was drawn all the more to him because both came from the same tribe. But in addition he was, like almost every Arab, covetous and ambitious. He had dreamed that he would be loaded with gold and made an emir at least; he had dreamed of military expeditions against the "Turks," of captured cities and spoils. Now, after what he had heard from el-Tadhil, he began to fear whether in the presence of far greater events, all his acts would not fade into insignificance, just as a drop of rain disappears in the sea. "Perhaps," he thought with bitterness, "nobody will pay attention to what I have accomplished, and Smain will not even be pleased that I have brought those children to him;" and he was gnawed by this thought. The morrow was to dispel or confirm those fears; so he awaited it with impatience.

The sun rose at six o'clock, and the bustle among the dervishes began. Nur el-Tadhil soon appeared and ordered them to prepare for the journey. He declared at the same time that they would go to the ferry on foot, beside his horse. To Stas' great joy, Dinah led Nell from an upper floor; after which they proceeded on the rampart, skirting the whole city, as far as the place at which the ferry boats stopped. Nur el-Tadhil rode ahead on horseback. Stas escorted Nell by the hand; after them came Idris, Gebhr, and Chamis, with Dinah and Saba, as well as thirty of the emir's soldiers. The rest of the caravan remained in Khartûm.

Stas, gazing around, could not understand how a city so strongly fortified, and lying in a fork formed by the White and Blue Niles, and therefore surrounded on three sides by water and accessible only from the south, could fall. Only later did he learn from a Christian slave that the river at that time had subsided and left a wide sandy strip, which facilitated access to the ramparts. The garrison, losing hope of relief and reduced by hunger, could not repel the assault of the infuriated savages, and the city was captured; after which a massacre of the inhabitants took place. Traces of the battle, though a month had already elapsed since the assault, could everywhere be seen along the ramparts; on the inside protruded the ruins of razed buildings against which the first impetus of the victors had been directed and on the outside the moat was full of corpses, which no one thought of burying. Before they reached the ferry Stas counted over four hundred. They did not, however, infect the air as the Sudânese sun dried them up like mummies; all had the hue of gray parchment, and were so much alike that the bodies of the Europeans, Egyptians, and negroes could not be distinguished from each other. Amid the corpses swarmed small gray lizards, which, at the approach of men, quickly hid under those human remains and often in the mouths or between the dried-up ribs.

Stas walked with Nell in such a manner as to hide this horrible sight from her, and told her to look in the direction of the city.

But from the side of the city many things transpired which struck the eyes and soul of the little girl with terror. The sight of the "English" children, taken into captivity, and of Saba led with a leash by Chamis attracted a throng, which as the procession proceeded to the ferry increased with each moment. The throng after a certain time became so great that it was necessary to halt. From all sides came threatening outcries. Frightfully tattooed faces leaned over Stas and over Nell. Some of the savages burst out into laughter at the sight of them and from joy slapped their hips with the palms of their hands; others cursed them; some roared like wild beasts, displaying their white teeth and rolling their eyes; finally they began to threaten and reach out towards them with knives. Nell, partly unconscious from fright, clung to Stas, while he shielded her as well as he knew how, in the conviction that their last hour was approaching. Fortunately this persistent molestation of the brutal swarm at last disgusted even Nur el-Tadhil. By his command between ten and twenty soldiers surrounded the children, while the others began, without mercy, to scourge the howling mob with courbashes. The concourse dispersed hurriedly, but on the other hand a mob began to gather behind the detachment and amid wild shrieks accompanied it to the boat.

The children breathed more freely during the passage over the river. Stas comforted Nell with the statement that when the dervishes became accustomed to the sight of them they would cease their threats, and he assured her that Smain would protect and defend both of them, and particularly her, for if any evil should befall them he would not have any one to exchange for his children. This was the truth, but the little girl was so terror-stricken by the previous assaults that, having seized Stas' hand, she did not want to let go of it for a moment, repeating continually, as if in a fever: "I am afraid! I am afraid!"

He with his whole soul wished to get as soon as possible
into the hands of Smain, who knew them of old, and
who in Port Said had displayed great friendship towards
them, or at least had pretended to display it.   At any rate
he was not so wild as the other Dongolese of the Sudân,
and captivity in his house would be more endurable.

The only concern now was whether they would find
him in Omdurmân.   Of this Idris spoke with Nur el-
Tadhil, who at last recollected that a year before, while
tarrying by the order of the caliph Abdullahi in Kordofân,
far from Khartûm, he had heard of a certain Smain,
who taught the dervishes how to fire from the cannons
captured from the Egyptians, and afterwards became a
slave hunter.   Nur suggested to Idris the following
method of finding him:

"At noon, when you hear the sounds of the umbajas,[1]
be with the children at the place of prayer, to which the
Mahdi repairs daily to edify the faithful with an example
of piety and to fortify them in the faith.   There besides
the sacred person of the Mahdi you will behold all the
'Nobles' and also the three caliphs as well as the pashas
and emirs; among the emirs you may find Smain."

"But what am I to do and where shall I stay until
the time of the afternoon prayer?"

"You will remain with my soldiers."

"And will you, Nur el-Tadhil, leave us?"

"I am going for orders to the caliph Abdullahi "

"Is he the greatest of caliphs?   I come from far and
though the names of the commanders have reached my
ears, nevertheless you may instruct me more definitely
about them."

"Abdullahi my commander is the Mahdi's sword."

"May Allah make him the son of victory."

[1] Umbajas — big trumpets of ivory tusk.

For some time the boat floated in silence. There could be heard only the grating of the oars on the boat's edges and once in a while a splash of water by a crocodile struck in the tail. Many of these ugly reptiles had swam down from the south to Khartûm, where they found an abundance of food, for the river teemed with corpses, not only of the people who were slaughtered after the capture of the city, but also of those who died of diseases which raged amidst the Mahdists and particularly among the slaves. The commands of the caliphs prohibited, indeed, "the contamination of the water," but they were not heeded, and the bodies which the crocodiles did not devour floated with the water, face downward, to the Sixth Cataract and even as far as Beber.

But Idris thought of something else, and after a while said:

"This morning we did not get anything to eat. I do not know whether we can hold out from hunger until the hour of prayer, and who will feed us later?"

"You are not a slave," replied Tadhil, "and can go to the market-place where merchants display their supplies. There you can obtain dried meat and sometimes dochnu (millet), but for a high price; as I told you, famine reigns in Omdurmân."

"But in the meantime wicked people will seize and kill those children."

"The soldiers will protect them, and if you give money to any one of them, he will willingly go for provisions."

This advice did not please Idris who had a greater desire to take money than to give it to any one, but before he was able to make reply the boat touched the bank.

To the children Omdurmân appeared different from Khartûm. In the latter place there were houses of several stories built of brick and stone; there was a "mudirya," that is, a Governor's palace in which the heroic Gordon had perished; there were a church, a hospital, missionary buildings, an arsenal, great barracks for the troops and a large number of greater and smaller gardens with magnificent tropical plants. Omdurmân, on the other hand, seemed rather a great encampment of savages. The fort which stood on the northern side of the settlement had been razed by command of Gordon. As a whole, as far as the eye could reach the city consisted of circular conical huts of dochnu straw. Narrow, thorny little fences separated these huts from each other and from the streets. Here and there could be seen tents, evidently captured from the Egyptians. Elsewhere a few palm mats under a piece of dirty linen stretched upon bamboo constituted the entire residence. The population sought shelter under the roofs during rain or exceptional heat; for the rest they passed their time, built fires, cooked food, lived, and died out-of-doors. So the streets were so crowded that in places the detachment with difficulty forced its way through the multitude. Formerly Omdurmân was a wretched village; at present, counting the slaves, over two hundred thousand people were huddled in it. Even the Mahdi and his caliphs were perturbed by this vast concourse, which was threatened with famine and disease. They continually despatched to the north new expeditions to subjugate localities and cities, loyal yet to the Egyptian Government.

At the sight of the white children here also resounded unfriendly cries, but at least the rabble did not threaten them with death. It may be that they did not dare to, being so close to the prophet's side, and perhaps because they were more accustomed to the sight of prisoners who were all transported to Omdurmân immediately after the capture of Khartûm. Stas and Nell, however, saw hell on earth. They saw Europeans and Egyptians lashed with courbashes until they bled; hungry, thirsty, bending under burdens which they were commanded to carry or under buckets of water. They saw European women and children, who were reared in affluence, at present begging for a handful of durra or a shred of meat; covered with rags, emaciated, resembling specters, with faces swarthy from want, on which dismay and despair had settled, and with a bewildered stare. They saw how the savages burst into laughter at the sight of these unfortunates; how they pushed and beat them. On all the streets and alleyways there were not lacking sights from which the eyes turned away with horror and aversion. In Omdurmân, dysentery and typhoid fever, and, above all, small-pox raged in a virulent form. The sick, covered with sores, lay at the entrances of the hovels, infecting the air. The prisoners carried, wrapped in linen, the bodies of the newly dead to bury them in the sand beyond the city, where the real charge of the funeral was assumed by hyenas. Above the city hovered flocks of vultures from whose wings fell melancholy shadows upon the illuminated sand. Stas, witnessing all this, thought that the best for him and Nell would be to die as soon as possible.

Nevertheless, in this sea of human wretchedness and malice there bloomed at times compassion, as a pale flower blooms in a putrid marsh. In Omdurmân there were a few Greeks and Copts whom the Mahdi had spared because he needed them. These not only walked about freely, but engaged in trade and various affairs, and some, especially those who pretended to change their faith, were even officers of the Mahdi, and this gave them considerable importance among the wild dervishes. One of these Greeks stopped the detachment and began to question the children as to how they happened to be there. Learning with amazement that they had just arrived, and that they had been kidnapped from far-away Fayûm, he promised to speak about them to the Mahdi and to inquire about them in the future. In the meantime he nodded his head compassionately at Nell and gave to each a few handfuls of dried wild figs and a silver dollar with an image of Maria Theresa. After which he admonished the soldiers not to dare to do any harm to the little girl, and he left, repeating in English: "Poor little bird!"

XVII

THROUGH tortuous little streets they finally arrived at
the market-place which was situated in the center of the
city. On the way they saw many men with a hand or
foot cut off. They were thieves or transgressors who had
concealed booty. The punishment meted by the caliphs
for disobedience or violation of the laws promulgated by
the prophet was horrible, and even for a trivial offense,
such as smoking tobacco, the delinquent was whipped
with courbashes until he bled or became unconscious.
But the caliphs themselves observed these commands
only seemingly; at home they indulged in everything, so
that the penalties fell upon the poor, who at one blow
were despoiled of all their goods. Afterwards there remained for them nothing to do but beg; and as in Omdurmân there was a scarcity of provisions they died of
starvation.

A large number of beggars also swarmed around the
provision stalls. The first object, however, which attracted the attention of the children was a human head
fastened on a high bamboo set up in the center of the
market-place. The face of this head was dried up and
almost black, while the hair on the skull and the chin
was as white as milk. One of the soldiers explained to
Idris that that was Gordon's head. Stas, when he heard
this, was seized by fathomless sorrow, indignation, and
a burning desire for revenge; at the same time terror

froze the blood in his veins. Thus had perished that hero,
that knight without fear and without reproach; a man,
just and kind, who was loved even in the Sudân. And
the English people had not come in time to his aid, and
later retired, leaving his remains without a Christian
burial, to be thus dishonored! Stas at that moment lost
his faith in the English people. Heretofore he naïvely
believed that England, for an injury to one of her citizens,
was always ready to declare war against the whole world.
At the bottom of his soul there had lain a hope that in
behalf of Rawlinson's daughter, after the unsuccessful
pursuit, formidable English hosts would be set in motion
even as far as Khartûm and farther. Now he became
convinced that Khartûm and that whole region was in
the hands of the Mahdi, and that the Egyptian Government and England were thinking rather of preserving
Egypt from further conquests than of delivering the
European prisoners from captivity.

He understood that he and Nell had fallen into an
abyss from which there was no escape, and these thoughts,
linked with the horrors which he witnessed on the streets
of Omdurmân, disheartened him completely. His customary energy gave way to total passive submission to
fate and a dread of the future. In the meantime he
began aimlessly to gaze about the market-place and at
the stalls at which Idris was bargaining for provisions.
The hucksters, mainly Sudânese women and negresses,
sold jubhas here, that is, white linen gowns, pieced together with many colored patches, acacia gum, hollow
gourds, glass beads, sulphur and all kinds of mats. There
were a few stalls with provisions and around all of them
the throng pressed. The Mahdists bought at high
prices principally dried strips of meat of domestic animals;
likewise of buffaloes, antelopes and giraffes. Dates, figs,

manioc, and durra were totally lacking. They sold here
and there water and honey of wild bees, and grains of
dochnu soaked in a decoction of tamarind fruit. Idris
fell into despair, for it appeared that in view of the prevail-
ing market-prices he would soon exhaust all the money
he had received from Fatma Smain for living expenses
and afterwards would, in all probability, have to beg.
His only hope now was in Smain, and strangely enough
Stas also relied solely upon Smain's assistance.

After a lapse of an hour Nur el-Tadhil returned from
the caliph Abdullahi. Evidently he had met with some
kind of disagreeable mishap there, for he returned in a
bad humor. So when Idris asked him if he had learned
anything about Smain, he replied testily:

"Fool, do you think that the caliph and I have nothing better to do than to seek Smain for you?"

"Well, what are you going to do with me?"

"Do what you please. I gave you a night's lodging
in my house and a few words of good advice, and now I
do not want to know anything more about you."

"That is well, but where shall I find shelter?"

"It is all the same to me."

Saying this he took the soldiers and went away. With
great difficulty Idris prevailed upon him to send to the
market-place the camels and the rest of the caravan, in-
cluding those Arabs who had joined it between Assuan
and Wâdi Halfa. These people did not come until the
afternoon, and it appeared that none of them knew
what they were going to do. The two Bedouins began to quarrel with Idris and Gebhr, claiming that they
had promised them an entirely different reception and
that they had cheated them. After a long dispute and
much deliberation they finally decided to erect at the
outskirts of the city huts of dochnu boughs and reeds as

shelter during the night, and for the rest to depend upon the will of providence, and wait.

After the erection of the huts, which employment does not require much time from Sudânese and negroes, all, excepting Chamis, who was to prepare the supper, repaired to the place of public prayer. It was easy for them to find it, as the swarm of all Omdurmân was bound thither. The place was spacious, encircled partly by a thorny fence and partly by a clay enclosure which was being built. In the center stood a wooden platform. The prophet ascended it whenever he desired to instruct the people. In front of the platform were spread upon the ground sheep hides for the Mahdi, the caliphs, and eminent sheiks. Planted at the sides were the flags of emirs, which fluttered in the air, displaying all colors and looking like great flowers. The four sides were surrounded by the compact ranks of dervishes. Around could be seen a bold, numberless forest of spears, with which almost all the warriors were armed.

It was real good fortune for Idris and Gebhr, and for the other members of the caravan, that they were taken for a retinue of one of the emirs. For that reason they could press forward to the first rows of the assembled throng. The arrival of the Mahdi was announced by the beautiful and solemn notes of umbajas, but when he appeared there resounded the shrill notes of fifes, the beating of drums, the rattle of stones shaken in empty gourds, and whistling on elephants' teeth, all of which combined created an infernal din. The swarm was swept by an indescribable fervor. Some threw themselves on their knees; others shouted with all their strength:

"Oh! Messenger of God!" "Oh! Victorious!" "Oh! Merciful'" "Oh! Gracious!" This continued until the Mahdi entered the pulpit. Then a dead stillness fell while he raised his hands, placed his big fingers to his ears, and for some time prayed.

The children did not stand far away, and could see him well. He was a middle-aged man, prodigiously obese as though bloated, and almost black. Stas, who had an unusually keen sight, perceived that his face was tattooed. In one ear he wore a big ivory ring. He was dressed in a white jubha and had a white cap on his head. His feet were bare, as on mounting the platform he shook off red half-boots and left them on the sheep's hide on which he was afterwards to pray. There was not the least luxury in his clothing. Only at times the wind carried a strong sandal [1] scent which the faithful present inhaled eagerly through their nostrils; at the same time they rolled their eyes from joy. On the whole Stas had pictured differently this terrible prophet, plunderer, and murderer of so many thousand people, and looking now at the fat face with its mild look, with eyes suffused with tears, and with a smile, as though grown to those lips, he could not overcome his astonishment. He thought that such a man ought to bear on his shoulders the head of a hyena or a crocodile, and instead he saw before him a chubby-faced gourd, resembling drawings of a full moon.

But the prophet began his instruction. His deep and resonant voice could be heard perfectly all over the place, so that his words reached the ears of all the faithful. He first spoke of the punishments which God meted out to those who disobey the commands of the Mahdi, and hide booty, get intoxicated upon merissa, spare the enemy in battles, and smoke tobacco. On account of these crimes Allah sends upon the sinners famine and

[1] From sandal wood, from which in the East a fragrant oil is derived.

that disease which changes the face into a honey-comb (small-pox). Temporal life is like a leaky leather bottle. Riches and pleasure are absorbed in the sand which buries the dead. Only faith is like a cow which gives sweet milk. But paradise will open only for the victorious. Whoever vanquishes the enemy wins for himself salvation. Whoever dies for the faith will rise from the dead for eternity. Happy, a hundredfold more happy are those who already have fallen.

"We want to die for the faith!" answered the swarm in one tumultuous shout.

And for a while an infernal uproar again prevailed. The umbajas and drums sounded. The warriors struck sword against sword, spear against spear. The martial ardor spread like a flame. Some cried: "The faith is victorious!" Others: "To paradise through death!" Stas now understood why the Egyptian army could not cope with this wild host.

When the hubbub had somewhat subsided, the prophet resumed his address. He told them of his visions and of the mission which he had received from God. Allah commanded him to purify the faith and spread it over the entire world. Whoever does not acknowledge him as the Mahdi, the Redeemer, is condemned to damnation. The end of the world is already near, but before that time it is the duty of the faithful to conquer Egypt, Mecca, and all those regions beyond the seas where the gentiles dwell. Such is the divine will which nothing can change. A great deal of blood will flow yet; many warriors will not return to their wives and children under their tents, but the happiness of those who fall no human tongue can describe.

After which he stretched out his arms towards the assembled throng and concluded thus:

"Therefore I, the Redeemer and servant of God, bless this holy war and you warriors. I bless your toils, wounds, death; I bless victory, and weep over you like a father who has conceived an affection for you."

And he burst into a flood of tears. When he descended from the pulpit a roar and a clamor resounded. Weeping became general. Below, the two caliphs Abdullahi and Ali Uled Helu took the prophet under the arms and escorted him to the sheep hide on which he knelt. During this brief moment Idris asked Stas feverishly whether Smain was not among the emirs.

"No!" replied the boy, who vainly sought the familiar face with his eyes "I do not see him anywhere. Perhaps he fell at the capture of Khartûm."

The prayers lasted long. During these the Mahdi threw his arms and legs about like a buffoon or raised his eyes in rapture, repeating "Lo! It is he!" "Lo! It is he!" and the sun began to decline towards the west, when he rose and left for his home. The children now could be convinced with what reverence the dervishes surrounded their prophet, for crowds eagerly followed him and scratched up the places which his feet touched. They even quarreled and came to blows for they believed that such earth protected the healthy and healed the sick.

The place of prayer was vacated gradually. Idris himself did not know what to do and was about to return with the children and his whole party to the huts and to Chamis for the night, when unexpectedly there stood before them that same Greek who in the morning had given Stas and Nell each a dollar and a handful of wild figs.

"I spoke with the Mahdi about you;" he said in Arabian, "and the prophet desires to see you."

"Thanks to Allah and to you, sir," exclaimed Idris. "Shall we find Smain at the prophet's side."

"Smain is in Fashoda," answered the Greek.

After which he addressed Stas in the English language.

"It may be that the prophet will take you under his protection as I endeavored to persuade him to do. I told him that the fame of his mercy would then spread among all the white nations. Here terrible things are taking place and without his protection you will perish from starvation and want of comforts, from sickness or at the hands of madmen. But you must reconcile him and that depends upon you."

"What am I to do?" Stas asked.

"In the first place, when you appear before him throw yourself upon your knees, and if he should tender his hand, kiss it with reverence and beseech him to take you two under his wings."

Here the Greek broke off and asked:

"Do any of these men understand English?"

"No. Idris and Gebhr understand only a few simple words and the others not even that."

"That is well. So listen further, for it is necessary to anticipate everything. Now the Mahdi will in all probability ask you whether you are ready to accept his faith. Answer at once that you are and that at the sight of him, from the first glance of the eye an unknown light of grace flowed upon you. Remember, 'an unknown light of grace.' That will flatter him and he will enroll you among his muzalems, that is, among his personal servants. You will then enjoy plenty and all the comforts which will shield you from sickness. If you should act otherwise you would endanger yourself, that poor little creature, and even me, who wishes your good. Do you understand?"

Stas set his teeth and did not reply, but his face was

icy and his eyes flashed up sullenly. Seeing which the Greek continued thus:

"I know, my boy, that this is a disagreeable matter, but it cannot be helped. All of those who were saved after the massacre in Khartûm accepted the Mahdi's doctrines. Only a few Catholic missionaries and nuns did not assent to it, but that is a different matter. The Koran prohibits the slaughter of priests, so though their fate is horrible, they are not at least threatened with death. For the secular people, however, there was no other salvation. I repeat, they all accepted Mohammedism; the Germans, Italians, Englishmen, Copts, Greeks — I myself."

And here, though Stas had assured him that no one in that crowd understood English, he nevertheless lowered his voice.

"Besides, I need not tell you that this is no denial of faith, no treason, no apostasy. In his soul every one remained what he was and God saw it. Before superior force it is necessary to bend, though seemingly. It is the duty of man to preserve life and it would be madness, and even a sin, to jeopardize it — for what? For appearances, for a few words, which at the same time you may disavow in your soul? And remember that you hold in your hands not only your life but the life of your little companion which it is not permissible for you to dispose of. In truth, I can guarantee to you if ever God saves you from these hands then you will not have anything to reproach yourself with, nor will any one find fault with you, as this is the case with all of us."

The Greek, speaking in this manner, perhaps deceived his own conscience, but Stas' silence deceived him also for in the end he mistook it for fear. He determined therefore to give the boy courage.

"These are the houses of the Mahdi," he said. "He prefers to live in the wooden sheds of Omdurmân rather than in Khartûm, though there he could occupy Gordon's palace. Well then, bravely! Don't lose your head! To the question reply firmly. They prize courage here. Also do not imagine that the Mahdi will at once roar at you like a lion! No! He always smiles, even when contemplating nothing good."

And saying this he began to shout at the crowd standing in front of the house to make way for the prophet's "guests."

XVIII

WHEN they entered the room, the Mahdi lay on a soft
cot, surrounded by his wives, two of whom fanned him
with great ostrich feathers and the other two lightly
scratched the soles of his feet. Besides his wives, there
were present only the caliph Abdullahi and the sheref
caliph, as the third, Ali Uled Helu, was despatching at that
time troops to the north, particularly to Beber and Abu
Hâmed, which already had been captured by the dervishes. At sight of the arrivals the prophet dismissed
his wives and sat up on the cot. Idris, Gebhr, and the
two Bedouins fell on their faces and afterwards knelt
with hands crossed on their breasts. The Greek beckoned
to Stas to do the same, but the boy, pretending not to
see the gesture, only bowed and remained standing erect.
His face was pale, but his eyes shone strongly and from
his whole posture and head, haughtily upraised, from
his tightly compressed lips it could easily be seen that
something had taken an ascendancy over him, that uncertainty and fear had passed away, that he had adopted
an inflexible resolution from which he would not recede
for anything. The Greek evidently understood this,
as great uneasiness was reflected on his features. The
Mahdi observed both children with a fleeting glance,
brightened his fat face with his customary smile, after
which he first addressed Idris and Gebhr:

"You came from the distant north," he said.

Idris struck the ground with his forehead.

"Yes, oh Mahdi! We belong to the tribe of Dongola; therefore we abandoned our homes in Fayûm in order to kneel at your blessed feet."

"I beheld you in the desert. That was a terrible journey but I sent an angel to guard and shield you from death at the hands of the infidels. You did not see this, but he watched over you."

"Thanks to thee, Redeemer."

"And you brought those children to Smain to exchange them for his own, that the Turks imprisoned together with Fatma in Port Said."

"Thee we desired to serve."

"Whoever serves me — serves his own salvation; therefore you have opened for yourselves the path to paradise. Fatma is my relative. But verily I say unto you that when we subjugate the whole of Egypt, then my relative and her posterity will anyway regain liberty."

"And therefore do with these children whatever thou desirest — oh blessed one."

The Mahdi closed his eyelids, after which he opened them, smiling kindly, and nodded at Stas.

"Approach, boy."

Stas advanced a few paces with an energetic, as if soldierly, stride; he bowed a second time after which he straightened as a chord and, looking straight into the Mahdi's eyes, waited.

"Are you delighted that you came to me?" the Mahdi asked.

"No, prophet. We were abducted in spite of our wills from our parents."

This plain answer created a certain sensation upon the ruler accustomed to flattery, and upon those present. Caliph Abdullahi frowned, the Greek gnawed his mustache, and began to wring his hands. The Mahdi, however, did not cease to smile.

"But," he said, "you are at the fountain of truth. Do you want to drink at that fountain?"

A moment of silence followed; so the Mahdi, thinking the boy did not understand the question, repeated it more plainly.

"Do you desire to accept my doctrines?"

To this Stas imperceptibly made a sign of the holy cross with his hand which he held at his breast, as though he was about to leap from a sinking ship into a watery chaos.

"Prophet," he said, "your doctrines I do not know; therefore if I accepted them, I would do it out of fear like a coward and a base man. Are you anxious that your faith should be professed by cowards and base people?"

And speaking thus he looked steadfastly in the eyes of the Mahdi. It became so quiet that only the buzz of flies could be heard. But at the same time something extraordinary had happened. The Mahdi became confused, and for the nonce did not know what reply to make. The smile vanished from his face, on which was reflected perplexity and displeasure. He stretched out his hand, took hold of the gourd, filled it with water and honey, and began to drink, but obviously only to gain time and to conceal his confusion.

And the brave boy, a worthy descendant of the defenders of Christianity, of the true blood of the victors at Khoczim and Vienna, stood with upraised head, awaiting his doom. On his emaciated cheeks, tanned by the desert winds, bloomed bright blushes, his eyes glittered, and his body quivered with the thrill of ardor. "All others," he soliloquized, "accepted his doctrines, but I have denied neither my faith nor my soul." And fear before what might

and was to follow at that moment was subdued in his
heart, and joy and pride overflowed it.

In the meantime the Mahdi replaced the gourd and
asked:

"So, you reject my doctrines?"

"I am a Christian like my father."

"Whoever closes his eyes to the voice of God," said
the Mahdi slowly in a changed voice, "is only fuel for
the flames."

At this the caliph Abdullahi, notorious for his ferocity
and cruelty, displayed his white teeth like a savage animal
and spoke out:

"The speech of this boy is insolent; therefore punish
him, lord, or permit me to punish him."

"It has happened!" Stas thought.

But the Mahdi always desired that the fame of his
mercy should spread not only among the dervishes but
over the whole world; therefore he thought that a too
severe sentence, particularly upon a small boy, might
injure that fame.

For a while he fingered the rosary beads and meditated,
and afterwards said:

"No.   These children were abducted for Smain; so,
though I do not want to enter into any negotiations with
the infidels, it is necessary to send them to Smain.   Such
is my will."

"It shall be obeyed," answered the caliph.

But the Mahdi pointed to Idris, Gebhr, and the
Bedouins and said:

"Reward these men for me, oh Abdullahi, for they
made a long and dangerous journey to serve God and
me."

After which he nodded in sign that the audience was
ended and at the same time ordered the Greek to leave

also. The latter, when they found themselves in the darkness on the place of prayer, seized Stas' arm and began to shake it with anger and despair.

"Accursed! You have sealed the doom of that innocent child," he said, pointing at Nell. "You have ruined yourself and perhaps me."

"I could not do otherwise," answered Stas.

"You could not? Know that you are condemned to a journey a hundredfold worse than the first. And that is death, — do you understand? In Fashoda the fever will kill you in the course of a week. The Mahdi knew why he sent you to Smain."

"In Omdurmân we also would perish."

"That is not true! You would not have perished in the house of the Mahdi, in plenty and comfort. And he was ready to take you under his wings. I know that he was. You also repaid me nicely for interceding for you. But do what you wish, Abdullahi will despatch the camel-post to Fashoda in about a week and during that time do whatever you please! You will not see me any more!"

Saying this he went away, but after a while returned. He, like all Greeks, was loquacious, and it was necessary for him to tell everything he had to say. He wanted to pour upon Stas' head all the bile which had accumulated within him. He was not cruel and did not possess a bad heart; he desired, however, that the boy should understand more thoroughly the awful responsibility which he had assumed in not heeding his advice and warnings.

"Who would have prevented you from remaining a Christian in your soul?" he said. "Do you think that I am not one? But I am not a fool. You on the other hand preferred to make a parade of your false heroism. Heretofore I have rendered great services to the white prisoners, but now I shall not be able to aid them for the

Mahdi has become incensed at me. All will perish. And your little companion in misfortune also: you have killed her! In Fashoda even adult Europeans die of the fever like flies, and what of such a child? And if they order you to go on foot beside the horses and camels, she will fall the first day. You did all this. Enjoy yourself now — you Christian!"

And he left them while they turned from the place of prayer towards the huts. They walked long, as the city was spread over an immense space. Nell, worn out by fatigue, hunger, fright, and the horrible impressions of the whole day, began to lag. Idris and Gebhr urged her to walk faster. But after a time her limbs became entirely numb. Then Stas, without reflection, took her in his arms and carried her. On the way he wanted to speak to her; he wanted to justify himself, but ideas were torpid, as if they were dead in his mind; so he only repeated in a circle, "Nell! Nell! Nell!" and he clasped her to his bosom, not being able to say anything more. After a few score paces Nell fell asleep in his arms from exhaustion; so he walked in silence amid the quiet of the slumbering little streets, interrupted only by the conversation of Idris and Gebhr, whose hearts overflowed with joy. This was fortunate for Stas, as otherwise they would have punished him for his insolent reply to the Mahdi. They were, however, so occupied with what they had seen that they could not think of anything else.

"I felt sick," said Idris, "but the sight of the prophet healed me."

"He is like a palm in the desert, and like cool water on a scorching day, and his words are like ripe dates," answered Gebhr.

"Nur el-Tadhil lied when he said that he would not

permit us to be admitted to his presence. He admitted us, blessed us, and ordered Abdullahi to lavish gifts upon us."

"Who will munificently enrich us, for the wish of the Mahdi is sacred."

"Bismillah! May it be as you say!" spoke out one of the Bedouins.

And Gebhr began to dream of whole herds of camels, horned cattle, and bags full of piastres.

From these dreams he was awakened by Idris who, pointing at Stas carrying the sleeping girl, asked:

"What shall we do with that hornet and that fly?"

"Ha! Smain ought to reward us for them, separately."

"Since the prophet says that he will not permit any negotiations with the infidels, Smain will have no interest in them."

"In such case I regret that they did not get into the hands of the caliph, who would have taught that whelp what it is to bark against the truth and the elect of the Lord."

"The Mahdi is merciful," answered Idris.

After which he pondered for a while and said:

"Nevertheless, Smain having both in his hands will be certain that neither the Turks nor the English people will kill his children and Fatma."

"So he may reward us?"

"Yes. Let Abdullahi's post take them to Fashoda. A weight will fall off our heads, and when Smain returns here we will demand recompense from him."

"You say then that we will remain in Omdurmân?"

"Allah! Have you not had enough in the journey from Fayûm to Khartûm? The time for rest has come."

The huts were now not far off. Stas, however, slackened his pace for his strength began to wane. Nell, though light, seemed heavier and heavier. The Sudânese, who were anxious to go to sleep, shouted at him to hurry and afterwards drove him on, striking him on the head with their fists. Gebhr even pricked him painfully in the shoulder with a knife. The boy endured all this in silence, protecting above all his little sister, and not until one of the Bedouins shoved him so that he almost fell, did he say to them through his set teeth:

"We are to arrive at Fashoda alive."

And these words restrained the Arabs, for they feared to violate the commands of the Mahdi. A yet more effective restraint, however, was the fact that Idris suddenly became so dizzy that he had to lean on Gebhr's arm. After an interval the dizziness passed away, but the Sudânese became frightened and said:

"Allah! Something ails me. Has not some sickness taken hold of me?"

"You have seen the Mahdi, so you will not fall sick," answered Gebhr.

They finally reached the huts. Stas, hurrying with the remnants of his strength, delivered sleeping Nell to the hands of old Dinah, who, though unwell also, nevertheless made a comfortable bed for her little lady. The Sudânese and the Bedouins, swallowing a few strips of raw meat, flung themselves, like logs, on the saddle-cloth. Stas was not given anything to eat, but old Dinah shoved into his hand a fistful of soaked durra, a certain amount of which she had stolen from the camels. But he was not in the mood for eating or sleeping, for the load which weighed on his shoulders was in truth too heavy. He felt that in rejecting the favor of the Mahdi, for which it was necessary to pay with denial of faith and soul, he had acted as he should have done; he felt that his father would have been proud and happy at his conduct, but at the same time he thought that he had caused the destruction of Nell, his companion in misfortune, his little beloved sister, for whom he would willingly have sacrificed his last drop of blood.

So when all had fallen asleep he burst into a flood of tears, and, lying on a piece of saddle-cloth, he wept long, like the child which, after all, he still was.

XIX

The visit to the Mahdi and the interview with him evidently did not heal Idris, as during the night he grew worse and in the morning became unconscious. Chamis, Gebhr, and the two Bedouins were summoned to the caliph who detained them some hours and praised their courage. But they returned in the worst humor and with rage in their souls for they had expected the Lord knows what rewards, and in the meantime Abdullahi gave each one an Egyptian pound[1] and a horse.

The Bedouins began a quarrel with Gebhr which almost resulted in a fight; in the end they announced that they would ride together with the camel-post to Fashoda to demand payment from Smain. They were joined by Chamis who expected that the patronage of Smain would be more beneficial to him than a sojourn in Omdurmân.

For the children a week of hunger and misery began, for Gebhr did not think of feeding them. Fortunately Stas had the two dollars with the effigy of Maria Theresa, which he got from the Greek; so he went to the city to buy dates and rice. The Sudânese did not oppose this trip as they knew that he could not escape from Omdurmân and that under no circumstances would he desert the little "bint." This experience did not pass without some adventures, however, for the sight of a boy in European dress buying provisions at the market-place, again

[1] About five dollars — *Translator's Note.*

attracted a crowd of semi-savage dervishes, who received
him with laughter and yells. Fortunately many knew
that he had been at the Mahdi's the previous day, and
they restrained those who wanted to assault him. Only
children threw sand and stones at him, but he paid no
attention to them.

At the market-place the prices were too high. Stas
could not obtain any dates at all and a considerable part
of the rice was taken away from him by Gebhr for "his
sick brother." The boy resisted with all his strength,
in consequence of which a scuffle and fight ensued, in
which the really weaker one came out with numerous
contusions and bruises. In addition the cruelty of Chamis
became manifest. The latter evinced an attachment for
Saba and fed him with raw meat; on the other hand, at
the distress of the children, whom he knew of old and who
had always been kind to him, he looked with the utmost
indifference, and when Stas addressed him with a request
that he should at least give Nell a morsel of food, he
replied, laughing:

"Go and beg."

And it finally came to the pass that Stas during the
following days, desiring to save Nell from death by
starvation, begged. Nor was he always unsuccessful.
At times some former soldier or officer of the Egyptian
Khedive gave him a few piastres or a few dried figs, and
promised to aid him on the following day. Once he happened to meet a missionary and a sister of charity, who,
hearing his story, bemoaned the fate of both children, and
though they themselves were wasted with hunger, shared
with him everything which they had. They also promised to visit them in the huts and did actually come the
next day in the hope that they might succeed in taking
the children with them until the time of the departure of

the post. But Gebhr with Chamis drove them away with courbashes. On the following day Stas met them again and received from them a little measure of rice together with two quinine powders, which the missionary instructed him to save most carefully in the expectation that in Fashoda fever inevitably awaited both.

"You will ride now," he said, "alongside of the dense floating masses in the White Nile or the so-called 'sudds.' The river, not being able to flow freely across the barriers composed of vegetation and weeds which the current of the water carries and deposits in the more shallow places, forms there extensive and infectious swamps, amid which the fever does not spare even the negroes. Beware particularly of sleeping on the bare ground without a fire."

"We already wish to die," answered Stas, almost with a moan.

At this the missionary raised his haggard face and for a while prayed; after which he made the sign of the cross over the boy and said:

"Trust in God. You did not deny Him; so His mercy and care will be over you."

Stas tried not only to beg, but to work. A certain day, seeing a crowd of men laboring at the place of prayer, he joined them, and began to carry clay for the palisade with which the place was to be surrounded. They jeered at and jostled him, but at evening the old sheik, who superintended the work, gave him twelve dates. Stas was immensely overjoyed at this compensation, for dates with rice formed the only wholesome nourishment for Nell and became more and more difficult to obtain in Omdurmân.

So he brought them with pride to his little sister, to whom he gave everything which he could secure; he sustained himself for a week almost exclusively upon durra taken from the camels. Nell was greatly delighted at the sight of her favorite fruit but wanted him to share it with her. So, tiptoeing, she placed her hands on his shoulders, and turning up her head, began to gaze into his eyes and plead:

"Stas! Eat a half, eat — "

To this he replied:

"I have already eaten. I have eaten. I have eaten my fill."

And he smiled, but immediately began to bite his lips in order not to weep, as he really was hungry. He promised himself that the following day he would go again and earn some more; but it happened otherwise. In the morning a muzalem from Abdullahi came with the announcement that the camel-post was to leave at night for Fashoda, and with the caliph's command that Idris, Gebhr, Chamis, and the two Bedouins should prepare to go with the children. This command amazed and aroused the indignation of Gebhr; so he declared that he would not go as his brother was sick and there was no one to attend to him, and even if he were well, both had decided to remain in Omdurmân.

But the muzalem replied:

"The Mahdi has only one will, and Abdullahi, his caliph and my master, never alters commands. Your brother can be attended by a slave, while you will depart for Fashoda."

"Then I shall go and inform him that I will not depart."

"To the caliph are admitted only those whom he himself desires to see. And if you without permission, and through violence, should force yourself into his presence, I will lead you to the gallows."

"Allah akbar! Then tell me plainly that I am a slave!"

"Be silent and obey orders!" answered the muzalem.

The Sûdanese had seen in Omdurmân gallows breaking under the weight of hanging men. By order of the ferocious Abdullahi these gallows were daily decorated with new bodies. Gebhr became terror-stricken. That which the muzalem told him, that the Mahdi commanded but once, was reiterated by all the dervishes. There was therefore no help; it was necessary to ride.

"I shall see Idris no more!" thought Gebhr.

In his tigerish heart was concealed a sort of attachment for his older brother, so that at the thought that he would have to leave him in sickness he was seized by despair. In vain did Chamis and the Bedouins represent to him that they might fare better in Fashoda than in Omdurmân, and that Smain in all probability would reward them more bountifully than the caliph had done. No words could assuage Gebhr's grief and rage, and the rage rebounded mainly upon Stas.

It was indeed a day of martyrdom for the boy. He was not permitted to go to the market-place, so he could not earn anything or beg, and was compelled to work as a slave at the pack-saddles, which were being prepared for the journey. This became a more difficult matter as from hunger and torture he weakened very much. He was certain that he would die on the road; if not under Gebhr's courbash, then from exhaustion.

Fortunately the Greek, who had a good heart, came in at the evening to visit the children and to bid them farewell, and at the same time to provide for them on the way. He brought a few quinine powders, and besides these a few glass beads and a little food. Finally, learning of Idris' sickness, he turned to Gebhr, Chamis, and the Bedouins.

"Know this," he said. "I come here by the Mahdi's command."

And when they heard this they smote with their fore-
heads and he continued:

"You are to feed the children on the way and treat
them well. They are to render a report of your behavior
to Smain. Smain shall write of this to the prophet. If
any complaint against you comes here, the next post
will carry a death sentence for you."

A new bow was the only reply to these words; in addition Gebhr and Chamis had the miens of dogs on which
muzzles are placed.

The Greek then ordered them away, after which he
thus spoke to the children in English:

"I fabricated all this, for the Mahdi did not issue any
new orders. But as he said that you were to go to Fashoda,
it is necessary that you should reach there alive. I also
reckoned upon this, that none of them will see either the
Mahdi or the caliph before their departure."

After which to Stas:

"I took umbrage at you, boy, and feel it yet. Do you
know that you almost ruined me? The Mahdi was
offended at me, and to secure his forgiveness I was forced
to surrender to Abdullahi a considerable portion of my
estate, and besides, I do not know for how long a time I
have saved myself. In any case I shall not be able to
assist the captives as I have heretofore done. But I felt
sorry for you, particularly for her (and here he pointed
at Nell). I have a daughter of the same age, whom I
love more than my own life, and for her sake I have
done everything which I have done. Christ will judge
me for this — Up to this time she wears under her dress,
on her breast, a silver cross. — Her name is the same as
yours, little one. Were it not for her, I would have preferred to die rather than to live in this hell."

He was deeply moved. For a while he was silent, after

which he rubbed his forehead with his hand and began to speak of something else.

"The Mahdi sends you to Fashoda with the idea that there you will die. In this manner he will revenge himself upon you for your stubbornness, boy, which touched him deeply, and he will not lose his fame for 'mercy.' He always acts thus. But who knows who is destined to die first? Abdullahi suggested to him the idea that he should order the dogs who kidnapped you, to go with you. He rewarded them miserably, and now he fears that they may publish it. Besides, they both preferred that the people should not be told that there are still in Egypt troops, cannons, money, and Englishmen. — It will be a hard road and distant. You will go into a country desolate and unhealthy. So guard, as the eye in the head, those powders which I gave to you."

"Sir, order Gebhr once more not to dare to starve or hit Nell," said Stas.

"Do not fear. I commended you to the old sheik who has charge of the post. He is an old acquaintance of mine. I gave him a watch and with that I gained his protection for you."

Saying this, be began to bid them farewell. Taking Nell in his arms, he pressed her to his bosom and repeated:

"May God bless you, my child."

In the meantime the sun descended and the night became starry. In the dusk resounded the snorting of horses and the groans of the heavily loaded camels.

XX

THE old sheik Hatim faithfully kept his promise given
to the Greek and watched over the children with great
solicitude. The journey up the White Nile was difficult.
They rode through Keteineh, Ed-Dueim, and Kawa; afterwards they passed Abba, a woody Nile island, on which
before the war the Mahdi dwelt, in a hollow tree as a
dervish hermit. The caravan often was compelled to
make a detour around extensive floating masses overgrown
with pyrus, or so-called "sudds," from which the breeze
brought the poisoned odor of decomposed leaves carried
by the current of water. English engineers had previously
cut through these barriers, and formerly steamboats
could ascend from Khartûm to Fashoda and farther. At
present the river was blocked again and, being unable to
run freely, overflowed on both sides. The right and left
banks of this region were covered by a high jungle amid
which stood hillocks of termites and solitary gigantic
trees; here and there the forest reached the river. In
dry places grew groves of acacias. During the first week
they saw Arabian settlements and towns composed of
houses with strange conical roofs made of dochnu straw,
but beyond Abba, from the settlement of Gôz Abu Guma
they rode in the country of the blacks. It was nearly
desolate, for the dervishes had almost totally carried away
the local negro population and sold it in the markets
of Khartûm, Omdurmân, Fasher, Dar, El-Obeid, and other

cities in the Sudân, Darfur, and Kordofân. Those inhabitants who succeeded in escaping slavery in thickets in the
forests were exterminated by starvation and small-pox,
which raged with unusual virulence along the White and
Blue Niles. The dervishes themselves said that whole
nations had died of it. The former plantations of sorghum,
manioc, and bananas were covered by a jungle. Only
wild beasts, not pursued by any one, multiplied plenti-
fully. Sometimes before the evening twilight the children
saw from a distance great herds of elephants, resembling
movable rocks, walking with slow tread to watering places
known only to themselves. At the sight of them Hatim,
a former ivory dealer, smacked his lips, sighed, and spoke
thus to Stas in confidence:

"Mashallah! How much wealth there is here! But
now it is not worth while to hunt, for the Mahdi has
prohibited Egyptian traders from coming to Khartûm,
and there is no one to sell the tusks to, unless to the emirs
for umbajas."

They met also giraffes, which, seeing the caravan, escaped hurriedly with heavy ambling pace, swinging their
long necks as if they were lame. Beyond Gôz Abu Guma
appeared, more and more frequently, buffaloes and whole
herds of antelopes. The people of the caravan when they
lacked fresh meat hunted for them, but almost always in
vain, for the watchful and fleet animals would not allow
themselves to be approached or surrounded.

Provisions were generally scarce, as owing to the de-
population of the region they could not obtain either
millet or bananas, or fish, which in former times were
furnished by the Shilluk and Dinka tribes who exchanged
them willingly for glass beads and brass wire. Hatim,
however, did not permit the children to die of starvation,
and what is more he kept a strict control over Gebhr;

and once, when the latter at about bed-time struck Stas while removing saddles from the camels, he ordered the Sudânese to be stretched upon the ground and whipped thirty times on each heel with a bamboo. For two days the cruel Sudânese could walk only on his toes and cursed the hour when he left Fayûm, and revenged himself upon a young slave named Kali, who had been presented to him.

Stas at the beginning was almost pleased that he had left infected Omdurmân and that he saw a country of which he always had dreamed. His strong constitution thus far endured perfectly the toils of the journey and the abundant food restored his energy. Several times during the journey and at the stops he whispered to his little sister that it was possible to escape even from beyond the White Nile, and that he did not at all abandon that design. But her health disquieted him. Three weeks after the day of their departure from Omdurmân Nell had not indeed succumbed to the fever, but her face grew thinner and instead of being tanned it became more and more transparent, and her little hands looked as if they were moulded of wax. She did not lack care and even such comforts as Stas and Dinah with the aid of Hatim could provide, but she lacked the salubrious desert air. The moist and torrid climate united with the hardships of the journey more and more undermined the strength of the child.

Stas, beginning at Gôz Abu Guma, gave her daily a half powder of quinine and worried terribly at the thought that this remedy, which could be obtained nowhere later, would not last him long. But it could not be helped, for it was necessary above all things to prevent the fever. At moments despair possessed him. He deluded himself, however, with the hope that Smain, if he desired to exchange them for his own children, would have to seek for them a more salubrious place than the neighborhood of Fashoda.

But misfortune seemed continually to pursue its victims. On the day before the arrival at Fashoda, Dinah, who while in Omdurmân felt weak, fainted suddenly at the untying of the small luggage with Nell's things taken from Fayûm, and fell from the camel. Stas and Chamis revived her with the greatest difficulty. She did not, however, regain consciousness, or rather she regained it at the evening only to bid a tearful farewell to her beloved little lady, and to die. After her death Gebhr insisted upon cutting off her ears in order to show them to Smain as proof that she died during the journey, and to demand of him a separate payment for her abduction. This was done with a slave who expired during the journey. But Hatim, at the entreaties of Stas and Nell, would not consent to this; so they buried her decently and her mound was safeguarded against hyenas with the assistance of stones and thorns. The children felt yet more lonely for they realized that in her they had lost the only near and devoted soul. This was a terrible blow, particularly for Nell, so Stas endeavored to comfort her throughout the whole night and the following day.

The sixth week of the journey arrived. On the next day at noon the caravan reached Fashoda, but they found only a pyre. The Mahdists bivouacked under the bare heaven or in huts hurriedly built of grass and boughs. Three days previously the settlement had been burnt down. There remained only the clay walls of the round hovels, blackened with smoke, and, standing close by the water, a great wooden shed, which during the Egyptian times served as a storage-place for ivory; in it at present lived the commander of the dervishes, Emir Seki Tamala. He was a distinguished personage among the Mahdists, a secret enemy of Abdullahi, but on the other hand a personal friend of Hatim. He received the old sheik and the children hospitably, but immediately at the introduction told them unfavorable news.

Smain was not in Fashoda. Two days before he had gone southeast from the Nile on an expedition for slaves, and it was not known when he would return, as the nearer localities were so depopulated that it was necessary to seek for human chattels very far. Near Fashoda, indeed, lay Abyssinia, with which the dervishes likewise waged war. But Smain having only three hundred men did not dare to cross its borders, guarded vigilantly, at present, by King John's warlike inhabitants and soldiers.

In view of this Seki Tamala and Hatim began to deliberate as to what was to be done with the children. The consultation was held mainly at supper, to which the emir invited Stas and Nell.

"I," he said to Hatim, "must soon start with all the men upon a distant expedition against Emin Pasha,[1] who is located at Lado, having steamers and troops there. Such is the command which you, Hatim, brought me. Therefore you must return to Omdurmân, for in Fashoda there will not remain a single living soul. Here there is no place in which to live, there is nothing to eat, and sickness is raging. I know, indeed, that the white people do not catch small-pox, but fever will kill those children within a month."

"I was ordered to bring them to Fashoda," replied Hatim, "so I brought them, and need not trouble myself

---

[1] Emin Pasha, by birth a German Jew, was after the occupation by Egypt of the region around Albert Nyanza, Governor of the Equatorial Provinces. His headquarters were at Wadelai. The Mahdists attacked it a number of times. He was rescued by Stanley, who conducted him with a greater part of his troops to Bagamoyo, on the Indian Ocean.

about them any more. But they were recommended to me by my friend, the Greek Kaliopuli; for that reason I would not want them to perish"

"And this will surely happen."

"Then what is to be done?"

"Instead of leaving them in desolate Fashoda, send them to Smain together with those men who brought them to Omdurmân. Smain went to the mountains, to a dry and high region where the fever does not kill the people as on the river."

"How will they find Smain?"

"By the trail of fire. He will set fire to the jungle, first, in order to drive the game to the rocky ravines in which it will be easy to surround and slaughter it, and then in order to scare out of the thickets the heathens, who hid in them before pursuit. Smain will not be hard to find — "

"Will they, however, overtake him?"

"He will at times pass a week in one locality to cure meat. Even though he rode away two or three days ago they surely will overtake him."

"But why should they chase after him? He will return to Fashoda anyway."

"No. If the slave-hunt is successful, he will take the slaves to the cities to sell them — "

"What is to be done?"

"Remember that both of us must leave Fashoda. The children, even though the fever does not kill them, will die of starvation."

"By the prophet! That is true."

And there really remained nothing else to do but to despatch the children upon a new wandering life. Hatim, who appeared to be a very good man, was only troubled about this: whether Gebhr, with whose cruel disposition he had become acquainted during the journey, would not treat them too harshly.   But the stern Seki Tamala, who aroused fear even in his own soldiers, commanded the Sudânese to be summoned, and announced to him that he was to convey the children alive and in good health to Smain, and at the same time to treat them kindly, as otherwise he would be hung.   The good Hatim entreated the emir to present to little Nell a female slave, who would serve her and take care of her during the journey and in Smain's camp.   Nell was delighted greatly with this gift as it appeared that the slave was a young Dinka girl with pleasant features and a sweet facial expression.

Stas knew that Fashoda was death, so he did not at all beg Hatim that he should not send them upon a new journey, the third in rotation.   In his soul, he thought also that riding in an easterly and southerly direction, he must approach the Abyssinian boundaries and that he might escape.   He had a hope that upon the dry table-land Nell would be safeguarded against the fever, and for these reasons he willingly and zealously entered into the preparation for the journey.

Gebhr, Chamis, and the two Bedouins also were not opposed to the expedition, reckoning that at Smain's side they would succeed in capturing a considerable number of slaves, and afterwards sell them profitably in the markets.   They knew that slave-dealers in time amass great fortunes; in any case they preferred to ride rather than to remain at that place under the immediate control of Hatim and Seki Tamala.

The preparations, however, consumed considerable time, particularly as the children had to recuperate.   The camels were unavailable now for this journey, so the Arabs, and Stas and Nell were to ride on horseback.   Kali,

Gebhr's slave, and Nell's maid, called Mea upon Stas'
suggestion, were to go on foot beside the horses. Hatim
also procured a donkey to carry a tent intended for the
little girl and provisions for three days for the children.
More Seki Tamala could not give them. For Nell, something in the nature of a ladies' saddle, made of saddle-
cloth, palm, and bamboo mats was constructed.

The children passed three days in Fashoda to rest, but
the countless number of mosquitoes above the river made
their stay unendurable.   During the daytime appeared
swarms of big blue flies, which did not indeed bite, but
were so vexing that they crept into the ears, filled the
eyes, and fell even into the mouths. Stas had heard
while in Port Said that the mosquitoes and flies spread
fever and an infection of the inflammation of the eyes.
Finally he himself entreated Seki Tamala to hurry the
expedition, particularly as the rainy spring season was
approaching.

XXI

"STAS, why are we riding and speeding and have not yet reached Smain?"

"I do not know. He undoubtedly is moving rapidly ahead, in order to reach as quickly as possible the region in which he can catch negroes. Are you anxious that we should join his detachment?"

The little girl nodded her pale-yellow little head in sign that she was very much concerned about it.

"Why should you be so anxious?" asked Stas.

"Because perhaps Gebhr will not dare in Smain's company to beat that poor Kali so cruelly."

"Smain probably is no better. They all have no mercy for their slaves."

"Is that so?"

And two little tears coursed over her emaciated cheeks.

It was the ninth day of the journey. Gebhr, who was now the leader of the caravan, in the beginning easily discovered traces of Smain's march. His way was indicated by a trail of burnt jungle and camping grounds strewn with picked bones and various remnants. But after the lapse of five days they came upon a vast expanse of burnt steppe, on which the wind had carried the fire in all directions. The trails became deceptive and confusing, as, apparently, Smain had divided his detachment into ten or more small divisions, in order to facilitate the surrounding of the game and the capture of provisions. Gebhr did not know in which direction to go, and often it happened that the caravan, after moving long in a circle, returned to the same place from which it started. Afterwards they chanced upon forests, and after passing through them they entered upon a rocky country where the ground was covered by smooth rocks or small stones, scattered over the immense expanse so thickly that the children were reminded of city pavements. The vegetation there was scant. Only here and there, in the crannies of rocks, grew euphorbias, mimosas, and thorny and scrubby plants and, more infrequently yet, a slender, light green tree, which Kali in the Kiswahili language called "m'ti" and with the leaves of which the horses were fed. In this locality little rivers and streams were lacking, but fortunately from time to time the rain began to fall, so they found water in the hollows and excavations of the rocks.

The game was driven away by Smain's detachment and the caravan would have died of starvation, were it not for a multitude of guinea-fowls which every little while started from under the horses' legs, and at evening encumbered the trees so thickly that it was sufficient to shoot in their direction to cause a few to fall to the ground. In addition they were not timid and permitted a close approach, and they rose so heavily and indolently that Saba, rushing ahead of the caravan, seized and choked some of them almost every day.

Chamis killed about a score of them daily with an old shotgun which he had bartered from one of the dervishes serving under Hatim during the trip from Omdurmân to Fashoda. He did not, however, have shot for more than twenty charges and he became uneasy at the thought of what would happen when the supply was exhausted. Indeed, notwithstanding the scaring away of the game, there appeared at times amidst the rocks herds of ariels, beautiful antelopes common in all Central Africa, but it was necessary to shoot at the ariels with the short rifle, while they did not know how to use Stas' gun and Gebhr did not want to place it in his hands.

The Sudânese likewise began to grow uneasy at the long journey. At times it occurred to him to return to Fashoda, because in case he and Smain should miss each other they might stray in wild regions in which, not to speak of starvation, they were in danger of attacks of wild animals, and savage negroes panting for revenge for the hunt which had been despatched against them. But as he did not know that Seki Tamala was preparing an expedition against Emin, for the conversation about this was not held in his presence, he was seized with terror at the thought of appearing before the face of the puissant emir, who had commanded him to convey the children to Smain and had given him a letter addressed to him and in addition had announced that if he did not acquit himself properly of his duty, he would be hung. All of this taken together filled his soul with bitterness and rage. He did not dare, however, to revenge himself for his disappointments upon Stas and Nell; instead the back of poor Kali was covered with blood under the courbash. The young slave approached his cruel master always trembling and in fear. In vain he embraced his feet and kissed his hands; in vain he fell upon his face before him. The stony heart was not moved either by humility or by groans, and the courbash gashed the body of the unhappy boy upon the most trivial cause and often for none whatever. At night his feet were placed in a wooden board with an opening to prevent him from running away. During the day he walked tied with a rope fastened to a horse; this amused Chamis very much. Nell shed tears over Kali's plight. Stas' heart raged and a number of times he passionately interceded for him, but when he perceived that this inflamed Gebhr still more, he set his teeth and remained silent.

But Kali understood that those two interceded for him, and he began to love them deeply with his afflicted heart.

For two days they rode in a stony ravine lined with high steep rocks. From the stones heaped and scattered in disorder it was easy to perceive that during the rainy season the ravine was filled with water, but at present its bed was entirely dry. On the walls, on both sides, grew small patches of grass, a great many thorns, and here and there even a tree. Gebhr directed his way by this stony gullet because it went continually upwards; so he thought that it would lead him to some eminence from which he could descry smoke during the daytime and Smain's camp-fires at night. In some places the ravine became so narrow that only two horses could go side by side; in other places it widened into small, round valleys, surrounded as if by high stone walls, on which sat big baboons, playing with each other, barking, and displaying their teeth at the caravan.

It was five o'clock in the afternoon. The sun already lowered towards the west. Gebhr thought of a resting place; he wanted only to reach some small valley in which he could construct a zareba, that is, enclose the caravan and horses with a fence of thorny mimosa and acacias, for protection against attacks of wild animals. Saba rushed ahead, barking at the baboons which at sight of him shook uneasily, and all of a sudden disappeared in the bend of the ravine. Echo repeated loudly his barking.

Suddenly, however, he became silent and after a while he came rushing to the horses with hair bristling on his back and tail curled under him. The Bedouins and Gebhr understood that something must have frightened him, but staring at each other and desiring to ascertain what it could be, they proceeded farther.

But riding around a small bend, the horses shied and stood still in one moment as if thunderstruck by the sight which met their eyes.

On a fair-sized rock situated in the middle of the ravine, which was quite wide at that place, lay a lion.

At most, a hundred paces separated him from them. The powerful beast, seeing the riders and horses, rose on his fore paws and began to gaze at them. The sun, which now stood low, illumined his huge head and shaggy breasts, and in that ruddy luster he was like one of those sphinxes which ornament the entrances to ancient Egyptian temples.

The horses began to sit upon their haunches, to wince and draw back. The amazed and frightened riders did not know what to do; so from mouth to mouth there flowed only the fearsome and helpless words, "Allah! Bismillah! Allah akbar!"

And the king of the wilderness gazed at them from above, motionless as if cast of bronze.

Gebhr and Chamis had heard from traders, who came to Egypt from the Sudân with ivory and gum, that lions sometimes lie down in the paths of caravans, which, on account of this, must turn aside. But here there was no place which they could turn to. It behoved them perhaps to turn about and fly. Yes! But in such case it was a certainty that the dreadful beast would rush after them in pursuit.

Again resounded the feverish interrogations:

"What is to be done?"

"Allah! Perhaps he will step aside."

"No, he will not."

And again a silence fell. Only the snorting of the horses and the quickened breathing of the human breasts could be heard.

"Untie Kali!" Chamis suddenly exclaimed to Gebhr, "and we will escape on the horses; the lion will first overtake him, and kill him only."

"Do that," repeated the Bedouins.

But Gebhr surmised that in such a case Kali, in the twinkling of an eye, would climb on the rocky wall and the lion would chase after the horses; therefore another horrible idea suggested itself to him. He would kill the boy with his knife and fling his body ahead of him and then the lion, dashing after them, would see on the ground the bleeding corpse and stop to devour it.

So he dragged Kali by the rope to the saddle and had already raised his knife, when in the same second Stas clutched the wide sleeve of his jubha.

"Villain! What are you doing?"

Gebhr began to tug and, if the boy had seized him by the hand, he would have freed it at once, but it was not so easy with the sleeve; so he began to tug, and splutter with a voice stifled with fury.

"Dog! if he is not enough, I shall stab you both! Allah! I shall stab you! I shall stab you!"

And Stas paled mortally, for like lightning the thought flashed through his mind that the lion chasing after the horses above all might actually overlook Kali, and in such case Gebhr with the greatest certainty would stab them both in turn.

So pulling the sleeve with redoubled strength he shouted:

"Give me the short rifle! I will kill the lion!"

These words astonished the Bedouins, but Chamis, who had witnessed Stas' shooting in Port Said, began at once to cry:

"Give him the rifle! He will kill the lion."

Gebhr recollected at once the shots on Lake Karûn and in view of the horrible danger, assented. With great haste he gave the boy the short rifle and Chamis, as quick as a thought, opened the cartridge box, from which Stas took a large fistful of cartridges, after which he leaped off his horse, inserted the cartridges in the barrels, and moved forward.

For the first few steps he was as though stupefied and saw only himself and Nell with throats cut by Gebhr's knife. But soon the nearer and more horrible danger commanded him to forget about everything else. He had a lion before him! At the sight of the animal his eyes grew dim. He felt a chill on his cheeks and nose, he felt that he had feet as if made of lead and he could scarcely breathe. Plainly he feared. In Port Said he had read during the recitation time of lion-hunts, but it was one thing to examine pictures in books and another to stand eye to eye with the monster, who now gazed at him as if with amazement, wrinkling his broad forehead which resembled a shield.

The Arabs held the breath in their breasts, for never in their lives had they seen anything like this. On the one side was a small boy, who amid the steep rocks appeared yet smaller, on the other a powerful beast, golden in the sun's rays, magnificent, formidable — "The lord with the great head," as the Sudânese say.

Stas overcame with the whole force of his will the inertness of his limbs and advanced farther. For a while yet it seemed to him that his heart had leaped up into his throat, and this feeling continued until he raised the rifle to his face. Then it was necessary to think of something else. Whether to approach nearer or to fire at once; where to aim. The smaller the distance the surer the shot — therefore nearer and nearer! — forty paces, too many yet; — thirty! — twenty! Already the breeze carried the pungent animal odor.

The boy stood.

"A bullet between the eyes, or it will be all over with me," he thought. "In the name of the Father and of the Son —!"

And the lion rose, stretched his body, and lowered his head. His lips began to open, his brows to contract over his eyes. This mite of being had dared to approach too closely — so he prepared for a leap, sitting with haunches quivering on his hind legs.

But Stas, during the twinkling of an eye, perceived that the bead of the rifle was in a direct line with the forehead of the animal — and pulled the trigger.

The shot pealed. The lion reared so that for a while he straightened out to his full height; after which he toppled over on his back with his four paws up.

And in the final convulsions he rolled off the rock onto the ground.

Stas for several minutes covered him with his rifle, but seeing that the quivering ceased and that the tawny body was stretched out inertly, he opened the rifle and inserted another cartridge.

The stony walls reverberated yet with the thunderous echo. Gebhr, Chamis, and the Bedouins could not at once descry what had happened, as on the previous night rain had fallen, and owing to the dampness of the weather the smoke veiled everything in the narrow ravine. Only when the smoke abated, did they shout with joy, and wanted to rush towards the boy, but in vain, as no power could force the horses to move ahead.

And Stas turned around, took in the four Arabs with his gaze and fixed his eyes on Gebhr.

"Ah! There has been enough of this!" he said through his set teeth. "You have exceeded the measure. You shall not torment Nell or any one else any more."

And suddenly he felt that his nose and cheeks turned pale, but this was a different chill, caused not by fright, but by a terrible and inflexible resolution from which the heart in the bosom becomes, for the time being, iron.

"Yes! It is imperative! These are mere villains, executioners, murderers, and Nell is in their hands!"

"You shall not murder her!" he repeated.

He approached them — again stood, and suddenly with the rapidity of lightning raised the rifle to his face.

Two shots, one after the other, jarred the ravine with an echo. Gebhr tumbled upon the ground, and Chamis swayed in the saddle and struck his horse's neck with his bleeding forehead.

The two Bedouins uttered a horrified cry of consternation and, springing from the horses, dashed at Stas. A bend was not far behind them, and if they had run in the other direction, which Stas in his soul desired, they could have saved their lives. But blinded by terror and fury they thought that they would reach the boy before he would be able to change the cartridges, and cut him to pieces with their knives. Fools! They ran barely a dozen paces when again the ill-omened rifle cracked; the ravine resounded with the echo of new shots and both fell with faces on the ground, flouncing about like fishes taken out of water. One of them, who in the haste was hurt the least, raised himself and propped himself on his hands, but at that moment Saba sunk his fangs in his throat.

And mortal silence ensued.

It was broken only by the moans of Kali, who threw himself on his knees and, stretching out his hands, exclaimed in the broken Kiswahili tongue:

"Bwana kubwa! (Great master!) Kill the lion! Kill bad people, but do not kill Kali!"

Stas, however, paid no heed to his cries. For some time he stood as if dazed; after which, observing Nell's pallid face and half-conscious eyes, opened widely from terror, he ran towards her.

"Nell, do not fear! — Nell, we are free!"

In fact they actually were free, but astray in a wild, uninhabited region, in the heart of the land of the Blacks.

PART SECOND

I

Before Stas and the young negro dragged the slain Arabs and the lion's heavy body to the side of the ravine the sun had descended still more and night was soon to fall. But it was impossible to sleep in the vicinity of the corpses; so, though Kali stroked his stomach and repeated, smacking with his tongue, "Msuri niama" (good meat), Stas did not permit him to busy himself with the "niama," and instead ordered him to catch the horses, which ran away after the shooting. The black boy did this with extraordinary skill. Instead of running after them in the ravine, in which case they would have sped away farther and farther, he climbed to the top and, shortening his way by avoiding the bends, he intercepted the startled steeds from the front. In this manner he easily caught two; and two more he drove towards Stas. Only Gebhr's and Chamis' horses could not be found, but at any rate four remained, not counting the lap-eared creature, loaded with the tent and things, who, in view of the tragic occurrences, displayed a true philosophical calm. They found him beyond a bend, cropping closely and without any haste the grass growing on the bottom of the ravine.

The medium-sized Sudânese horses are accustomed generally to the sight of wild animals, but they fear lions, so it was with considerable difficulty that they were led past the rock which was blackened with a puddle of blood. The horses snorted, dilating their nostrils and stretching their necks towards the blood-stained stones; nevertheless, when the donkey, only pricking his ears a little, passed by calmly, they also passed on. Night had already fallen; they nevertheless rode over half a mile, and halted only in a place where the ravine widened again into a small amphitheatrical vale, overgrown with dense thorns and prickly mimosa trees.

"Master," said the young negro, "Kali will make a fire — a big fire."

And taking the broad Sudânese sword, which he had removed from Gebhr's corpse, he began to cut with it thorns and even little trees. After building the fire, he continued to cut until he secured a supply which would suffice for the whole night, after which with Stas he pitched the tent for Nell, under a steep perpendicular wall of the ravine, and later they surrounded it with a semi-circular, broad and prickly fence, or a so-called zareba.

Stas knew from descriptions of African travels that travelers in this manner safeguarded themselves against the attacks of wild animals. The horses could not be placed within the fence; so the boy, unsaddling them and removing the tin utensils and bags, only hobbled them so that they should not stray too far in seeking grass or water. Mea finally found water near-by in a stony cavity, forming as it were a little basin under the opposite rocks. There was so copious a supply that it sufficed for the horses and the cooking of the guinea-fowls which were shot that morning by Chamis. In the pack-saddles, which the donkey bore, they also found about three pots of durra, a few fistfuls of salt, and a bunch of dried manioc roots.

This sufficed for a bounteous supper. Kali and Mea mainly took advantage of it. The young negro whom Gebhr had starved in a cruel manner ate such an amount

of food as would have sated two men. But for this
he was grateful with his whole heart to his new master
and mistress, and immediately after supper he fell on
his face before Stas and Nell in token that he desired to
remain their slave to the end of his life, and afterwards
he also prostrated himself with due humility before Stas'
short rifle, understanding that it was the best policy to
conciliate so formidable a weapon. After this he announced that during the slumber of the "great master"
and the "bibi" he, alternately with Mea, would watch
that the fire should not go out, and squatted near it,
mumbling quietly something in the nature of a song, in
which every little while was repeated the refrain, "Simba
kufa, simba kufa," which in the Kiswahili language
means, "The lion is killed."

But the "great master" and the little "bibi" were not
inclined to sleep. Nell, at Stas' urgent request, barely
swallowed a few pieces of guinea-fowl and a few grains of
boiled durra. She said that she did not care to eat or
sleep but only to drink. A fear seized Stas that she might
be suffering from fever, but he soon became satisfied that
her hands were cool and even too cold. He persuaded her
to enter the tent where he prepared bedding for her,
first searching carefully in the grass for scorpions. He
himself sat upon a stone with short rifle in hand to defend
her from attacks by wild beasts, if the fire did not afford
sufficient protection. He was beset by great fatigue and
exhaustion. In his soul he repeated to himself, "I killed
Gebhr and Chamis; I killed the Bedouins; I killed the
lion, and we are free." But it was as if those words were
whispered to him by some one else and as if he himself did
not comprehend their full meaning. He had not a feeling
that they were free, but that something awful at the same
time had happened which filled him with uneasiness and

weighed upon his bosom like a heavy stone. Finally his thoughts began to grow blunt. For a long time he gazed at the big moths hovering above the flame and in the end he nodded and dozed. Kali also dozed, but awoke every little while and threw twigs into the fire.

The night became dark and, what is a rare occurrence under the tropics, very still. They could hear only the cracking of the burning thorns and the hissing of flames which illumined the overhanging rocks forming a semi-circle. The moon did not shine into the depths of the ravine, but above twinkled a swarm of unknown stars. The air became so cool that Stas shook off his drowsiness and began to worry whether the chill would not incommode little Nell.

But he became reassured, when he recollected that he left her under the tent upon the plaid cloth, which Dinah took with her from Fayûm. It also occurred to him that riding continuously from the Nile upwards, though imperceptibly, they must have ridden, through so many days, quite high; therefore to a region which was not threatened with fever as are the low river banks. The penetrating night chill appeared to confirm this supposition.

And this thought encouraged him. He went for a moment to Nell's tent to listen whether she slept peacefully; after which he returned, sat nearer the fire, and again began to doze and even fell into a sound slumber.

Suddenly he was awakened by the growling of Saba, who previously had lain down to sleep close by his feet.

Kali awoke also and both began to look about uneasily at the mastiff, who, stretching out like a chord, pricked his ears, and with quivering nostrils scented in the direction from which they had come, gazed fixedly at the same time into the darkness. The hair bristled on his neck and back and his breasts heaved from air which during the growling he inhaled into his lungs.

The young slave flung dry twigs into the fire as speedily as possible.

"Master," he whispered. "Take the rifle! Take the rifle!"

Stas took the rifle and moved before the fire to see better in the dusky depth of the ravine. Saba's growls changed into barks. For a long time nothing could be heard, after which, however, from the distance there reached the ears of Kali and Stas a hollow, clattering sound as if some great animals were rushing in the direction of the fire. This sound reverberated in the stillness with an echo against the stony walls, and became louder and louder.

Stas realized that a dire danger was drawing near. But what could it be? Buffaloes, perhaps? Perhaps a pair of rhinoceroses seeking an exit from the ravine? In such case if the report of the shot did not scare them and turn them back, nothing could save the caravan, for those animals, not less ferocious and aggressive than rapacious beasts, do not fear fire and tread under foot everything in their way.

If, however, it should be a division of Smain's forces who, having encountered the corpses in the ravine, are pursuing the murderers? Stas did not know which would be better — a sudden death or new captivity? In addition it flitted through his mind that if Smain himself was in the division, he might spare them, but if he was not, then the dervishes would at once kill them or, what is worse, torture them in a horrible manner before their death. "Ah," he thought, "God grant that these are animals, not men!"

In the meantime the clatter increased and changed

into a thunder of hoof-beats until finally there emerged out of the darkness glittering eyes, dilated nostrils, and wind-tossed manes.

"Horses!" cried Kali.

In fact they were Gebhr's and Chamis' horses. They came running, driven evidently by fright, but dashing into the circle of light and seeing their fettered companions, they reared on their hind legs; after which, snorting, they implanted their hoofs in the ground and remained for a while motionless.

But Stas did not lower his rifle. He was certain that at any moment after the horses a shaggy-haired lion or a flat-skulled panther would appear. But he waited in vain. The horses quieted slowly, and what was more, Saba after a certain time ceased to scent. Instead, he turned about a few times on the spot as dogs usually do, lay down, rolled himself into a ball and closed his eyes. Apparently, if any rapacious animal had chased the horses, then, having smelt the smoke or seen the reflection of the fire on the rocks, it had retreated into the distance.

"Something must have frightened them badly," Stas said to Kali, "since they did not fear to rush by the body of the lion and the men's corpses."

"Master," answered the boy, "Kali can guess what happened. Many, many hyenas and jackals entered the ravine to get at the corpses. The horses ran before them, but the hyenas are not chasing them, for they are eating Gebhr and those others — "

"That may be, but do you now unsaddle the horses; remove the utensils and bags and bring them here. Do not fear, for the rifle will protect you."

"Kali does not fear," answered the boy.

And pushing aside the thorns close by the rocks, he

slipped out of the zareba. In the meantime Nell came out of the tent.

Stas rose at once and, pressing his nose close to her, claimed his usual caress. But she, extending at first her hand, withdrew it at once as if with aversion.

"Stas, what has happened?" she asked.

"Nothing. Those two horses came running up. Did their hoof-beats awaken you?"

"I was awake before then and even wanted to come out of the tent, but — "

"But what?"

"I thought that you might get angry."

"I? At you?"

And Nell raised her eyes and began to gaze at him with a peculiar look with which she had never eyed him before. Great astonishment stole over Stas' face, for in her words and gaze he plainly read fear.

"She fears me," he thought.

And in the first moment he felt something like a gleam of satisfaction. He was flattered by the thought that, after what he had accomplished, even Nell regarded him not only as a man fully matured, but as a formidable warrior spreading alarm about. But this lasted only a short time, for misfortune had developed in him an observing mind and talent; he discerned, therefore, that in those uneasy eyes of the little girl could be seen, besides fright, abhorrence, as it were, of what had happened, of the bloodshed and the horrors which she that day had witnessed. He recalled how, a few moments before, she withdrew her hand, not wishing to pat Saba, who had finished, by strangling, one of the Bedouins. Yes! Stas himself felt an incubus on his breast. It was one thing to read in Port Said about American trappers, killing in the far west red-skinned Indians by the dozens, and another to accomplish that personally and see men, alive a short while before, struggling in their death-throes, in a pool of blood. Yes, Nell's heart undoubtedly was full of fear and at the same time aversion which would always remain with her. "She will fear me," Stas thought, "and in the depths of her heart, involuntarily, she will not cease holding it ill of me, and this will be my reward for all that I have done for her."

At this thought great bitterness swelled in his bosom, for it was apparent to him that if it were not for Nell he would either have been killed or would have escaped. For her he suffered all that he had endured; and those tortures and that hunger resulted only in this, that she now stood before him frightened, as if she was not the same little sister, and lifted her eyes towards him not with former trustfulness, but with a strange fear. Stas suddenly felt very unhappy. For the first time in his life he understood what it was to be moved to tears. In spite of his will tears flowed to his eyes and were it not for the fact that it did not under any circumstances become "a formidable warrior" to weep, he might perhaps have shed tears.

He restrained himself, however, and, turning to the little girl, asked:

"Do you fear, Nell?"

And she replied in a low voice:

"Somehow — it is so horrible!"

At this Stas ordered Kali to bring the saddle-cloths from a saddle and, covering with one of them a rock on which he had previously dozed, he spread the other upon the ground and said:

"Sit here beside me near the fire. How chilly the night is! If sleep overcomes you, rest your head upon me and you will fall asleep."

But Nell repeated:

"Somehow — it is so horrible!"

Stas wrapped her carefully in plaids and for some time they sat in silence, supporting each other and illuminated by a rosy luster which crept over the rocks and sparkled on the mica plates with which the stony fissures were bespangled.

Beyond the zareba could be heard the snorting of horses and the crunching of grass in their teeth.

"Listen, Nell," Stas spoke out. "I had to do that — Gebhr threatened that he would stab us both if the lion would not be content with Kali and should continue to pursue them. Didn't you hear him? Think of it; he threatened by that not only me, but you. And he would have done it. I tell you sincerely that if it were not for that threat, though formerly I already was thinking of it, I would not have shot at them. I think I could not — But he exceeded the measure. You saw how cruelly before that time he treated Kali. And Chamis? How vilely he betrayed us. Besides, do you know what would have happened if they did not find Smain? Gebhr would likewise have vented his anger upon us — upon you. It is dreadful to think that he would have whipped you daily with the courbash, and would have tortured us both to death, and after our death he would return to Fashoda and say that we died of fever. Nell, I did not do that from fiendishness, but I had to think of this, how to save you — I was concerned only about you — "

And his face plainly reflected that affliction which overflowed in his heart. Nell evidently understood this, as she pressed yet more closely to him, while he, momentarily mastering his emotions, continued thus:

"I, of course, shall not change, and shall guard and watch over you as before. As long as they lived there was no hope of rescue. Now we may fly to Abyssinia. The Abyssinians are black and wild, but Christians and foes of the dervishes. If you only retain your health, we shall succeed, for it is not so very far to Abyssinia. And even though we do not succeed, though we fall into Smain's hand, do not think that he will revenge himself upon us. He never in his life saw either Gebhr or the Bedouins; he knew only Chamis, but what was Chamis to him? Besides, we need not tell Smain that Chamis was with us. If we succeed in reaching Abyssinia, then we are saved, and if not, you will not fare any worse, but better, for tyrants worse than those men probably cannot be found in the world. Do not fear me, Nell."

And desiring to win her confidence and at the same time cheer her, he began to stroke her little yellow head. The little maid listened, raising timidly her eyes to him. Evidently she wanted to say something but hesitated and feared. Finally she leaned her head so that her hair entirely covered her face and asked in a yet lower and slightly quivering voice:

"Stas —"

"What is it, dear?"

"They will not come here?"

"Who?" Stas asked with amazement.

"Those — killed."

"What are you talking about, Nell?"

"I am afraid! I am afraid!"

And her pallid lips began to quiver.

Silence ensued. Stas did not believe that the slain could rise from the dead, but as it was night and their bodies lay not far away, he became depressed in spirit; a chill passed over his back.

"What are you saying, Nell?" he repeated. "Then Dinah taught you to fear ghosts — The dead do not —"

And he did not finish, for at that moment something awe-inspiring occurred. Amid the stillness of the night, in the depths of the ravine, from the direction in which the corpses lay suddenly resounded a kind of inhuman, frightful laughter in which quivered despair, and joy, and cruelty, and suffering, and pain, and sobbing, and derision; the heart-rending and spasmodic laughter of the insane or condemned.

Nell screamed, and with her whole strength embraced Stas with her arms. Stas' hair stood on end. Saba started up suddenly and began to growl.

But Kali, sitting at some distance, quietly raised his head and said almost gleefully:

"Those are hyenas gloating over Gebhr and the lion —"

II

THE great events of the preceding day and the sensations of the night so tired out Stas and Nell that when finally slumber overcame them they fell into a deep sleep, and the little girl did not appear outside the tent until about noon-time. Stas rose somewhat earlier from a saddle-cloth spread near the camp-fire, and in expectation of his little companion he ordered Kali to prepare a breakfast, which in view of the late hour was to form at the same time their dinner.

The bright light of the day dispelled the terrors of the night; both awoke not only well rested, but refreshed in spirit. Nell looked better and felt stronger. As both wanted to ride away as far as possible from the place where the slain Sudânese were lying, immediately after the refreshments they mounted their horses and moved ahead.

At that time of the day all travelers in Africa stop for the noon rest, and even caravans composed of negroes seek shelter under the shade of great trees; for they are the so-called white hours, hours of heat and silence, during which the sun broils unmercifully and, looking from above, seems to seek whom to slay. Every beast at such times burrows itself in the greatest thicket, the song of birds ceases, the buzz of insects stops, and all nature falls into silence, secreting itself as if desirous of guarding against the eye of a wicked divinity. But they rode on in the ravine in which one of the walls cast a deep shadow, enabling them to proceed without exposing themselves to the scorching heat. Stas did not want to leave the ravine, firstly, because, above, they might be espied from a distance by Smain's detachments, and then it was easier to find, in rocky crevices, water, which in uncovered places soaked into the ground or under the influence of the sun's rays was transformed into steam.

The road continuously but imperceptibly led upwards. On the rocky walls could be seen from time to time yellow traces of sulphur. The water in the clefts was saturated with its odor, which reminded both children unpleasantly of Omdurmân and the Mahdists, who smeared their heads with fat mixed with sulphur powder. In some places muskcats could be smelt; but there, where from high, overhanging rocks magnificent cascades of lianas fell to the bottom of the ravine, came an intoxicating scent of vanilla. The little wanderers willingly stopped in the shade of these tapestries embroidered with purple flowers and lilies, which with the leaves provided food for the horses.

Animals could not be seen; only from time to time on the crests of rocks monkeys squatted, resembling on the blue background those fantastic idols which in India adorn the borders of temples. Big males with long manes displayed their teeth at Saba or stretched out their jaws in sign of amazement and rage, and at the same time jumped about, blinking with their eyes and scratching their sides. But Saba, accustomed already to the sight of them, did not pay much heed to their menaces.

They rode briskly. Joy at recovering liberty drove away from Stas' breast that incubus which had throttled him during the night. His mind was now occupied with the thought of what was to be done farther; how to lead

Nell and himself from a locality in which they were threatened by new captivity with the dervishes; what measures to adopt during the long journey through the wilderness in order not to die of hunger and thirst, and finally, whither to go? He knew already from Hatim that the Abyssinian boundary in a direct line from Fashoda was not more than five days' journey, and he calculated that this would be about one hundred English miles. Now from their departure from Fashoda almost two weeks had elapsed; so it was clear that they had not gone by the shortest route, but in seeking Smain must have turned considerably towards the south. He recollected that on the sixth day they crossed a river which was not the Nile, and that afterwards, before the country began to rise, they rode around great swamps. At school in Port Said, the geography of Africa was taught very thoroughly and in Stas' memory remained the name of Ballor, designating an expansion of the little-known river Sobat, a tributary of the Nile. He was not indeed certain whether they had passed that expansion, but assumed that they had. It occurred to him that Smain, desiring to capture slaves, could not seek for them directly west of Fashoda, as that country was already entirely depopulated by dervishes and small-pox; but that he would have to go to localities which heretofore were not visited by an expedition. Stas deduced from this that they were following Smain's trail, and the thought frightened him in the first moments.

He therefore reflected whether it would not be better to abandon the ravine which turned more and more plainly towards the south and go directly eastward. But after a moment's consideration he relinquished the plan. On the contrary, to follow the tracks of Smain's band at two or three days' distance appeared to him

to be the safest course as it was very improbable that
Smain would return with his human wares by way of
the same circuitous route instead of making his way
directly for the Nile. Stas understood also that Abyssinia could be reached only from the southern side where
that country borders on a great wilderness and not from
the eastern boundary which was carefully guarded by
dervishes.

As a result of these thoughts he determined to venture
as far as possible towards the south. They might encounter negroes, either refugees from the banks of the
White Nile or natives. But of the two evils Stas preferred
to have dealings with the blacks rather than with Mahdists.
He reckoned too that in the event of meeting refugees
or natives Kali and Mea might prove useful. It was
enough to glance at the young negress to surmise that
she belonged to the Dinka or Shilluk tribe, for she had
uncommonly long and thin limbs, so characteristic of
both of those tribes, dwelling on the banks of the Nile
and wading like cranes and storks, during its inundation.
Kali, on the other hand, though under Gebhr's hand he
became like a skeleton, had an entirely different stature.
He was short and thick and strongly built; he had powerful shoulders and his feet in comparison with Mea's feet
were relatively small.

As he did not speak Arabian at all and spoke poorly
the Kiswahili language with which one can converse
almost anywhere in Africa and which Stas had learned
fairly well from the natives of Zanzibar, working on the
Canal, it was evident that he came from some distant
region.

Stas determined to sound him upon this point.

"Kali, what is the name of your people?" he asked.

"Wahima," answered the young negro.

"Is that a great nation?"

"Great, which is making war upon the bad Samburus and takes their cattle."

"Is that country like this?"

"No. There are mountains and great water."

"How is that water called?"

"We call it 'The Dark Water.'"

Stas thought that the boy might come from the neighborhood of the Albert Nyanza, which up to that time had been in the hands of Emin Pasha; so, desiring to confirm this, he asked further:

"Does not a white chief live there who has black smoking boats and troops?"

"No, the old men with us say that they saw white men, (here Kali parted his fingers) one, two, three. Yes. There were three of them in long white dresses. They were looking for tusks. Kali did not see them for he was not in the world, but Kali's father received them and gave them many cows."

"What is your father?"

"The king of Wahima."

Stas was flattered a little by the idea that he had a Prince Royal for a servant.

"Would you like to see your father?"

"Kali wants to see his mother."

"What would you do if we met the Wahimas, and what would they do?"

"The Wahimas would fall on their faces before Kali."

"Lead us to them; then you shall remain with them and rule after your father, and we will go farther to the sea."

"Kali cannot find the way to them, and cannot remain, for Kali loves the great master and the daughter of the moon."

Stas turned merrily to his companion and said:

"Nell, you have become the daughter of the moon."

But, glancing at her, he saddened suddenly, for it occurred to him that the emaciated girl actually looked with her pale and transparent countenance more like a lunar than an earthly being.

The young negro became silent for a while; then he repeated:

"Kali loves Bwana kubwa, for Bwana kubwa did not kill Kali, only Gebhr, and gives Kali a great deal to eat."

And he began to stroke his breast, repeating with evident delight:

"A great deal of meat! a great deal of meat!"

Stas wanted to ascertain how Kali became the slave of the dervishes; it appeared that from the night when he was caught in a pit, dug for zebras, he had gone through so many hands that Stas could not tell from his statements what countries he had passed through and by what route he had been conducted to Fashoda. Stas was much impressed by what he said about the "dark water," for if he came from the region of Albert Nyanza, Albert Edward Nyanza, or even Victoria Nyanza, near which lay the kingdoms of the Unyoro and the Uganda, he would undoubtedly have heard something about Emin Pasha, about his troops, and about the steamers, which aroused the wonder and fear of the negroes. Tanganyika was too far away; there remained only the supposition that Kali's nation had its seat somewhere nearer. For this reason their meeting with the Wahimas was not an utter improbability.

After a few hours' ride, the sun began to descend. The heat decreased considerably. They chanced upon a wide valley in which they found water and a score or more of wild fig trees. So they stopped to rest their horses and partake of provisions. As the rocky walls at that place were lower, Stas ordered Kali to climb to the top and ascertain whether smoke could not be seen in the vicinity.

Kali complied with the order and in the twinkling of an eye reached the edge of the rocks. Peering around carefully in all directions he slid down a thick liana stalk and announced that there was no smoke, but that there were "niama." It was easy to surmise that he was speaking not of guinea-fowl but of some bulkier game, for he pointed at Stas' short rifle and afterwards put his fingers on his head to indicate horned game.

Stas in turn climbed up and, leaning his head carefully over the edge, began to look ahead. Nothing obstructed his view of the expanse, as the old, high jungle was burnt away and the new, which had already sprouted from the blackened ground, was barely a few inches high. As far as the eye could reach could be seen sparsely growing great trees, with trunks singed by the fire. Under the shade of one of them grazed a flock of antelopes which from the shape of their bodies resembled horses, and from their heads buffaloes. The sun penetrating through the baobab leaves cast quivering bright spots upon their brown backs. There were ten of them. The distance was not more than one hundred paces, but the wind blew from the animals towards the ravine, so they grazed quietly, not suspecting any danger. Stas, desiring to replenish his supplies with meat, shot at the nearest one, which tumbled on the ground as if struck by lightning. The rest of the flock ran away, and with them a great buffalo, which he did not perceive before, as he lay hidden behind a stone. The boy, not from necessity, but from a sporting vein, choosing the moment when the animal turned his side somewhat, sent a bullet after him. The buffalo staggered greatly after the shot, drew in his haunches, but rushed away, and before Stas was able to reload disappeared in the unevenness of the ground.

Before the smoke blew away, Kali sat upon the antelope and cut open its abdomen with Gebhr's knife. Stas walked towards him, desiring to inspect more closely the animal, and great was his surprise when after a while the young negro with blood-stained hands handed to him the reeking liver of the antelope.

"Why are you giving me that?" he asked.

"Msuri, msuri! Bwana kubwa eat at once."

"Eat it yourself," replied Stas, indignant at the proposition.

Kali did not allow this command to be repeated, but immediately began to tear the liver with his teeth, and greedily gulp down the raw pieces; seeing that Stas gazed at him with loathing he did not cease between one gulp and another to repeat: "Msuri! msuri!"

In this manner he ate over half of the liver; after which he started to dress the antelope. He did this with uncommon quickness and skill, so that soon the hide was flayed and the haunches were separated from the backbone. Then Stas, somewhat surprised that Saba was not present at this work, whistled for him to come to a bounteous feast of the fore parts of the animal.

But Saba did not appear at all. Instead, Kali, who was bending over the antelope, raised his head and said:

"The big dog ran after the buffalo."

"Did you see him?" Stas asked.

"Kali saw."

Saying this, he placed the loin of the antelope on his head and the two haunches on his shoulders and started for the ravine. Stas whistled a few times more and

waited, but seeing that he was doing this in vain, followed
Kali. In the ravine Mea was already engaged in cutting
the thorns for a zareba, while Nell, picking with her
little fingers the last guinea-fowl, asked:

"Did you whistle for Saba? He ran after you."

"He ran after a buffalo which I wounded with a shot,
and I am worried," Stas answered. "Those animals are
terribly ferocious and so powerful that even a lion fears
to attack them. Saba may fare badly if he begins a fight
with such an adversary."

Hearing this Nell became alarmed and declared that
she would not go to sleep until Saba returned. Stas,
seeing her grief, was angry at himself because he had
not concealed the danger from her and began to comfort
her:

"I would go after them with the rifle," he said, "but
they must now be very far away, and soon the night will
fall and the tracks will be invisible. The buffalo is badly
wounded, and I have a hope that he will fall. In any case
he will weaken through loss of blood, and if he should
rush at Saba, Saba will be able to run away. Yes! he
may return during the night, but he surely will return."

Although he said this, he did not greatly believe his
own words, for he remembered what he had read of the
extraordinarily revengeful nature of the African buffalo,
which, though heavily wounded, will run about in a circuit and lie in ambush near a path over which the hunter
goes and afterwards attack him unexpectedly, pin him on
its horns, and toss him into the air. Something similar
might happen to Saba; not to speak of other dangers
which threatened him on the return to the camp during
the night.

In fact night soon fell. Kali and Mea put up a zareba,
built a fire, and prepared supper. Saba did not return.

Nell became more and more worried and finally began to cry.

Stas with difficulty persuaded her to lie down, promising her that he would wait for Saba, and as soon as the day should break, he himself would search for the dog and bring him back. Nell indeed entered the tent, but at intervals she put out her little head from under its folds, asking whether the dog had not returned. Sleep overcame her only after midnight, when Mea came out to relieve Kali, who watched the fire.

"Why does the daughter of the moon weep?" the young negro asked Stas, when both lay down on the saddle-cloths. "Kali does not want that."

"She is sorry for Saba, whom the buffalo has surely killed."

"But perhaps he did not kill him," replied the black boy.

After this they became silent and Stas fell into a deep sleep. It was still dark, however, when he awoke, for the chill began to incommode him. The fire was partly extinct. Mea, who was to watch the fire, dozed and after a time had ceased throwing fuel upon the flames.

The saddle-cloth on which Kali slept was unoccupied.

Stas himself threw brushwood onto the fire, after which he shook the negress and asked:

"Where is Kali?"

For a time she stared at him unconsciously; afterwards coming to her senses, she said:

"Kali took Gebhr's sword and went beyond the zareba. I thought he wanted to cut more brushwood, but he did not return at all."

"Did he go long ago?"

"Long."

Stas waited for some time, but as the negro did not return, he involuntarily propounded to himself the question:

"Did he run away?"

And his heart was oppressed by the disagreeable feeling which human ingratitude always arouses. Why! he had interceded for this Kali and defended him when Gebhr vented his rage upon him for whole days, and afterwards he had saved the slave's life. Nell was always kind to him and had wept over his unhappy lot, and both treated him in the best possible manner. Now he ran away! He himself had said that he did not know in which direction the Wahima settlements were situated, and though he would be unable to find them, he nevertheless ran away. Stas again recollected those "African Travels" in Port Said, and the narratives of travelers about the stupidity of negroes, who, throwing away packages, run away although in their escape they are threatened by inevitable death. In fact, Kali, having as his only weapon Gebhr's Sudânese sword, must die of starvation, or if he did not fall again into the captivity of the dervishes would become the prey of wild animals.

Ah! Ingrate and fool!

Stas then began to meditate over this; — how far more difficult and vexatious the journey without Kali would be for them, and how much heavier the work. To water the horses and fetter them for the night, to pitch the tent, build zarebas, watch during the journey that none of the supplies and packets with things were lost, to flay and dress the slain animals, all this for want of the young negro was to fall upon him and he admitted in his soul that as to some of these employments, flaying the hides of animals, for instance, he did not have the slightest knowledge.

"Ha! it will be hard," he said, "but necessary."

In the meantime the sun emerged from beyond the horizon and, as usually happens in the tropics, in a

moment it was day. Somewhat later the water for bathing, which Mea had prepared during the night for the
little lady, began to splash, which meant that Nell had
risen and was dressing herself. In fact, she soon appeared,
already dressed, with a comb in her hand and her hair
still unkempt.

"And Saba?" she asked.

"He has not come yet."

The lips of the little girl at once began to quiver.

"He may yet return," said Stas. "You remember that
on the desert sometimes he was not seen for two days,
and afterwards he always overtook us."

"You said that you would go and search for him."

"I cannot."

"Why, Stas?"

"I cannot leave you in the ravine alone with Mea."

"And Kali?"

"Kali is not here."

Stas was silent, not knowing whether to tell her the
whole truth; but as the matter could not be concealed
he thought it best to divulge it at once.

"Kali took Gebhr's sword," he said, "and in the night
went away; I do not know where. Who knows whether
he has not run away? The negroes often do that, even
to their own destruction   I am sorry for him — But he
may understand that he has acted like a fool and — "

Further words were interrupted by Saba's joyful barking which filled the whole ravine. Nell threw the comb
on the ground and wanted to rush out to meet him. She
was prevented, however, by the thorns of the zareba.

Stas, with the greatest haste, began to scatter them about,
but before he had opened a passage Saba appeared and
after him Kali, as shiny and wet from the dew as if after
the greatest rain.

Immense joy possessed both children, and when Kali, out of breath from fatigue, came inside the enclosure, Nell flung her white hands around his black neck and hugged him with all her strength.

And he said:

"Kali did not want to see the 'bibi' cry, so Kali found the dog."

"Good boy, Kali!" answered Stas, slapping him on the shoulders. "Did you not fear in the night that you would meet a lion or a panther?"

"Kali feared, but Kali went," answered the boy.

These words gained still more the hearts of the children. Stas, at Nell's request, took out from one of the small pieces of luggage a string of glass beads with which they had been provided by the Greek, Kaliopuli, on their departure from Omdurmân; with it he decorated Kali's splendid throat; while the latter, overjoyed with the gift, glanced at once with pride at Mea and said:

"Mea has no beads and Kali has, for Kali is 'the great world.'"

In this manner was the devotion of the black boy rewarded. On the other hand Saba received a sharp rebuke, from which, for the second time in Nell's service, he learned that he was perfectly horrid, and that if he once more did anything like that he would be led by a string like a puppy. He heard this, wagging his tail in quite an equivocal manner. Nell, however, claimed that it could be seen from his eyes that he was ashamed and that he certainly blushed; only this could not be seen because his mouth was covered with hair.

After this followed breakfast, consisting of excellent wild figs and a rump of venison. During the breakfast Kali related his adventures, while Stas interpreted them in English for Nell who did not understand the Kiswahili language. The buffalo, as it appeared, fled far. It was difficult for Kali to find the tracks as it was a moonless night. Fortunately, rain had fallen two days before and the ground was not too hard; in consequence of this the heavy animal's hoofs left deep imprints upon it. Kali sought them with the aid of his toes and walked a long distance. The buffalo finally fell and must have dropped dead as there was no sign of a fight between him and Saba. When Kali found them Saba already had devoured the greater part of the fore quarter of the buffalo, and although he was fully sated he would not permit the approach of two hyenas and about a dozen of jackals, which stood waiting until the more powerful rapacious creature finished his feast and left. The boy complained that the dog also growled at him, but he then threatened him with the anger of the "great master" and the "bibi," after which he grabbed him by the collar and dragged him from the buffalo, and did not let go of him until they reached the ravine.

With this ended the narrative of Kali's nocturnal adventures, after which all in good humor mounted their horses and proceeded on their journey.

One alone, long-limbed Mea, though quiet and meek, gazed with envy at the young negro's necklace and Saba's collar, and with sorrow in her heart thought:

"Both of them are 'the great world,' and I have only a brass ring on one leg."

III

DURING the following three days they rode continuously in the ravine and always upwards. The days were as a rule scorching, the nights alternately cool or sultry; the rainy season was approaching. From beyond the horizon here and there emerged clouds, white as milk but deep and heavy. At the sides could already be seen stripes of rain and distant rainbows. Towards the morning of the third day one of these clouds burst above their heads like a barrel from which the hoops had flown off and sprinkled them with a warm and copious rain which fortunately was of brief duration. Afterwards the weather became fine and they could ride farther. Guinea-fowls again appeared in such numbers that Stas shot at them without dismounting from his horse, and in this manner got five, which more than sufficed for one meal, even counting Saba. Travel in the refreshed air was not burdensome, and the abundance of game and water removed fears of hunger and thirst. On the whole everything passed more easily than they had anticipated. So then good humor did not desert Stas, and, riding beside the little girl, he chattered merrily with her and at times even joked.

"Do you know, Nell," he said, when for a while he stopped the horses under a great bread-fruit tree from which Kali and Mea cut off fruit resembling huge melons, "at times it seems to me that I am a knight-errant."

"And what is a knight-errant?" asked Nell, turning her pretty head towards him.

"Long, long ago in the mediæval days there were knights who rode over the world, looking for adventure. They fought with giants and dragons, and do you know that each one had his lady, whom he protected and defended?"

"And am I such a lady?"

Stas pondered for a while, after which he replied:

"No, you are too small. All those others were grown up."

And it never occurred to him that probably no knight-errant had ever performed as much for his lady as he had done for his little sister. Plainly it appeared to him that whatever he had done was done as a matter of course.

But Nell felt aggrieved at his words; so with a pout she said:

"And you once said in the desert that I acted like a person of thirteen. Aha!"

"Well, that was once. But you are eight."

"Then after ten years I shall be eighteen."

"A great thing! And I shall be twenty-four! At such age a man does not think of any ladies for he has something else to do; that is self-evident."

"And what will you do?"

"I shall be an engineer or a sailor or, if there is a war in Poland, I shall go to fight, just as my father did."

While she asked uneasily:

"But you will return to Port Said?"

"We both must return there first."

"To papa!" the little girl replied.

And her eyes were dimmed with sorrow and longing. Fortunately there flew at that moment a small flock of wonderfully fine parrots, gray, with rosy heads, and a rosy lining under their wings. The children at once forgot about their previous conversation and began to follow the flight with their eyes.

The little flock circled about a group of euphorbias and lighted upon sycamores, growing at some distance, amidst the branches of which resounded voices similar to a wordy conference or a quarrel.

"Those are parrots which are very easily taught to talk," Stas said. "When we stop at a place for a length of time, I will try to catch one for you."

"Oh, Stas, thank you!" answered Nell gleefully. "I will call it Daisy."

In the meantime Mea and Kali, having cut off fruit from the bread-fruit tree, loaded the horses with it, and the little caravan proceeded. In the afternoon it began to cloud and at times brief showers occurred, filling the crevices and the depressions in the earth. Kali predicted a great downpour, so it occurred to Stas that the ravine, which was becoming narrower and narrower, would not be a safe shelter for the night, for it could change into a torrent. For this reason he determined to pass the night above, and this decision delighted Nell, particularly when Kali, who was sent to reconnoitre, returned and announced that not far away was a small grove composed of various trees, and in it many monkeys, not as ugly as the baboons which up to that time they had met.

Chancing thereafter upon a place at which the rocky walls were low and sloped gradually, he led the horses out, and before it grew dark they built a barricade for the night. Nell's tent stood on a high and dry spot close to a big white-ant hillock, which barred the access from one side and for that reason lessened the labor of building the zareba.

Near-by stood a large tree with widely spread boughs

which, covered by dense foliage, furnished shelter against rain. In front of the zareba grew single clumps of trees and further a thick forest entangled with climbing plants, beyond which loftily shot out crowns of strange palm trees resembling gigantic fans or outspread peacock tails.

Stas learned from Kali that before the second rainy season, that is, in autumn, it was dangerous to pass the night under these palm trees, for the huge fruit, at that time ripe, breaks off unexpectedly and falls from a considerable distance with such force that it can kill a person or even a horse. At present, however, the fruit was in bud, and in the distance before the sun set there could be seen, under the crowns, agile little monkeys, which, leaping gaily, chased each other.

Stas, with Kali, prepared a great supply of wood, sufficient for the whole night, and, as at times strong blasts of hot air broke out, they reinforced the zareba with pickets which the young negro whittled with Gebhr's sword and stuck in the ground. This precaution was not at all superfluous, as a powerful whirlwind could scatter the thorny boughs with which the zareba was constructed and facilitate an attack by beasts of prey.

However, immediately after sunset the wind ceased, and instead, the air became sultry and heavy. Through the rifts in the clouds the stars glittered here and there, but afterwards the night became so utterly dark that one could not see a step ahead. The little wanderers grouped about the fire, while their ears were assailed by the loud cries and shrieks of monkeys who in the adjacent forest created a veritable bedlam. This was accompanied by the whining of jackals and by various other voices in which could be recognized uneasiness and fright before something which under the cover of darkness threatened every living being in the wilderness.

Suddenly the voices subsided for in the dusky depths resounded the groans of a lion. The horses, which were pastured at some distance on the young jungle, began to approach the fire, starting up suddenly on their fettered fore legs, while the hair on Saba, who usually was so brave, bristled, and with tail curled under him, he nestled close to the people, evidently seeking their protection.

The groaning again resounded, as though it came from under the ground; deep, heavy, strained, as if the beast with difficulty drew it from its powerful lungs. It proceeded lowly over the ground, alternately increased and subsided, passing at times into a hollow, prodigiously mournful moan.

"Kali, throw fuel into the fire," commanded Stas.

The negro threw upon the camp-fire an armful of boughs so hastily that at first whole sheaves of sparks burst out, after which a high flame shot up.

"Stas, the lion will not attack us, will he?" whispered Nell, pulling the boy by the sleeve.

"No, he will not attack us. See how high the zareba is."

And speaking thus, he actually believed that danger did not threaten them, but he was alarmed about the horses, which pressed more and more closely to the fence and might trample it down.

In the meantime the groans changed into the protracted, thunderous roar by which all living creatures are struck with terror, and the nerves of people, who do not know what fear is, shake, just as the window-panes rattle from distant cannonading.

Stas cast a fleeting glance at Nell, and seeing her quivering chin and moist eyes, said:

"Do not fear; don't cry."

And she answered as if with difficulty:

"I do not want to cry — only my eyes perspire — oh!"

The last ejaculation burst from her lips because at that moment from the direction of the forest thundered a second roar even stronger than the first for it was nearer. The horses began to push upon the zareba and were it not for the long and hard-as-steel thorns of the acacia branches, they would have demolished it. Saba growled and at the same time trembled like a leaf, while Kali began to repeat with a broken voice:

"Master, two! two! two!"

And the lions, aware of each other's presence, did not cease roaring, and the horrible concert continued in the darkness incessantly, for when one beast became silent the other began again. Stas soon could not distinguish from where the sounds came, as the echoes repeated them in the ravine; rock sent them back to rock, they ascended and descended, filling the forest and the jungle, and the entire darkness with thunder and fear.

To the boy one thing seemed certain, and that was that they approached nearer and nearer. Kali perceived likewise that the lions ran about the encampment making a smaller circle each moment, and that, prevented from making an attack only by the glare of the flames, they were expressing their dissatisfaction and fear by their roar.

Evidently, however, he thought that danger threatened only the horses, as, spreading his fingers, he said:

"The lions will kill one, two, not all! not all!"

"Throw wood into the fire," repeated Stas.

A livelier flame burst forth; the roars suddenly ceased. But Kali, raising his head and gazing upwards, began to listen.

"What is it?" Stas asked.

"Rain," replied the negro.

Stas in turn listened. The branches of the tree mantled the tent and the whole zareba so that not a drop of rain fell upon the ground, but above could be heard the rustle of leaves. As the sultry air was not stirred by the slightest breeze, it was easy to surmise that it was the rain which began to murmur in the jungle.

The rustle increased with each moment and after a time the children saw drops flowing from the leaves, similar in the luster of the fire to ruddy pearls. As Kali had forecast, a downpour began. The rustle changed into a roar. Ever-increasing drops fell, and finally through the dense foliage whole streams of water began to penetrate.

The camp-fire darkened. In vain Kali threw whole armfuls into it. On the surface the wet boughs smoked only, and below, the burning wood began to hiss and the flame, however much it was replenished, began to be extinguished.

"When the downpour quenches the fire, the zareba will defend us," Stas said to pacify Nell.

After which he conducted the little girl into the tent and wrapped her in plaids, but he himself went out as quickly as possible as the briefly interrupted roars had broken out again. This time they sounded considerably nearer and as if they were gleeful.

The downpour intensified with each moment. The rain pattered on the hard leaves and splashed. If the camp-fire had not been under the shelter of the boughs, it would have been quenched at once, but as it was there hovered over it mainly smoke, amid which narrow, blue little flames glittered. Kali gave up the task and did not add any more deadwood. Instead he flung a rope around the tree and with its aid climbed higher and higher on the trunk.

"What are you doing?" Stas asked.

"Kali climbs the tree."

"What for?" shouted the boy, indignant at the negro's selfishness.

Bright, dreadful flashes of lightning rent the darkness and Kali's reply was drowned by a peal of thunder which shook heaven and the wilderness. Simultaneously a whirlwind broke out, tugged the boughs of the tree, swept away in the twinkling of an eye the camp-fire, seized the embers, still burning under the ashes, and carried them with sheaves of sparks into the jungle.

Impenetrable darkness temporarily encompassed the camp. A terrible tropical storm raged on earth and in the sky. Thunder followed thunder, lightning, lightning. The gory zigzags of thunderbolts rent the sky, black as a pall. On the neighboring rocks appeared strange blue balls, which sometimes rolled along the ravine and then burst with a blinding light and broke out with a peal so terrible that it seemed as if the rocks would be reduced to powder from the shock.

Afterwards darkness again followed.

Stas became alarmed about Nell and went groping in the darkness to the tent. The tent, protected by the white-ant hillock and the giant tree-trunk, stood yet, but the first strong buffet of the whirlwind might pull out the ropes and carry it the Lord knows where. And the whirlwind subsided, then broke out again with a fury, carrying waves of rain, and clouds of leaves, and branches broken off in the adjacent forest. Stas was beset with despair. He did not know whether to leave Nell in the tent or lead her out of it. In the first case she might get entangled in the ropes and be seized with the linen folds, and in the other she would get a thorough drenching and also would be carried away, as Stas, though beyond comparison stronger, with the greatest difficulty could keep on his feet.

The problem was solved by the whirlwind which a moment later carried away the top of the tent. The linen walls now did not afford any shelter. Nothing else remained to do but to wait in the darkness in which the lions lurked, until the storm passed away.

Stas conjectured that probably the lions had sought shelter from the tempest in the neighboring forest, but he was certain that after the storm they would return. The danger of the situation increased because the wind had totally swept away the zareba.

Everything was threatened with destruction. The rifle could not avail for anything, nor could his energy. In the presence of the storm, thunderbolts, hurricane, rain, darkness, and the lions, which might be concealed but a few paces away, he felt disarmed and helpless. The linen walls tugged by the wind splashed them with water from all sides, so, enclosing Nell in his arms, he led her from the tent; after which both nestled close to the trunk of the tree, awaiting death or divine mercy.

At this moment, between one blow of the wind and another, Kali's voice reached them, barely audible amidst the splashing of the rain.

"Great master! Up the tree! up the tree!"

And simultaneously the end of a wet rope, lowered from above, touched the boy's shoulder.

"Tie the 'bibi,' and Kali will pull her up!" the negro continued to shout.

Stas did not hesitate a moment. Wrapping Nell in a saddle-cloth in order that the rope should not cut her body, he tied a girdle around her; after which he lifted her and shouted:

"Pull!"

The first boughs of the tree were quite low so Nell's aerial journey was brief. Kali soon seized her with his powerful arms and placed her between the trunk and a giant bough, where there was sufficient room for half a dozen of such diminutive beings. No wind could blow her away from there and in addition, even although water flowed all over the tree, the trunk, about fifteen feet thick, shielded her at least from new waves of rain borne obliquely by the wind.

Having attended to the safety of the little "bibi," the negro again lowered the rope for Stas, but he, like a captain who is the last to leave a sinking ship, ordered Mea to go ahead of him.

Kali did not at all need to pull her as in a moment she climbed the rope with skill and agility as if she were the full sister of a chimpanzee. For Stas it was considerably more difficult, but he was too well-trained an athlete not to overcome the weight of his own body together with the rifle and a score of cartridges with which he filled his pockets.

In this manner all four found themselves in the tree. Stas was so accustomed to think of Nell in every situation that now he was occupied, above all, in ascertaining whether she was not in danger of falling, whether she had sufficient room and whether she could lie down comfortably. Satisfied in this respect, he began to wrack his brains as to how to protect her from the rain. But for this there was no help. It would have been easy to construct during the daytime some kind of roof over her head, but now they were enveloped in such darkness that they could not see each other at all. If the storm at last passed away and if they succeeded in starting the fire again, they might dry Nell's dress! Stas, with despair, thought that the little girl, soaked to the skin, would undoubtedly on the following day suffer from the first attack of fever.

He feared that towards the morning, after the storm, it would be as cool as it was on the previous night. Thus far the wind was rather warm and the rain as though heated. Stas was surprised at its persistence as he knew that the more strongly a storm raged the shorter was its duration.

After a long time the thunder abated and the buffets of the wind weakened, but the rain continued to fall, less copious, indeed, than before, but so heavy and thick that the leaves did not afford any protection against it. From below came the murmur of water as if the whole jungle were transformed into a lake. Stas thought that in the ravine certain death would have awaited them. Immense sorrow possessed him at the thought of what might have become of Saba, and he did not dare to speak of him to Nell. He, nevertheless, had a slight hope that the intelligent dog would find a safe haven among the rocks projecting above the ravine. There was not, however, a possibility of going to him with any aid.

They sat, therefore, one beside the other amid the expanding boughs, drenched and waiting for the day. After the lapse of a few more hours the air began to cool and the rain finally ceased. The water too flowed down the slope to a lower place as they could not hear a splash or a murmur. Stas had observed on the previous days that Kali understood how to stir up a fire with wet twigs, so it occurred to him to order the negro to descend and try whether he would not succeed this time. But at the moment in which he turned to him something happened which froze the blood in the veins of all four.

The deep silence of the night was rent suddenly by the squeaking of horses, horrible, shrill, full of pain, fears, and mortal dismay. Some mischief was afoot in the darkness; there resounded short rattlings in the throat, afterwards hollow groans, a snorting, a second squeak yet more penetrating, after which all was quiet.

"Lions, great Master! Lions killing horses!" whispered Kali.

There was something so horrible in this night attack, in the superior force of the monsters, and in the sudden slaughter of the defenseless animals that Stas for a time was struck with consternation, and forgot about the rifle. What, after all, would it have availed him to shoot in such darkness? Unless for this, that those midnight assassins, if the flash and report should frighten them, would abandon the horses already killed, and start after those which were scared away and had run from the camp as far as their fettered legs would permit them.

Stas' flesh began to creep at the thought of what would have happened if they had remained below. Nell, nestling close to him, shook as if she already were suffering the first attack of fever, but the tree at least protected them from an attack of lions. Kali plainly had saved their lives.

It was, however, a horrible night — the most horrible in the entire journey.

They sat like drenched birds on a twig, listening to what was happening below. And there for some time a deep silence continued, but soon came a peculiar sound as though of lapping, smacking of torn-off pieces of flesh, together with the horses' heavy breathing and the groans of the monsters.

The odor of the raw meat and blood reached up to the tree, as the lions feasted not farther than twenty paces from the zareba.

And they feasted so long that in the end anger seized

Stas. He seized the rifle and fired in the direction of the sounds.

But he was answered only by a broken, irritated roar, after which resounded the cracking of bones, rattling in powerful jaws. In the depths glared the blue and red eyes of hyenas and jackals waiting for their turn.

And thus the long hours of the night passed away.

IV

THE sun finally rose and illuminated the jungle, groups
of trees, and the forest. The lions had disappeared
before the first ray began to gleam on the horizon. Stas
commanded Kali to build a fire. Mea was ordered to
take Nell's clothes out of the leather bag in which they
were packed, to dry them, and to dress anew the little
girl as soon as possible; while Stas himself, taking his
rifle, proceeded to visit the camp and at the same time
to view the devastation wrought by the storm and the
two midnight assassins.

Immediately beyond the zareba, of which only the
pickets remained, lay the first horse almost half devoured;
about a hundred paces farther the second, barely touched,
and immediately behind him the third, disemboweled,
and with crushed head. All presented a horrible sight;
their eyes were open, full of settled terror, and their teeth
were bared. The ground was trampled upon; in the depressions were whole puddles of blood. Stas was seized
with such rage that at the moment he almost wished that
the shaggy head of a marauder, sluggish after the nocturnal feast, would emerge from some cluster of trees
that he might put a bullet in him. But he had to postpone his revenge to a later time for at present he had
something else to do. It was necessary to find and capture the remaining horses. The boy assumed that they
must have sought shelter in the forest, and that the same

was true of Saba, whose body was nowhere to be seen. The hope that the faithful companion in misfortune had not fallen a victim to the predaceous beasts pleased Stas so much that he gained more courage. His happiness was yet augmented by the discovery of the donkey. It appeared that the sagacious, long-eared creature did not wish to fatigue himself by a too distant flight. He had ensconced himself outside of the zareba in a corner formed by the white-ant hillock and the tree and there, having his head and sides protected, had awaited developments, prepared in an emergency to repel an attack by kicking heroically with his heels. But the lions, apparently, did not perceive him at all, so when the sun rose and danger passed away he deemed it proper to lie down and rest after the dramatic sensations of the night.

Stas, strolling about the camp, finally discovered upon the softened ground the imprint of horses' hoofs. The tracks led in the direction of the forest and afterwards turned towards the ravine. This was a favorable circumstance for the capture of the horses in the ravine did not present any great difficulties. Between ten and twenty paces farther he found in the grass the fetters which one of the horses had broken in his escape. This one must have run away so far that for the time being he must be regarded as lost. On the other hand, the two espied by Stas were behind a low rock, not in the hollow itself, but on the brink. One of them was rolling about, while the other was cropping the new light-green grass. Both looked unusually exhausted, as if after a long journey. But the daylight had banished fear from their hearts, so they greeted Stas with a short, friendly neigh. The horse which was rolling about started to his feet. The boy observed that this one also had freed himself from his fetters, but fortunately he apparently preferred to remain with his companion instead of running away wherever his eyes should lead him.

Stas left both horses near the rock and went to the brink of the ravine to ascertain whether a farther journey by way of it was feasible. And he saw that owing to the great declivity the water had flowed away and the bottom was almost dry.

After a while his attention was attracted to a white object entangled in the climbing plants in the recess of the opposite rocky wall. It appeared that it was the top of the tent which the wind had carried as far as that and driven into the thicket so that the water could not carry it away. The tent, at any rate, assured Nell of a better protection than a hut hurriedly constructed of boughs; so its recovery greatly delighted Stas.

But his joy increased still more when from a lower recess partly hidden by lianas Saba sprang out, holding in his teeth some kind of animal whose head and tail hung from his jaws. The powerful dog, in the twinkling of an eye, reached the top, and laid at Stas' feet a striped hyena with broken back and gnawed foot. After which he began to wag his tail and bark joyfully as if he wanted to say:

"I admit that I behaved like a coward before the lions, but to tell the truth, you sat perched on the tree like guinea-fowls. Look, however! I did not waste the night altogether."

And he was so proud of himself that Stas was barely able to induce him to leave the bad-smelling animal on the spot and not to carry it as a gift to Nell.

When they both returned a good fire was burning in the camp; water was bubbling in the utensils in which boiled durra grain, two guinea-fowls, and smoked strips of venison. Nell was already attired in a dry dress but looked so wretched and pale that Stas became alarmed about her, and, taking her hand to ascertain whether she had a fever, asked:

"Nell, what ails you?"

"Nothing, Stas; only I do want to sleep so much."

"I believe you! After such a night! Thank God, your hands are cool. Ah, what a night it was! No wonder you want to sleep. I do also. But don't you feel sick?"

"My head aches a little."

Stas placed his palm on her head. Her little head was as cold as her hands; this, however, only proved great exhaustion and weakness, so the boy sighed and said:

"Eat something warm and immediately afterwards lie down to sleep and you will sleep until the evening. To-day, at least, the weather is fine and it will not be as it was yesterday."

And Nell glanced at him with fear.

"But we will not pass the night here."

"No, not here, for there lie the gnawed remains of the horses; we will select some other tree, or will go to the ravine and there will build a zareba such as the world has not seen. You will sleep as peacefully as in Port Said."

But she folded her little hands and began to beg him with tears that they should ride farther, as in that horrible place she would not be able to close her eyes and surely would become ill. And in this way she begged him, in this way she repeated, gazing into his eyes, "What, Stas? — Well?" so that he agreed to everything.

"Then we shall ride by way of the ravine," he said, "for there is shade there. Only promise me that if you feel weak or sick, you will tell me."

"I am strong enough. Tie me to the saddle and I will sleep easily on the road."

"No. I shall place you on my horse and I shall hold you. Kali and Mea will ride on the other and the donkey will carry the tent and things."

"Very well! very well!"

"Immediately after breakfast you must take a nap. We cannot start anyway before noon. It is necessary to catch the horses, to fold the tent, to rearrange the packs. Part of the things we shall leave here for now we have but two horses altogether. This will require a few hours and in the meantime you will sleep and refresh yourself. To-day will be hot, but shade will not be lacking under the tree."

"And you — and Mea and Kali? I am so sorry that I alone shall sleep while you will be tiring yourselves —"

"On the contrary, we shall have time to nap. Don't worry about me. In Port Said during examination time I often did not sleep whole nights; of which my father knew nothing. My classmates also did not sleep. But a man is not a little fly like you. You have no idea how you look to-day — just like glass. There remain only eyes and tufts of hair; there is no face at all."

He said this jestingly, but in his soul he feared, as by the strong daylight Nell plainly had a sickly countenance and for the first time he clearly understood that if it continued thus the poor child not only might, but must, die. At this thought his legs trembled for he suddenly felt that in case of her death he would not have anything to live for, or a reason for returning to Port Said.

"For what would I then have to do?" he thought.

For a while he turned away in order that Nell might not observe the grief and fear in his eyes, and afterwards went to the things deposited under the tree. He threw aside the saddle-cloth with which the cartridge box was covered, opened it, and began to search for something.

He had hidden there in a small glass bottle the last of the quinine powders and had guarded it like an "eye in the head" for "the black hour," that is, for the emergency when Nell should be fever-stricken. But now he was almost certain that after such a night the first attack would come, so he determined to prevent it. He did this with a heavy heart, thinking of what would happen later, and were it not that it did not become a man and the leader of a caravan to weep, he would have burst into tears over this last powder.

So, desiring to conceal his emotion, he assumed a very stern mien and, addressing the little girl, said:

"Nell, before you eat, take the rest of the quinine."

She, on the other hand, asked:

"But if you catch the fever?"

"Then I will shiver. Take it, I tell you."

She took it without further resistance, for from the time he killed the Sudânese she feared him a little, notwithstanding all his efforts for her comfort and the kindness he evinced towards her. Afterwards they sat down to breakfast, and after the fatigue of the night, the hot broth of guinea-fowl tasted delicious. Nell fell asleep immediately after the refreshment and slept for several hours. Stas, Kali, and Mea during that time put the caravan in order. They brought from the ravine the top of the tent, saddled the horses, and put the packages on the donkey and buried under the roots of the tree those things which they could not take with them. Drowsiness terribly assailed them at the work, and Stas, from fear that they should fall asleep, permitted himself and them to take short naps in turn.

It was perhaps two o'clock when they started on their further journey. Stas held Nell before him; Kali rode with Mea on the other horse. They did not ride at once down the ravine, but proceeded between its brink and the forest. The young jungle had grown considerably during the rainy night; the soil under it, however, was black and bore traces of fire. It was easy to surmise that Smain had passed that way with his division, or that the fire driven from far by a strong gale had swept over the dry jungle and, finally encountering a damp forest, had passed on by a not very wide track between it and the ravine. Stas wanted to ascertain whether traces of Smain's camp or imprints of hoofs could not be found on this track; and with pleasure he became convinced that nothing resembling them could be seen. Kali, who was well versed in such matters, claimed positively that the fire must have been borne by the wind and that since that time at least a fortnight must have elapsed.

"This proves," observed Stas, "that Smain, with his Mahdists, is already the Lord knows where, and in no case shall we fall into his hands."

Afterwards he and Nell began to gaze curiously at the vegetation, as thus far they had not ridden so close to a tropical forest. They rode now along its very edge in order to have the shade over their heads. The soil here was moist and soft, overgrown with dark-green grass, moss, and ferns. Here and there lay decomposed trunks, covered as though with a carpet of most beautiful orchids, with flowers brightly colored like butterflies and brightly colored cups in the center of the crown. Wherever the sun reached, the ground was gilded by other odd orchids, small and yellow, in which two petals protruding on the sides of a third petal created a resemblance to the head of a little animal with big ears ending abruptly. In some places the forest was lined with bushes of wild jasmine draped in garlands with thin, climbing plants, blooming rose-colored. The shallow hollows and de-

pressions were overgrown with ferns, compressed into
one impenetrable thicket, here low and expansive, there
high, entwined with climbing plants, as though distaffs,
reaching up to the first boughs of the trees and spreading
under them in delicate green lace.   In the depths there
was a great variety of trees; date, raffia, fan-palm, sycamore, bread-fruit, euphorbia, immense varieties of senna,
acacia; trees with foliage dark and glittering and light
or red as blood grew side by side, trunk by trunk, with
entangled branches from which shot yellow and purple
flowers resembling candlesticks.   In some groups the
tree-tops could not be seen as the climbing plants covered
them from top to bottom, and leaping from trunk to trunk
formed the letters W and M and hung in form of fes-
toons, portières, and whole curtains.   Caoutchouc lianas
just strangled the trees with thousands of serpentine
tendrils and transformed them into pyramids, buried
with white flowers like snow.   About the greater lianas the
smaller entwined and the medley became so thick that
it formed a wall through which neither man nor animal
could penetrate.   Only in places where the elephants,
whose strength nothing can resist, forced their way,
were there beaten down in the thicket deep and winding
passageways, as it were.

The song of birds which so pleasantly enlivens the
European forest could not be heard at all; instead, on
the tree-tops resounded the strangest calls, similar to the
sound of a saw, to the beating of a drum, to the clatter of
a stork, to the squeaking of old doors, to the clapping of
hands, to caterwauling, or even to the loud, excited talk
of men.   From time to time soared above the trees flocks
of parrots, gray, green, white, or a small bevy of gaudily
plumaged toucans in a quiet, wavy flight.   On the snowy
background of the rubber climbing plants glimmered like

sylvan sprites, little monkey-mourners, entirely black with the exception of white tails, a white girdle on the sides, and white whiskers enveloping faces of the hue of coal.

The children gazed with admiration at this virgin forest which the eyes of a white man perhaps had never beheld. Saba every little while plunged into the thicket from which came his happy barks. The quinine, breakfast, and sleep had revived little Nell. Her face was animated and assumed bright colors, her eyes sparkled. Every moment she asked Stas the names of various trees and birds and he answered as well as he could. Finally she announced that she wanted to dismount from the horse and pluck a bunch of flowers.

But the boy smiled and said:

"The siafu would eat you at once."

"What is a siafu? Is it worse than a lion?"

"Worse and not worse. They are ants which bite terribly. There are a great many of them on the branches from which they fall on people's backs like a rain of fire. But they also walk on the ground. Dismount from the horse and try merely to walk a little in the forest and at once you will begin to jump and whine like a monkey. It is easier to defend one's self against a lion. At times they move in immense ranks and then everything gives way to them."

"And would you be able to cope with them?"

"I? Of course. With the help of fire or boiling water."

"You always know how to take care of yourself," she said with deep conviction.

These words flattered Stas greatly; so he replied conceitedly and at the same time merrily:

"If you were only well, then as to the rest depend upon me."

"My head does not even ache now."

"Thank God! Thank God!"

Speaking thus they passed the forest, but one flank of which reached the hollow way. The sun was still high in the heaven and broiled intensely, as the weather cleared and in the sky not a cloud could be seen. The horses were covered with sweat and Nell began to complain of the heat. For this reason Stas, having selected a suitable place, turned to the ravine in which the western wall cast a deep shadow. It was cool there, and the water remaining in the depressions after the downpour was also comparatively cool. Over the little travelers' heads continually flew from one brink of the ravine to the other toucans with purple heads, blue breasts and yellow wings; so the boy began to tell Nell what he knew from books about their habits.

"Do you know," he said, "there are certain toucans which during the breeding season seek hollows in trees; there the female lays eggs and sits upon them, while the male pastes the opening with clay so that only her head is visible, and not until the young are hatched does the male begin to peck with his long beak and free the mother."

"And what does she eat during that time?"

"The male feeds her. He continually flies about and brings her all kind of berries."

"And does he permit her to sleep?" she asked in a sleepy voice. Stas smiled.

"If Mrs. Toucan has the same desire that you have at this moment, then he permits her."

In fact, in the cold ravine an unconquerable drowsiness oppressed the little girl, as from morning until early in the afternoon she had rested but little. Stas had a sincere desire to follow her example, but could not as he had to hold her, fearing that she might fall; besides, it was immensely uncomfortable for him to sit man-fashion on the flat and wide saddle which Hatim and Seki Tamala had provided for the little one in Fashoda. He did not dare to move and rode the horse as slowly as possible in order not to awaken her.

She, in the meantime, leaning backwards, supported her little head upon his shoulder and slept soundly.

But she breathed so regularly and calmly that Stas ceased to regret the last quinine powder. He felt that danger of fever was removed and commenced to reason thus:

"The ravine continually leads upwards and even now is quite steep. We are higher and the country is drier and drier. It is necessary only to find some sort of elevation, well shaded, near some swift stream, and there establish quarters and give the little one a few weeks' rest, and perhaps wait through the whole massica (the spring rainy season). Not every girl could endure even one tenth of these hardships, but it is necessary that she should rest! After such a night another girl would have been stricken with fever and she — how soundly she sleeps! — Thank God!"

And these thoughts brought him into a good humor; so looking down at Nell's little head resting on his bosom, he said to himself merrily and at the same time with certain surprise:

"It is odd, however, how fond I am of this little fly! To tell the truth, I always liked her, but now more and more."

And not knowing how to explain such a strange symptom he came to the following conclusion:

"It is because we have passed together through so much and because she is under my protection."

In the meantime he held that "fly" very carefully with his right hand around her waist in order that she should not slip from the saddle and bruise her little nose. They advanced slowly in silence; only Kali hummed under his nose — a song in praise of Stas.

"Great master kills Gebhr, kills a lion and a buffalo! Yah! Yah! Much meat! Much meat! Yah! Yah!"

"Kali," Stas asked in a low tone, "do the Wahimas hunt lions?"

"The Wahimas fear lions but the Wahimas dig pits and if in the night time the lion falls in, then the Wahimas laugh."

"What do you then do?"

"The Wahimas hurl lot of spears until lion is like a hedgehog. Then they pull him out of the pit and eat him. Lion is good." And according to his habit, he stroked his stomach.

Stas did not like this method of hunting; so he began to ask what other game there was in the Wahima country and they conversed further about antelopes, ostriches, giraffes, and rhinoceroses until the roar of a waterfall reached them.

"What is that?" Stas exclaimed. "Are there a river and waterfall ahead of us?"

Kali nodded his head in sign that obviously such was the fact.

And for some time they rode more quickly, listening to the roar which each moment became more and more distinct.

"A waterfall!" repeated Stas, whose curiosity was aroused.

But they had barely passed one or two bends when their way was barred by an impassable obstruction.

Nell, whom the motion of the horse had lulled to sleep, awoke at once.

"Are we already stopping for the night?" she asked.

"No, but look! A rock closes the ravine."

"Then what shall we do?"

"It is impossible to slip beside it for it is too close there; so it will be necessary that we turn back a little, get on top, and ride around the obstruction; but it is yet two hours to night; therefore we have plenty of time. Let us rest the horses a little. Do you hear the waterfall?"

"I do."

"We will stop near it for the night."

After which he turned to Kali, ordered him to climb to the brink of the ridge and see whether, beyond, the ravine was not filled with similar obstructions; he himself began to examine the rock carefully, and after a while he exclaimed:

"It broke off and tumbled down not long ago. Nell, do you see that fragment? Look how fresh it is. There is no moss on it, nor vegetation. I already understand, I understand!"

And with his hand he pointed at a baobab tree growing on the brink of the ravine whose huge roots hung over the wall and were parallel with the fragment.

"That root grew in a crevice between the wall and the rock, and growing stronger, it finally split the rock. That is a singular matter for stone is harder than wood; I know, however, that in mountains this often happens. After that anything can shake such a stone which barely keeps its place, and the stone falls off."

"But what could shake it?"

"It is hard to say. Maybe some former storm, perhaps yesterday's."

At this moment Saba, who previously had remained behind the caravan, came running up; he suddenly stood still as if pulled from behind by the tail, scented; afterwards squeezed into the narrow passage between the wall

and the detached rock, but immediately began to retreat
with bristling hair.

Stas dismounted from the horse to see what could
have scared the dog.

"Stas, don't go there," Nell begged; "a lion might
be there."

The boy, who was something of a swashbuckler and
who from the previous day had taken extraordinary
offense at lions, replied:

"A great thing. A lion in daylight!"

However, before he approached the passageway, Kali's
voice resounded from above:

"Bwana kubwa! Bwana kubwa!"

"What is it?" Stas asked.

The negro slid down the stalk of the climbing plant
in the twinkling of an eye. From his face it was easy to
perceive that he brought some important news.

"An elephant!" he shouted.

"An elephant?"

"Yes," answered the young negro, waving his hands;
"there thundering water, here a rock. The elephant
cannot get out. Great master kill the elephant and Kali
will eat him. Oh, eat, eat!"

And at this thought he was possessed by such joy
that he began to leap, slapping his knees with his palms
and laughing as if insane, in addition rolling his eyes and
displaying his white teeth.

Stas at first did not understand why Kali said that
the elephant could not get out of the ravine. So, desiring
to see what had happened, he mounted his horse and
entrusting Nell to Mea in order to have his hands free
in an emergency, he ordered Kali to sit behind him; after
which they all turned back and began to seek a place
by which they could reach the top. On the way Stas

questioned him how the elephant got into such a place and from Kali's replies he ascertained more or less what had happened.

The elephant evidently ran before the fire by way of the ravine during the burning of the jungle; on the way he forcibly bumped against a loosened rock, which tumbled down and cut off his retreat. After that, having reached the end of the hollow, he found himself on the edge of a precipice below which a river ran, and in this manner was imprisoned.

After a while they discovered an outlet but so steep that it was necessary to dismount from the horses and lead them after. As the negro assured them that the river was very near they proceeded on foot. They finally reached a promontory, bounded on one side by a river, on the other by the hollow, and glancing downward they beheld on the bottom of a dell an elephant.

The huge beast was lying on its stomach and to Stas' great surprise did not start up at the sight of them. Only when Saba came running to the brink of the dell and began to bark furiously did he for a moment move his enormous ears and raise his trunk, but he dropped it at once.

The children, holding hands, gazed long at him in silence, which finally was broken by Kali.

"He is dying of hunger," he exclaimed.

The elephant was really so emaciated that his spine protruded, his sides were shrunken, his ribs were distinctly outlined notwithstanding the thickness of his hide, and it was easy to conjecture that he did not rise because he did not now have sufficient strength.

The ravine, which was quite wide at its opening, changed into a dell, locked in on two sides by perpendicular rocks, and on its bottom a few trees grew. These trees were broken; their bark was peeled and on the branches there was not a leaf. The climbing plants hanging from the rocks were torn to pieces and gnawed, and the grass in the dell was cropped to the last blade.

Stas, examining the situation thoroughly, began to share his observations with Nell, but being impressed with the inevitable death of the huge beast he spoke in a low tone as if he feared to disturb the last moments of its life.

"Yes, he really is dying of starvation. He certainly has been confined here at least two weeks, that is, from the time when the old jungle was burnt. He ate everything that there was to eat and now is enduring torments, particularly as, here above, bread-fruit trees and acacias with great pods are growing, and he sees them but cannot reach them."

And for a while they again gazed in silence. The elephant from time to time turned towards them his small, languid eyes and something in the nature of a gurgle escaped from his throat.

"Indeed," the boy declared, "it is best to cut short his pangs."

Saying this, he raised the rifle to his face, but Nell clutched his jacket and, braced upon both of her little feet, began to pull him with all her strength away from the brink of the hollow.

"Stas! Don't do that! Stas, let us give him something to eat! He is so wretched! I don't want you to kill him! I don't want it! I don't!"

And stamping with her little feet, she did not cease pulling him, and he looked at her with great astonishment and, seeing her eyes filled with tears, said:

"But, Nell!—"

"I don't want it. I won't let him be killed! I shall get the fever if you kill him."

For Stas this threat was sufficient to make him forego his murderous design in regard to the elephant before them and in regard to anything else in the world. For a time he was silent, not knowing what reply to make to the little one, after which he said:

"Very well! very well! I tell you it is all right! Nell, let go of me!"

And Nell at once hugged him and through her tear-dimmed eyes a smile gleamed. Now she was concerned only about giving the elephant something to eat as quickly as possible. Kali and Mea were greatly astonished when they learned that the Bwana kubwa not only would not kill the elephant, but that they were to pluck at once as many melons from the bread-fruit trees, as many acacia pods, and as much of all kinds of weeds as they were able. Gebhr's two-edged Sudânese sword was of great use to Kali at this labor, and were it not for that the work would not have proceeded so easily. Nell, however, did not want to wait for its completion and when the first melon fell from the tree she seized it with both her hands and, carrying it to the ravine, she repeated rapidly as if from fear that some one else might want to supplant her:

"I! I! I!"

But Stas did not in the least think of depriving her of this pleasure, but from fear that through too much zeal she might fall over with the melon, he seized her by the belt and shouted:

"Throw!"

The huge fruit rolled over the steep declivity and fell close to the elephant's feet, while the latter in the twinkling of an eye stretched out his trunk and seized it; afterwards he bent his trunk as if he wanted to place the melon under his throat and this much the children saw of him.

"He ate it!" exclaimed the happy girl.

"I suppose so," answered Stas, laughing.

And the elephant stretched out his trunk towards them as if he wanted to beg for more and emitted in a powerful tone:

"Hruumf!"

"He wants more!"

"I suppose so!" repeated Stas.

The second melon followed in the track of the first and in the same manner afterwards disappeared in a moment a third, fourth, tenth; later acacia pods and whole bundles of grass and great leaves began to fly down. Nell did not allow any one to take her place, and when her little hands grew tired from the work, she shoved new supplies with her little feet; while the elephant ate and, raising his trunk, from time to time trumpeted his thunderous "hruumf" as a sign that he wanted to eat still more, but Nell claimed that it was a sign of gratitude.

But Kali and Mea finally were fatigued with the work which they performed with great alacrity under the impression that Bwana kubwa wanted first to fatten the elephant and afterwards to kill him. At last, however, Bwana kubwa ordered them to stop, as the sun was setting and it was time to start the construction of the zareba. Fortunately this was not a difficult matter, for two sides of the triangular promontory were utterly inaccessible, so that it was necessary only to fence in the third. Acacias with big thorns also were not lacking.

Nell did not retire a step from the ravine and, squatting upon its brink, announced from a distance to Stas what the elephant was doing. At frequent intervals her thin little voice resounded:

"He is searching about with his trunk!"

Or: "He is moving his ears. What big ears he has!"

"Stas! Stas! He is getting up! Oh!"

Stas approached hurriedly and seized Nell's hand.

The elephant actually rose, and now the children could observe his immense size. They had previously seen huge elephants which were carried on vessels through the Suez Canal bound from India to Europe, but not one of them could compare with this colossus, who actually looked like a huge slate-colored rock walking on four feet. He differed from the others in the size of his tusks which reached five or more feet and, as Nell already observed, his ears, which were of fabulous proportions. His fore legs were high but comparatively thin, which was undoubtedly due to the fast of many days.

"Oh, that is a Lilliputian!" laughed Stas. "If he should rear himself and stretch out his trunk, he might catch you by the feet."

But the colossus did not think of rearing or catching any one by the feet. With an unsteady gait he approached the egress of the ravine, gazed for a while over the precipice, at the bottom of which water was seething; afterwards he turned to the wall close to the waterfall, directed his trunk towards it, and, having immersed it as best he could, began to drink.

"It is his good fortune," Stas said, "that he can reach the water with his trunk. Otherwise he would have died."

The elephant drank so long that finally the little girl became alarmed.

"Stas, won't he harm himself?" she asked.

"I don't know," he replied, laughing, "but since you have taken him under your care, warn him now."

So Nell leaned over the edge and cried:

"Enough, dear elephant, enough!"

And the dear elephant, as if he understood what was the matter, stopped drinking at once, and instead, began to splash water over himself. First he splashed water on his feet, then on his back, and afterwards on both sides.

But in the meantime it grew dark; so Stas conducted the little girl to the zareba where supper already awaited them.

Both were in excellent humor — Nell because she had saved the elephant's life and Stas because he saw her eyes sparkling like two stars and her gladdened face which was ruddier and healthier than it had been at any time since their departure from Khartûm. A promise of a quiet and perfect night also conduced to the boy's contentment. The two inaccessible sides of the promontory absolutely secured them from attacks from those directions, and on the third side Kali and Mea reared so high a wall of thorny branches of acacias and of passion flowers that there could be no thought of any predacious beasts being able to surmount such a barrier. In addition the weather was fine and the heavens immediately after sunset were studded with countless stars. The air, which was cool, owing to the proximity of the waterfall, and which was saturated with the odor of the jungle and newly broken branches, was agreeable to breathe.

"This fly will not get the fever here," Stas thought joyfully.

Afterwards they commenced to converse about the elephant, as Nell was incapable of talking of anything else and did not cease going into transports over his stature, trunk, and tusks, which in reality were prodigious. Finally she asked:

"Honestly, Stas, is n't he wise?"

"As Solomon," answered Stas. "But what makes you think so?"

"Because when I asked him not to drink any more, he obeyed me at once."

"If before that time he had not taken any lessons in English and nevertheless understands it, that really is miraculous."

Nell perceived that Stas was making merry with her, so she gave him a scolding; after which she said:

"Say what you wish, but I am sure that he is very intelligent and will become tame at once."

"Whether at once I don't know, but he may be tamed. The African elephants are indeed more savage than the Asiatic; nevertheless, I think that Hannibal, for instance, used African elephants."

"And who was Hannibal?"

Stas glanced at her indulgently and with pity.

"Really," he said, "at your age, you are not supposed to know such things. Hannibal was a great Carthaginian commander, who used elephants in his war with the Romans, and as Carthage was in Africa, he must have used African —"

Further conversation was interrupted by the resounding roar of the elephant, who, having eaten and drunk his fill, began to trumpet; it could not be known whether from joy or from longing for complete freedom. Saba started up and began to bark, while Stas said:

"There you have it! Now he is calling companions. We will be in a nice predicament if he attracts a whole herd here."

"He will tell them that we were kind to him," Nell responded hastily.

But Stas, who indeed was not alarmed, as he reckoned that even if a herd should rush towards them, the glare of the fire would frighten them away, smiled spitefully and said:

"Very well! very well! But if the elephants appear, you won't cry, oh no! Your eyes will only perspire as they did twice before."

And he began to tease her:

"I do not cry, only my eyes perspire —"

Nell, however, seeing his happy mien, conjectured that no immediate danger threatened them.

"When he gets tame," she said, "my eyes will not perspire, though ten lions should roar."

"Why?"

"For he will defend us."

Stas quieted Saba, who would not stop replying to the elephant; after which he deliberated somewhat and spoke thus:

"You did not think of one thing, Nell. Of course, we will not stay here for ages but will proceed farther; I do not say at once. On the contrary, the place is good and healthy; I have decided to stop here — a week, perhaps, — perhaps two, for you, and all of us as well, are entitled to a rest. Well, very good! As long as we stay here we will feed the elephant, though that will be a big task for us all. But he is locked up and we cannot take him with us. Well then, what later? We shall go and he will remain here and again will endure the pangs of hunger until he dies. Then we shall be all the more sorry for him."

Nell saddened very much and for some time sat in silence, evidently not knowing what reply to make to these just remarks, but after a while she raised her head and, brushing aside the tufts of hair which fell over her eyes, turned her gaze, full of confidence, on the boy.

"I know," she said, "that if you want to, you will get him out of the ravine."

"I?"

And she stretched out her little finger, touched Stas' hand with it, and repeated:

"You."

The sly little woman understood that her confidence would flatter the boy and from that moment he would ponder on how to free the elephant.

V

THE night passed quietly and though, on the southern side of the sky, big clouds gathered, the morning was beautiful. By Stas' orders, Kali and Mea, immediately after breakfast, began to gather melons and acacia pods as well as fresh leaves and all kinds of fodder, which they deposited upon the brink of the ravine.

As Nell firmly insisted upon feeding her new friend herself, Stas cut for her from a young bifurcated fig tree something in the shape of a pitchfork in order to make it easier for her to shove down the supplies to the bottom of the ravine. The elephant trumpeted from morn, evidently calling for his refreshments, and when afterwards he beheld on the brink that same little white being who had fed him the previous day, he greeted her with a joyful gurgle and at once stretched out his trunk towards her. In the morning light he appeared to the children still more prodigious than on the preceding day. He was lean but already looked brisker and turned his small eyes almost joyfully on Nell. Nell even claimed that his fore legs had grown thicker during the night, and began to shove fodder with such zeal that Stas had to restrain her and in the end when she got out of breath too much, take her place at the work. Both enjoyed themselves immensely; the elephant's "whims" amused them especially. In the beginning he ate everything which fell at his feet, but soon, having satisfied the first cravings of hunger, he began to grow fastidious. Chancing upon a plant which was not to his taste, he beat it over his fore leg and afterwards tossed it upwards with his trunk, as if he wanted to say, "Eat this dainty yourselves;" finally, after having appeased his hunger and thirst, he began to fan with his prodigious ears with evident contentment.

"I am sure," said Nell, "that if we went down to him he would not hurt us."

And she began to call to him:

"Elephant, dear elephant, is n't it true you would not do any harm to us?"

And when the elephant nodded his trunk in reply she turned to Stas:

"There, you see he says 'Yes.'"

"That may be," Stas replied. "Elephants are very intelligent animals and this one undoubtedly understands that we both are necessary to him. Who knows whether he does not feel a little gratitude towards us? But it would be better not to try yet, and particularly not to let Saba try, as the elephant surely would kill him. But with time they become even friendly."

Further transports over the elephant were interrupted by Kali who, foreseeing that he should have to work every day to feed the gigantic beast, approached Stas with an ingratiating smile and said:

"Great master, kill the elephant, and Kali will eat him instead of gathering grass and branches."

But the "great master" was now a hundred miles from a desire to kill the elephant and, as in addition he was impulsive, he retorted:

"You are a donkey."

Unfortunately he forgot the Kiswahili word for donkey and said it in English. Kali, not understanding English, evidently took it for some kind of compliment or praise for himself, as a moment later the children heard how he, addressing Mea, boastfully said:

"Mea has a dark skin and dark brain, but Kali is a donkey."

After which he added with pride:

"The great master himself said that Kali is a donkey."

In the meantime Stas, ordering both to tend the little lady as the eye in the head and in case of any accident to summon him at once, took the rifle and went to the detached rock which blocked the ravine. Arriving at the place he inspected it attentively, examined all its cracks, inserted a stick into a crevice which he found near the bottom, and carefully measured its depths; afterwards he returned slowly to the camp and, opening the cartridge box, began to count the cartridges.

He had barely counted three hundred when from a baobab tree growing about fifty paces from the tent Mea's voice resounded.

"Master! Master!"

Stas approached the giant tree, whose trunk, hollowed through decay near the ground, looked like a tower, and asked:

"What do you want?"

"Not far away can be seen zebras, and further on antelopes are feeding."

"Good! I will take a rifle and go, for it is necessary to cure meat. But why did you climb the tree, and what are you doing there?"

The girl answered in her sad, melodious voice:

"Mea saw a nest of gray parrots and wanted to bring a young one to the little lady, but the nest is empty, so Mea will not get any beads for her neck."

"You will get them because you love the little lady."

The young negress came down the rugged bark as

quickly as possible, and with eyes glistening with joy began to repeat:

"Oh! Yes! Yes! Mea loves her very much — and beads also."

Stas gently stroked her head, after which he took the rifle, closed the cartridge box, and started in the direction in which the zebras were pastured. After a half hour the report of a shot reached the camp, and an hour later the young hunter returned with the good news that he had killed a young zebra and that the locality was full of game; that he saw from a height besides zebras, a numerous herd of ariel antelopes as well as a group of water-bucks pasturing in the vicinity of the river.

Afterwards he ordered Kali to take a horse, and despatched him for the slaughtered game, while he himself began to inspect carefully the gigantic baobab trunk, walk around it, and knock the rugged bark with the barrel of his rifle.

"What are you doing?" Nell asked him. He replied:

"Look what a giant! Fifteen men holding each other's hands could not encircle that tree, which perhaps remembers the times of the Pharaohs. But the trunk at the bottom is decayed and hollow. Do you see that opening? Through it one can easily reach the middle. We can there arrange a room in which we all can live. This occurred to me when I saw Mea among the branches, and afterwards when I stalked the zebra I was continually thinking of it."

"Why, we are to escape to Abyssinia."

"Yes. Nevertheless it is necessary to recuperate, and I told you yesterday that I had decided to remain here a week, or even two. You do not want to leave your elephant, and I fear for you during the rainy season, which has already commenced and during which fever is certain. To-day the weather is fine; you see, however, that the clouds are gathering thicker and thicker and who knows whether it will not pour before night? The tent will not protect you sufficiently and in the baobab tree if it is not rotten to the top, we can laugh at the greatest downpour. It will be also safer in it than in the tent for if in the evening we protect this opening with thorns and make a little window to afford us light, then as many lions as want to may roar and hover around. The spring rainy season does not last longer than a month and I am more and more inclined to think that it will be necessary to wait through it. And if so, it is better here than elsewhere, and better still in that gigantic tree than under the tent."

Nell always agreed to everything that Stas wanted; so she agreed now; the more so, as the thought of remaining near the elephant and dwelling in a baobab tree pleased her immensely. She began now to think of how she would arrange the rooms, how she would furnish them, and how they would invite each other to "five o'clocks" and dinners. In the end they both were amused greatly and Nell wanted at once to inspect her new dwelling, but Stas, who with each day acquired more experience and prudence, restrained her from too sudden housekeeping.

"Before we live there," he said, "it is first necessary to bid the present tenants to move out, if any such are found there."

Saying this, he ordered Mea to throw into the interior of the baobab tree a few lighted boughs, which smoked profusely because the branches were fresh.

In fact, it appeared that he did well as the gigantic tree was occupied by housekeepers upon whose hospitality no reliance could be placed.

VI

THERE were two apertures in the tree, one large, about a half a yard from the ground; the other smaller, and about as high as the first story of a city residence. Mea had scarcely thrown the lighted, smoking branches into the lower one when immediately out of the upper one big bats began to fly; squeaking and blinded by the luster of the sun, they flew aimlessly about the tree. But after a while from the lower opening there stole out, like lightning, a real tenant, in the person of a monstrous boa, who evidently, digesting the remnants of the last feast in a semi-somnolent state, had not become aroused and did not think of safety until the smoke curled in his nostrils. At the sight of the strong body, which, like a monstrous spring, darted out of the smoking interior of the tree, Stas grabbed Nell in his arms and began to run with her in the direction of the open jungle. But the reptile, itself terror-stricken, did not think of pursuing them; instead, winding in the grass and among the scattered packages, it slid away with unheard-of speed in the direction of the ravine, seeking to hide amid the rocky fissures and crannies. The children recovered their composure. Stas placed Nell on the ground and rushed for his rifle, and afterwards pursued the snake in the direction of the ravine, Nell following him. But after going a score of paces such an extraordinary spectacle struck their eyes that they stood still as if thunderstruck. Now high above the ravine appeared in the twinkling of an eye the body of the snake, and, describing a zigzag in the air, it fell again to the bottom. After a while it appeared a second time and again fell. The children, reaching the brink, saw with amazement that their new friend, the elephant, was amusing himself in this manner, for having first despatched the snake twice upon an aerial journey, at present he was crushing its head with his prodigious foot which resembled a log. Having finished this operation, he again lifted the still quivering body with his trunk; this time, however, he did not toss it upwards, but directly into the waterfall. After this, nodding both ways and fanning himself with his ears, he began to gaze keenly at Nell, and finally stretched out his trunk towards her as if claiming a reward for his heroic and, at the same time, sensible deed.

Nell ran at once to the tent and returning with a box full of wild figs, began to throw a few at a time to him, while he searched for them in the grass and placed one after another in his mouth. Those which fell in deeper crevices, he blew out with such force that, with the figs, stones the size of a man's fist flew up. The children received this exhibition with applause and laughter. Nell went back several times for new supplies, not ceasing to contend with each fig that the elephant was entirely tamed and that they could even at that moment go down to him.

"You see, Stas; we now shall have a defender. For he is afraid of nobody in the desert — neither lion, nor snake, nor crocodile. And he is very good and surely loves us."

"If he is tamed," said Stas, "and if I can leave you under his care, then really I can go hunting in perfect peace, for a better defender for you I could not find in all Africa."

After a while he added:

"The elephants of this place are wild, but I have read that Asiatic elephants, for instance, have a strange weakness for children. It has never occurred in India that an elephant has harmed a child, and if one falls in a rage, as sometimes happens, the native keepers send children to pacify him."

"Ah, you see! You see!"

"In any case you did well in not allowing me to kill him."

At this Nell's pupils flashed with joy like two little greenish flames. Standing on tiptoe, she placed both her hands on Stas' shoulders and, tilting her head backward, asked, gazing into his eyes:

"I acted as if I had how many years? Tell me! As if I had how many years?"

And he replied:

"At least seventy."

"You are always joking."

"Get angry, get angry, but who will free the elephant?"

Hearing this, Nell began at once to fawn like a little kitten.

"You — and I shall love you very much and he will also."

"I am thinking of that," Stas said, "but it will be hard work and I shall not do it at once, but only when we are ready to start upon a farther journey."

"Why?"

"Because if we should free him before he is entirely tame and becomes attached to us, he would go away at once."

"Oh! He won't go away from me."

"You think that he already is like me," retorted Stas with impatience.

Further conversation was checked by the arrival of

Kali, who brought with him the slain zebra and its colt, which had been partly devoured by Saba. It was the good fortune of the mastiff that he rushed after Kali, and was not present at the encounter with the python for he would have chased after him and, overtaking him, would have perished in his murderous coils before Stas could come to his aid. For eating the zebra he received, however, from Nell a tongue-lashing which after all he did not take too much to heart as he did not even hide his lolling tongue, with which he came running in from the hunt.

Stas announced in the meantime to Kali that he intended to arrange a dwelling in the interior of the tree and related to him what had occurred during the smoking out of the trunk, as well as how the elephant had handled the snake. The idea of living in the baobab tree, which would afford a protection not only against the rain but also against the wild animals, pleased the negro very much; but on the other hand the conduct of the elephant did not meet his approval.

"The elephant is foolish," he said, "so he threw the nioka (snake) into the thundering water, but Kali knows that nioka is good; so he will search for it in the thundering waters, and bake it as Kali is wise — and is a donkey."

"It is agreed that you are a donkey," Stas answered, "but of course you will not eat the snake."

"Nioka is good," repeated Kali. And pointing at the slain zebra, he added:

"Better than that niama."

After which both went into the baobab tree and occupied themselves in arranging the dwelling. Kali, having found on the river-side a flat stone the size of a sieve, placed it in the trunk, heaped burning coals upon it, and afterwards continually added more fuel, watching only that the decayed wood on the inside did not ignite and cause the conflagration of the whole tree. He said that he did this in order that "nothing should bite the great master and the bibi." In fact it appeared that this was not a useless precaution, for as soon as smoke filled the interior of the tree and spread even on the outside there began to creep out of the cracks in the bark a great variety of creatures; scarabees, black and cherry-colored, shaggy spiders big as plums, caterpillars of the thickness of a finger, covered as though with thorns, and loathsome and at the same time venomous scolopendras whose bite may even cause death. In view of what was occurring on the outside of the trunk it was easy to surmise how many similar creatures must have perished from the fumes of the smoke on the inside. Those which fell from the bark and lower branches upon the grass were crushed unmercifully with a stone by Kali, who was continually gazing at the upper and lower openings as if he feared that at any moment something strange might appear in either of them.

"Why are you looking so?" Stas asked. "Do you think that another snake is hiding in the tree?"

"No, Kali fears Mzimu!"

"What is a Mzimu?"

"An evil spirit."

"Did you ever in your life see a Mzimu?"

"No, but Kali has heard the horrible noise which Mzimu makes in the huts of fetish-men."

"Nevertheless your fetish-men do not fear him."

"The fetish-men know how to exorcise him, and afterwards go to the huts and say that Mzimu is angry; so the negroes bring them bananas, honey, pombe (beer made of sorghum plant), eggs, and meat in order to propitiate the Mzimu."

Stas shrugged his shoulders.

"I see that it is a good thing to be a fetish-man among your people. Perhaps that snake was Mzimu?"

Kali shook his head.

"In such case the elephant could not kill the Mzimu, but the Mzimu would kill the elephant. Mzimu is death."

Some kind of strange crash and rumble within the tree suddenly interrupted his reply. From the lower aperture there burst out a strange ruddy dust, after which there resounded a second crash, louder than the former one.

Kali threw himself in the twinkling of an eye upon his face and began to cry shrilly:

"Aka! Mzimu! Aka! Aka! Aka!"

Stas at first stepped back, but soon recovered his composure, and when Nell with Mea came running up he began to explain what might have happened.

"In all probability," he said, "a whole mass of decayed wood in the interior of the trunk, expanding from the heat, finally tumbled down and buried the burning wood. And he thinks that it was Mzimu. Let Mea, however, pour water a few times through the opening; if the live embers are not extinct for want of air and the decayed wood is kindled, the tree might be consumed by fire."

After which, seeing that Kali continued lying down and did not cease repeating with terror, "Aka! Aka!" he took the rifle with which he usually shot at guinea-fowl and, firing into the opening, said, shoving the boy with the barrel:

"Your Mzimu is killed. Do not fear."

And Kali raised his body, but remained on his knees.

"Oh, great master! great! You do not even fear Mzimu!"

"Aka! Aka!" exclaimed Stas, mimicking the negro.

And he began to laugh.

The negro became calm after a time and when he sat down to partake of the food prepared by Mea, it appeared that the temporary fright had not at all deprived him of his appetite, for besides a portion of smoked meat he consumed the raw liver of the zebra colt, not counting the wild figs, which a sycamore growing in the neighborhood furnished in great abundance. Afterwards with Stas they returned to the tree, about which there was yet a good deal of work to do.   The removal of the decayed wood and the ashes, with hundreds of broiled scarabees and centipedes, together with a score of baked bats occupied over two hours' time. Stas was also surprised that the bats could live in the immediate neighborhood of the snake. He surmised, however, that the gigantic python either despised such trifling game or, not being able to wind himself around anything in the interior of the trunk, could not reach them. The glowing coals, having caused the fall of layers of decayed wood, cleaned out the interior splendidly, and its appearance delighted Stas, for it was as wide as a large room and could have given shelter not merely to four persons, but to ten men. The lower opening formed a doorway and the upper a window, thanks to which in the huge trunk it was neither dark nor stifling. Stas thought of dividing the whole, by means of the tent canvas, into two rooms, of which one was to be assigned to Nell and Mea and the other to himself, Kali, and Saba. The tree was not decayed to the top of the trunk; the rain, therefore, could not leak to the center, but in order to be protected completely, it was sufficient to raise and prop bark above both openings in such manner that it should form two eaves. The bottom of the interior he determined to strew with sand from the river bank which had been grilled by the sun, and to carpet its surface with dry moss.

The work was really hard, especially for Kali, for he had, in addition, to cure the meat, water the horses, and think of fodder for the elephant who was incessantly trumpeting for it. But the young negro proceeded to work about the new abode with great willingness and even ardor; the reason for this he explained the same day to Stas in the following manner:

"When the great master and the 'bibi,'" he said, holding his arms akimbo, "live in the tree, Kali will not have to build big zarebas for the night and he can be idle every night."

"Then you like to be idle?" Stas asked.

"Kali is a man, so Kali loves to be idle, as only women ought to work."

"But you see, however, that I work for the 'bibi.'"

"But because when the 'bibi' grows up she will have to work for the great master, and, if she does not want to, the great master will whip her."

But Stas, at the very thought of whipping the "bibi," jumped as if scalded and shouted in anger:

"Fool, do you know who the 'bibi' is?"

"I do not," replied the black boy with fear.

"Bibi — is — is — a good Mzimu."

And Kali cowered.

After finishing his work he approached Nell bashfully; then he fell on his face and began to repeat, not indeed in a terror-stricken, but in an entreating voice:

"Aka! Aka! Aka!"

And the "Good Mzimu" stared at him, with her beautiful, sea-green eyes wide open, not understanding what had happened nor what was the matter with Kali.

VII

THE new abode, which Stas named "Cracow," was completed in the course of three days. But before that time the principal luggage was deposited in the "men's quarters" and during great downpours the young quartette staid in the gigantic trunk, perfectly sheltered. The rainy season began in earnest but it was not one of our long autumn rains during which the heavens are heavy with dark clouds and the tedious, vexatious bad weather lasts for weeks. There, about a dozen times during the day, the wind drives over the sky the swollen clouds, which water the earth copiously, after which the sun shines brightly, as if freshly bathed, and floods with a golden luster the rocks, the river, the trees, and the entire jungle. The grass grew almost before their eyes. The trees were clad with more abundant leaves, and, before the old fruit fell, buds of the new germinated. The air, owing to the tiny drops of water suspended in it, grew so transparent that even distant objects became entirely distinct and the view extended into the immeasurably far expanse. On the sky hung charming, seven-colored rainbows and the waterfall was almost continually attired with them. The brief dawn and twilight played with thousands of lights of such brilliance that the children had not seen anything like it, even on the Libyan Desert. The lower clouds, those nearest the earth, were dyed cherry-colored, the upper, better illuminated, overflowed in the shape of a lake of purple and gold, and the tiny woolly cloudlets changed colors like rubies, amethysts, and opals. During the night time, between one downpour of rain and another, the moon transformed into diamonds the drops of dew which clung on the mimosa and acacia leaves, and the zodiacal light shone in the refreshed transparent air more brightly than at any other season of the year.

From the overflow which the river formed below the waterfall came the uneasy croaking of frogs and the doleful piping of toads, and fireflies, resembling shooting stars, flew from bank to bank amid the clumps of bamboo and arum.

But when clouds covered the starry heaven and the rain began to fall it became very dusky and the interior of the baobab tree was as dark as in a cellar. Desiring to avoid this, Stas ordered Mea to melt the fat of the killed game and make a lamp of a small plate, which he placed beneath the upper opening, which was called a window by the children. The light from this window, visible from a distance in the darkness, drove away the wild animals, but on the other hand attracted bats and even birds so much that Kali finally was compelled to construct in the opening something in the nature of a screen of thorns similar to the one with which he closed the lower opening for the night.

However, in daytime, during fair weather, the children left "Cracow" and strolled over the promontory. Stas started after antelope-ariels and ostriches, of which numerous flocks appeared near the river below, while Nell went to her elephant, who in the beginning trumpeted only for food and later trumpeted when he felt lonesome without his little friend. He always greeted her with sheer delight and pricked his enormous ears as

soon as he heard from the distance her voice or her foot-
steps.

Once, when Stas went hunting and Kali angled for fish
beyond the waterfall, Nell decided to go to the rock which
closed the ravine, to see whether Stas had done anything
about its removal. Mea, occupied with preparations
for dinner, did not observe her departure; while on the
way, the little maid, gathering flowers, particularly begonia
which grew abundantly in the rocky clefts, approached
the declivity by which they at one time left the ravine
and descending found herself near the rock. The great
stone, detached from its native walls, obstructed the
ravine as it had previously done. Nell, however, noticed
that between the rock and the wall there was a passage
so wide that even a grown-up person could pass through
it with ease. For a while she hesitated, then she went in
and found herself on the other side. But there was a bend
there, which it was necessary to pass in order to reach
the wide egress of the locked-in waterfall. Nell began
to meditate. "I will go yet a little farther. I will peer
from behind the rocks; I will take just one look at the
elephant who will not see me at all, and I will return."
Thus meditating, she advanced step by step farther and
farther, until finally she reached a place where the ravine
widened suddenly into a small dell and she saw the elephant. He stood with his back turned towards her,
with trunk immersed in the waterfall, and drank. This
emboldened her, so pressing closely to the wall, she advanced a few steps, and a few more yet, and then the
huge beast, desiring to splash his sides, turned his head,
saw the little maid, and, beholding her, moved at once
towards her.

Nell became very much frightened, but as there was
no time now for retreat, pressing knee to knee, she curt-

sied to the elephant as best she could; after which she stretched out her little hand with the begonias and spoke in a slightly quivering voice.

"Good day, dear elephant. I know you won't harm me; so I came to say good day — and I have only these flowers —"

And the colossus approached, stretched out his trunk, and picked the bunch of begonias out of Nell's little fingers, and putting them into his mouth he dropped them at once as evidently neither the rough leaves nor the flowers were to his taste. Nell now saw above her the trunk like a huge black snake which stretched and bent; it touched one of her little hands and then the other; afterwards both shoulders and finally descending it began to swing gently to and fro.

"I knew that you would not harm me," the little girl repeated, though fear did not leave her.

Meanwhile the elephant drew back his fabulous ears, winding and unwinding alternately his trunk and gurgling joyfully as he always gurgled when the little girl approached the brink of the ravine.

And as at one time Stas and the lion, so now these two stood opposite each other — he, an enormity, resembling a house or a rock, and she a mite whom he could crush with one motion, not indeed in rage but through inadvertence.

But the good and prudent animal did not make angry or inadvertent motions, but evidently was pleased and happy at the arrival of the little guest.

Nell gained courage gradually and finally raised her eyes upwards and, looking as though onto a high roof she asked timidly, raising her little hand:

"May I stroke your trunk?"

The elephant did not, indeed, understand English, but

from the motion of her hand discerned at once what she wanted and shoved under her palm the end of his trunk, which was over two yards in length.

Nell began to stroke the trunk; at first carefully with one hand, afterwards with both, and finally embraced it with both arms and hugged it with perfectly childish trust.

The elephant stepped from one foot to the other and continually gurgled from joy.

After a while he wound the diminutive body of the girl with his trunk and, lifting her up, began to swing her lightly right and left.

"More! More!" cried Nell, intensely amused.

And the play lasted quite a long time and afterwards the little girl, now entirely bold, invented a new one.

Finding herself on the ground, she tried to climb on the elephant's fore legs, as on a tree, or, hiding behind them, she asked whether he could find her. But at these frolics she observed one thing, namely, that numerous thorns were stuck in his hind legs; from these the powerful beast could not free himself, first because he could not conveniently reach his hind legs with his trunk, and again because he evidently feared to wound the finger with which the trunk ended and without which he would lose his skill and cleverness. Nell was not at all aware that such thorns in the feet are a real plague to elephants in India and still more in the African jungles composed mainly of thorny plants. As, however, she felt sorry for the honest giant, without any thought, having squatted near his foot, she began to extract delicately at first the bigger splinters and afterwards the smaller, at which work she did not cease to babble and assure the elephant that she would not leave a single one. He understood excellently what she was concerned with, and bending his legs at the knee showed in this manner that on the soles between the hoofs covering his toes there were also thorns which caused him still greater pain.

In the meantime Stas came from the hunt and at once asked Mea where the little lady was. Receiving a reply that she undoubtedly was in the tree, he was about to enter the interior of the baobab tree when at that moment it seemed to him that he heard Nell's voice in the depth of the ravine. Not believing his own ears, he rushed at once to the edge and, glancing down, was astounded. The little girl sat near the foot of the colossus which stood so quietly that if he did not move his trunk and ears, one would think that he was hewed out of stone.

"Nell!" Stas shouted.

And she, engaged with her work, answered merrily:

"At once! At once!"

To this the boy, who was not accustomed to hesitate in the presence of danger, lifted his rifle with one hand in the air and with the other grabbed a dry liana stalk, which was stripped of its bark, and, winding his legs about it, slid to the bottom of the ravine.

The elephant moved his ears uneasily, but at that moment Nell rose and, hugging his trunk, cried hurriedly:

"Don't be afraid, elephant! That is Stas."

Stas perceived at once that she was in no danger, but his legs yet trembled under him, his heart palpitated violently, and before he recovered from the sensation, he began to speak in a choking voice, full of grief and anger:

"Nell! Nell! How could you do this?"

And she began to explain that she did not do anything wrong, for the elephant was good and was already entirely tamed; that she wanted to take only one look at him and return, but he stopped her and began to play with her, that he swung her very carefully, and if Stas wanted he would swing him also.

Saying this, she took hold of the end of the trunk with one hand and drew it to Stas, while she waved the other hand right and left, saying at the same time to the elephant:

"Elephant! Swing Stas also."

The wise animal surmised from her gesture what she wanted of him, and Stas, caught by the belt of his trousers, in one moment found himself in mid-air. In this there was such a strange and amusing contrast between his still angry mien and this rocking above the earth that the little "Mzimu" began to laugh until the tears came, clapping all the time her hands and shouting as before:

"More! More!"

And as it is impossible to preserve an appropriate dignity and deliver a lecture on deportment at a time when one is suspended from the end of an elephant's trunk and involuntarily goes through the motions of a pendulum, the boy in the end began to laugh also. But after a certain time, noticing that the motions of the trunk were slackening and the elephant intended to deposit him on the ground, a new idea unexpectedly occurred to him, and, taking advantage of the moment at which he found himself close to the prodigious ear, he grabbed it with both hands and in the twinkling of an eye climbed over it onto the head and sat on the elephant's' neck.

"Aha!" he exclaimed from above to Nell; "let him understand that he must obey me."

And he began to stroke the elephant's head with his palm with the mien of a ruler and master.

"Good!" cried Nell from below, "but how will you get down now?"

"That is small trouble," Stas answered.

And slinging his legs over the elephant's forehead, he

entwined the trunk with them and slid over it as if down a tree.

"That is how I come down."

After which both began to pick out the rest of the thorns from the legs of the elephant who submitted with the greatest patience.

In the meantime the first drops of rain fell; so Stas decided to escort Nell to "Cracow"; but here an unexpected obstacle presented itself. The elephant did not want to part from her and every time she attempted to go away he turned her about with his trunk and drew her towards him. The situation became disagreeable, and the merry play in view of the stubbornness of the elephant might have ended unfortunately. The boy did not know what to do as the rain became each moment heavier and a downpour threatened them. Both withdrew, indeed, somewhat towards the egress, but gradually, and the elephant followed them.

Finally Stas stood between him and Nell. He fixed his gaze upon the elephant's eyes and at the same time said to Nell in an undertone:

"Don't run, but continually draw back to the narrow passageway."

"And you, Stas?" the little maid asked.

"Draw back!" repeated Stas with emphasis, "otherwise I shall have to shoot the elephant."

The little maid, under the influence of this threat, obeyed the command; the more so as, having already unbounded confidence in the elephant, she was sure that under no circumstances would he do any harm to Stas.

But the boy stood about four paces from the giant, not removing his eyes from him for a moment.

In this manner a few minutes passed; a moment full of danger followed. The ears of the elephant moved a score of times, his little eyes glittered strangely, and suddenly his trunk was raised.

Stas felt that he was turning pale.

"Death!" he thought.

But the colossus turned his trunk unexpectedly toward the brink where he was accustomed to see Nell and began to trumpet more mournfully than he had ever done before.

Stas went peacefully to the passageway and behind the rock found Nell, who did not want to return to the tree without him.

The boy had an uncontrollable desire to say to her: "See what you have done! On account of you I might have been killed." But there was no time for reproof as the rain changed into a downpour and it was necessary to return as quickly as possible. Nell was drenched to the skin though Stas wrapped her in his clothing.

In the interior of the tree he ordered the negress to change Nell's dress while he himself unleashed Saba, whom previously he had tied from fear that in following his tracks he might scare away the game; afterwards he began to ransack all the clothing and luggage in the hope that he might find some overlooked pinch of quinine.

But he did not find anything. Only at the bottom of the small gallipot which the missionary had given him in Khartûm there lay a little white powder which would scarcely suffice for whitening the tip of a finger. He nevertheless determined to fill the gallipot with hot water and give this gargle to Nell to drink.

Then when the downpour had passed away and the sun began to shine again, he left the tree to look at the fish which Kali had brought. The negro had caught about twenty upon a line of thin wire. Most of them were small, but there were three about a foot long, silver speckled and surprisingly light. Mea, who was bred upon the

banks of the Blue Nile, was conversant with these fishes;
she said that they were good to eat and towards evening
they leap very high above the water. In fact, at the
scaling and cleaning of the first it appeared that they
were so light because they had big air bladders. Stas
took one of them about the size of an apple and brought
it to show to Nell.

"Look!" he said. "This was in the fish. We could
make a panè for our window from about a dozen of these.

And he pointed at the upper opening in the tree.

But reflecting for a time he added:

"And even something more."

"What is it?" asked Nell.

. "A kite."

"Such as you used to send up in Port Said? Oh good!
Do."

"I will. With thin, cut pieces of bamboo I will make a
frame and I will use these membranes instead of paper
for they are lighter and the rain will not soak them. Such
a kite will go away up in the air and with a powerful wind
will fly the Lord knows where —"

Here he suddenly struck his forehead.

"I have an idea."

"What is it?"

"You shall see. As soon as I figure it out better, I
will tell you. Now that elephant of yours is making such
a racket that one cannot even talk."

Indeed, the elephant, from longing for Nell, and perhaps for both children, trumpeted so that the whole ravine
shook, together with the adjacent trees.

"We must show ourselves to him," Nell said. "That
will quiet him."

And they strolled to the ravine. But Stas, entirely
absorbed in his thoughts, began in an undertone to say:

"'Nelly Rawlinson and Stanislas Tarkowski of Port Said, having escaped from the dervishes in Fashoda, are at —'"

And stopping abruptly, he asked:

"How to designate the place?"

"What, Stas?"

"Nothing, nothing. I already know, — 'are about a month's journey west of the Blue Nile and beg for immediate aid.' When the wind blows to the north or to the west I will send twenty, fifty, a hundred of such kites and you, Nell, shall help me to paste them."

"Kites?"

"Yes, and I tell you that they can be of greater service to us than ten elephants."

In the meantime they reached the brink. And now began the shuffling of the elephant's feet, the nodding, the movements of the ears, the gurgling, and again the mournful trumpeting when Nell attempted to retire even for a moment. In the end the little maid began to explain to the "dear elephant" that she could not be with him all the time, for, of course, she had to sleep, eat, work, and keep house in "Cracow." But he became quiet only when she shoved down to him with a pitchfork provisions prepared by Kali; at night he again began to trumpet.

The children that same evening named him "The King," as Nell was sure that before he got caught in the ravine he undoubtedly was the king of all the elephants in Africa.

VIII

DURING the few days following Nell passed all the moments during which the rain did not fall with the King, who did not oppose her departure, having understood that the little maiden would return a few times daily. Kali, who as a rule feared elephants, gazed at this one with amazement but in the end came to the conclusion that the mighty, "Good Mzimu" had bewitched the giant, so he began to visit him also.

The King was well disposed in his behavior towards Kali as well as towards Mea, but Nell alone could do with him whatever she pleased, so that after a week she ventured even to bring Saba to him. For Stas this was a great relief as he could with perfect peace leave Nell under the protection, or, as he expressed it, "under the trunk of the elephant," and without any fear he went hunting and even at times took Kali with him. He was certain now that the noble animal would not desert them under any circumstances and began to consider how to free him from his confinement.

And to speak properly, he long ago had discovered a way, but it required such sacrifices that he wrestled with his thoughts as to whether he would use it and afterwards postponed doing it from day to day. As he had no one to speak to about this, he finally decided to acquaint Nell with his intentions, though he regarded her as a mere child.

"The rock can be blasted with powder, but for that it is necessary to spoil a great number of cartridges; that is, to extract the bullets, pour out the powder, and make one big charge out of it all. Such a charge I will insert in the deepest fissure which I can find in the middle; afterwards I will plug it and light a fire. Then the rock will burst into a few or even a score of pieces and we can lead the King out."

"But if there is a great explosion, will he not get scared?"

"Let him get scared," answered Stas quickly. "That bothers me the least. Really, it is not worth while to talk to you seriously."

Nevertheless he continued, or rather thought aloud:

"But if I do not use enough cartridges the rock will not burst and I shall waste them in vain; if I use a sufficient number, then not many will remain. And if I should be in want of them before the end of the journey, death clearly threatens us. For with what will I hunt, with what will I defend you in case of àn attack? You well know, of course, that if it were not for this rifle and the cartridges we would have perished long ago, either at Gebhr's hands or from starvation. And it is very fortunate too that we have horses for without them we could not have carried all these things and the cartridges."

At this Nell raised her finger and declared with great positiveness:

"When I tell the King, he will carry everything."

"How will he carry the cartridges, if very few of them remain?"

"As to that, he will defend us."

"But he won't fire from his trunk as I do from the rifle."

"Then we can eat figs and big gourds which grow on the trees, and Kali will catch fish."

"That is, as long as we stay near the river. We still have to pass the rainy season here, as these continual downpours would surely prostrate you with the fever. Remember, however, that later we shall start upon a further journey and we might chance upon a desert."

"Such as Sahara?" Nell asked in alarm.

"No; one where there are neither rivers, nor fruit-trees, and only low acacias and mimosas grow. There one can live only upon what is secured by hunting. The King will find grass there and I antelopes, but if I do not have anything to shoot them with, then the King will not catch them."

And Stas, in reality, had something to worry about, as by that time, when the elephant was already tamed and had become friendly it was impossible to abandon him and doom him to death by starvation; and to liberate him meant the loss of a greater portion of the ammunition and exposing themselves to unavoidable destruction.

So Stas postponed the work from day to day, repeating to himself in his soul each evening:

"Perhaps to-morrow I may devise some other scheme."

In the meantime to this trouble others were added. At first Kali was stung at the river below by wild bees to which he was led by a small gray-greenish bird, well-known in Africa and called bee-guide. The black boy, through indolence, did not smoke out the bees sufficiently and returned with honey, but so badly stung and swollen that an hour later he lost all consciousness. The "Good Mzimu," with Mea's aid, extracted stings from him until night and afterwards plastered him with earth upon which Stas poured water. Nevertheless, towards morning it seemed as if the poor negro were dying. Fortunately, the nursing and his strong constitution overcame the danger; he did not, however, recover his health until the lapse of ten days.

The second mishap was met by the horses. Stas, who during Kali's sickness had to fetter the horses and lead them to water, observed that they began to grow terribly lean. This could not be explained by a lack of fodder as in consequence of the rains grass shot up high and there was excellent pasturage near the ford. And yet the horses wasted away. After a few days their hair bristled, their eyes became languid, and from their nostrils a thick slime flowed. In the end they ceased to eat and instead drank eagerly, as if fever consumed them. When Kali regained his health they were merely two skeletons. But he only glanced at them and understood at once what had happened.

"Tsetse!" he said, addressing Stas. "They must die."

Stas also understood, for while in Port Said he had often heard of the African fly, called "tsetse," which is such a terrible plague in some regions that wherever it has its permanent habitat the negroes do not possess any cattle at all, and wherever, as a result of temporary favorable conditions it multiplies unexpectedly, cattle perish. A horse, ox, or donkey bitten by a tsetse wastes and dies in the course of a fortnight or even in a few days. The local animals understand the danger which threatens them, for it happens that whole herds of oxen, when they hear its hum near a waterfall, are thrown into a wild stampede and scamper in all directions.

Stas' horses were bitten; these horses and the donkey Kali now rubbed daily with some kind of plant, the odor of which resembled that of onions and which he found in the jungles. He said that the odor would drive away the tsetse, but notwithstanding this preventative remedy the horses grew thinner. Stas, with dread, thought of what might happen if all the animals should succumb; how then could he convey Nell, the saddle-cloth, the tent, the cartridges and the utensils? There was so much of them that only the King could carry them all. But to liberate the King it was necessary to sacrifice at least two-thirds of the cartridges.

Ever-increasing troubles gathered over Stas' head like the clouds which did not cease to water the jungle with rain. Finally came the greatest calamity, in the presence of which all the others dwindled — fever!

IX

One night at supper Nell, having raised a piece of smoked meat to her lips, suddenly pushed it away, as if with loathing, and said:

"I cannot eat to-day."

Stas, who had learned from Kali where the bees were and had smoked them out daily in order to get their honey, was certain that the little one had eaten during the day too much honey, and for that reason he did not pay any attention to her lack of appetite. But she after a while rose and began to walk hurriedly about the campfire describing an ever larger circle.

"Do not get away too far, for something might seize you," the boy shouted at her.

He really, however, did not fear anything, for the elephant's presence, which the wild animals scented, and his trumpeting, which reached their vigilant ears, held them at a respectable distance. It assured safety alike to the people and to the horses, for the most ferocious beasts of prey in the jungle, the lion, the panther, and the leopard, prefer to have nothing to do with an elephant and not to approach too near his tusks and trunk.

Nevertheless, when the little maid continued to run around, more and more hurriedly, Stas followed her and asked:

"Say, little moth! Why are you flying like that about the fire?"

He asked still jestingly, but really was uneasy and his uneasiness increased when Nell answered:

"I don't know. I can't sit down in any place."

"What is the matter with you?"

"I feel so strangely —"

And then suddenly she rested her head on his bosom and as though confessing a fault, exclaimed in a meek voice, broken by sobs:

"Stas, perhaps I am sick —"

"Nell!"

Then he placed his palm upon her forehead which was dry and icy. So he took her in his arms and carried her to the camp-fire.

"Are you cold?" he asked on the way.

"Cold and hot, but more cold —"

In fact her little teeth chattered and chills continually shook her body. Stas now did not have the slightest doubt that she had a fever.

He at once ordered Mea to conduct her to the tree, undress her and place her on the ground, and afterwards to cover her with whatever she could find, for he had seen in Khartûm and Fashoda that fever-stricken people were covered with sheeps' hide in order to perspire freely. He determined to sit at Nell's side the whole night and give her hot water with honey to drink. But she in the beginning did not want to drink. By the light of the little lamp hung in the interior of the tree he observed her glittering eyes. After a while she began to complain of the heat and at the same time shook under the saddle-cloth and plaids. Her hands and forehead continued cold, but had Stas known anything about febrile disorders, he would have seen by her extraordinary restlessness that she must have a terrible fever. With fear he observed that when Mea entered with hot water the little girl gazed at her as though with a certain amazement and even fear and did not seem to recognize her. With him she spoke consciously. She said to him that she could not lie down and begged him to permit her to rise and run about; then again she asked whether he was not angry at her because she was sick, and when he assured her that he was not, her eyelashes were suffused with the tears which surged to her eyes, and she assured him that on the morrow she would be entirely well.

That evening, or that night, the elephant was somehow strangely disturbed and continually trumpeted so as to awake Saba and cause him to bark. Stas observed that this irritated the patient; so he left the tree to quiet them. He silenced Saba easily, but as it was a harder matter to bid the elephant to be silent, he took with him a few melons to throw to him, and stuff his trunk at least for a time. Returning, he observed, by the light of the camp-fire, Kali who, with a piece of smoked meat on his shoulders, was going in the direction of the river.

"What are you doing there, and where are you going?" he asked the negro.

And the black boy stopped, and when Stas drew near to him said with a mysterious countenance:

"Kali is going to another tree to place meat for the wicked Mzimu."

"Why?"

"That the wicked Mzimu should not kill the 'Good Mzimu.'"

Stas wanted to say something in reply, but suddenly grief seized his bosom; so he only set his teeth and walked away in silence.

When he returned to the tree Nell's eyes were closed, her hands, lying on the saddle-cloth, quivered indeed strongly, but it seemed that she was slumbering. Stas sat down

near her, and from fear of waking her he sat motionless.
Mea, sitting on the other side, readjusted every little
while pieces of ivory protruding out of her ears, in order
to defend herself in this manner from drowsiness. It
became still; only from the river below, from the direction
of the overflow, came the croaking of frogs and the melancholy piping of toads.

Suddenly Nell sat up on the bedding.

"Stas!"

"I am here, Nell."

And she, shaking like a leaf in the breeze, began to
seek his hands and repeat hurriedly:

"I am afraid! I am afraid! Give me your hand!"

"Don't fear. I am with you."

And he grasped her palm which this time was heated
as if on fire; not knowing what to do he began to cover
that poor, emaciated hand with kisses.

"Don't be afraid, Nell! don't be afraid!"

After which he gave her water with honey to drink,
which by that time had cooled. This time Nell drank
eagerly and clung to the hand with the utensil when he
tried to take it away from her lips. The cool drink seemed
to soothe her.

Silence ensued. But after the lapse of half an hour
Nell again sat up on the bedding and in her wide-open
eyes could be seen terrible fright.

"Stas!"

"What is it, dear?"

"Why," she asked in a broken voice, "do Gebhr and
Chamis walk around the tree and peer at me?"

To Stas in an instant it seemed as if thousands of ants
were crawling over him.

"What are you saying, Nell?" he said. "There is
nobody here. That is Kali walking around the tree."

But she, staring at the dark opening, cried with chattering teeth:

"And the Bedouins too! Why did you kill them?"

Stas clasped her with his arms and pressed her to his bosom.

"You know why! Don't look there! Don't think of that! That happened long ago!"

"To-day! To-day!"

"No, Nell, long ago."

In fact it was long ago, but it had returned like a wave beaten back from the shore and again filled with terror the thoughts of the sick child.

All words of reassurance appeared in vain. Nell's eyes widened more and more. Her heart palpitated so violently that it seemed that it would burst at any moment. She began to throw herself about like a fish taken out of the water, and this continued almost until morning. Only towards the morning was her strength exhausted and her head dropped upon the bedding.

"I am weak, weak," she repeated. "Stas, I am flying somewhere down below."

After which she closed her eyes.

Stas at first became terribly alarmed for he thought that she had died. But this was only the end of the first paroxysm of the dreadful African fever, termed deadly, two attacks of which strong and healthy people can resist, but the third no one thus far had been able to withstand. Travelers had often related this in Port Said in Mr. Rawlinson's home, and yet more frequently Catholic missionaries returning to Europe, whom Pan Tarkowski received hospitably. The second attack comes after a few days or a fortnight, while if the third does not come within two weeks it is not fatal as it is reckoned as the first in the recurrence of the sickness. Stas knew that the only medicine which could break or keep off the attack was quinine in big doses, but now he did not have an atom of it.

For the time being, however, seeing that Nell was breathing, he became somewhat calm and began to pray for her. But in the meantime the sun leaped from beyond the rocks of the ravine and it was day. The elephant already demanded his breakfast and from the direction of the overflow which the river made resounded the cries of aquatic birds. Desiring to kill a brace of guinea-fowl for broth for Nell, the boy took his gun and strolled along the river towards a clump of shrubs on which these birds usually perched for the night. But he felt the effect of lack of sleep so much and his thoughts were so occupied with the little girl's illness that a whole flock of guinea-fowl passed close by him in a trot, one after another, bound for the watering place, and he did not observe them at all. This happened also because he was continually praying. He thought of the slaying of Gebhr, Chamis, and the Bedouins, and lifting his eyes upwards he said with a voice choking with tears:

"I did this for Nell, oh Lord, for Nell! For I could not free her otherwise; but if it is a sin, punish me, but let her regain her health."

On the way he met Kali, who had gone to see whether the wicked Mzimu ate the meat offered to him the previous night. The young negro, loving the little "bibi," prayed also for her, but he prayed in an entirely different fashion. He particularly told the wicked Mzimu that if the "bibi" recovered her health he would bring him a piece of meat every day, but if she died, though he feared him and though he might afterwards perish, he would first so flay his hide that the wicked Mzimu would remember it for ages. He felt greatly encouraged when the meat deposited the previous night disappeared. It might indeed have been carried away by some jackal, but the Mzimu might assume the shape of a jackal.

Kali informed Stas of this propitious incident; the latter, however, stared at him as if he did not understand him at all and went on further. Passing a clump of shrubs in which he did not find any guinea-fowl, he drew nearer the river. Its banks were overgrown with tall trees from which were suspended like long stockings the nests of titmice, beautiful little yellow birds with black wings, and also wasps' nests resembling big roses, but colored like gray blotting-paper. In one place the river formed an expansion a few score paces wide, overgrown in part by papyrus. On this expansion aquatic birds always swarmed. There were storks just like our European storks, and storks with thick bills ending with a hook, and birds black as velvet, with legs red as blood, and flamingoes and ibises, and white spoon-bills with bills like spoons, and cranes with crowns on their heads, and a multitude of curlews, variegated and gray as mice, flying quickly back and forth as if they were tiny sylvan sprites on long, thin, snipe-like legs.

Stas killed two large ducks, beautiful, cinnamon colored, and treading upon dead butterflies, of which thousands strewed the bank, he first looked around carefully to see whether there were any crocodiles in the shallows, after which he waded into the water and lifted his quarry. The shots had dispersed the birds; there remained only two marabous, standing between ten and twenty paces away and plunged in reverie. They were like two old men with bald heads pressed between the shoulders. They did not move at all. The boy gazed for a while at the loathsome fleshy pouches hanging from their breasts, and afterwards, observing that the wasps were beginning to circle around him more and more frequently, he returned to the camping place.

Nell still slept; so handing the ducks to Mea, he flung himself upon a saddle-cloth and fell into a sound sleep. They did not wake until the afternoon — he first and Nell later. The little girl felt somewhat stronger and the strong broth revived her strength still more; she rose and left the tree, desiring to look at the King and at the sun.

But only now in the daylight could be seen what havoc that one night's fever had wrought in her. Her complexion was yellow and transparent; her lips were black; there were circles furrowed under her eyes, and her face was as though it had aged. Even the pupils of her eyes appeared paler than usual. It appeared also, despite her assurances to Stas that she felt quite strong and notwithstanding the large cup of broth which she drank immediately after awakening, that she could barely reach the ravine unaided. Stas thought with despair of the second attack and that he had neither medicine nor any remedy by which he could prevent it.

In the meantime the rain poured a dozen or more times a day, increasing the humidity of the air.

X

Days of suspense, heavy and full of fear, began. The second attack did not come until a week after and was not so strong as the first, but after it Nell felt still weaker. She wasted and grew so thin that she no longer was a little girl, but the shadow of a little girl. The flame of her life flickered so faintly that it appeared sufficient to blow at it to extinguish it. Stas understood that death did not have to wait for a third attack to take her and he expected it any day or any hour.

He himself became emaciated and black, for misfortune exceeded his strength and his reason. So, gazing on her waxen countenance, he said to himself each day: "For this I guarded her like the eye in the head; in order to bury her here in the jungle." And he did not understand why it should be so. At times he reproached himself that he had not guarded her enough, that he had not been sufficiently kind to her, and at such moments such sorrow seized his heart that he wanted to gnaw his own fingers. Clearly there was too much of woe.

And Nell now slept almost continuously and it may be that this kept her alive. Stas woke her a few times a day to give her nourishment. Then, as often as it did not rain, she begged him to carry her into the open air for now she could not stand on her own feet. It happened, moreover, that she fell asleep in his arms. She knew now that she was very sick and might at any moment die.

In moments of greater animation she spoke of this to Stas, and always with tears, for she feared death.

Once she said: "I shall not now return to papa, but tell him that I was very, very sorry — and beg him to come to me."

"You will return," Stas answered.

And he could not say anything more as he wanted to wail.

And Nell continued in a scarcely audible, dreamy voice:

"And papa will come and you will come sometime, will you not?"

At this thought a smile brightened the little wan face, but after a while she said in a still lower tone:

"But I am so sorry!"

Saying this she rested her little head upon his shoulder and began to weep. He mastered his pain, pressed her to his bosom, and replied with animation:

"Nell, I will not return without you — and I do not at all know what I would do in this world without you."

Silence followed, during which Nell again fell asleep.

Stas carried her to the tree, but he had barely gone outside when from the summit of the promontory Kali came running and waving his hands; he began to shout, with an agitated and frightened face:

"Great master! Great master!"

"What do you want?" Stas asked.

And the negro, stretching out his hand and pointing to the south, said:

"Smoke!"

Stas shaded his eyes with his palm and straining his sight in the direction indicated really saw in the ruddy luster of the sun, which now stood low, a streak of smoke rising far in the jungle, amid the top of two still more distant hills which were quite high.

Kali trembled all over, for he well remembered his horrible slavery with the dervishes; he was certain that this was their camping place. To Stas, also, it seemed that this could not be any one else than Smain, and at first he too became terribly frightened. Only this was wanting! Besides Nell's fatal disease, the dervishes! And again slavery, and again a return to Fashoda or to Khartûm, under the hand of the Mahdi or the lash of Abdullahi. If they caught them Nell would die at once, while he would remain a slave the rest of the days of his life; and if he did escape of what use was liberty to him without Nell? How could he look into the eyes of his father or Mr. Rawlinson, if the dervishes after her death should fling her to the hyenas. He himself would not even be able to say where her grave was.

Such thoughts flitted through his head like lightning. Suddenly he felt an insurmountable desire to look at Nell, and directed his steps towards the tree. On the way he instructed Kali to extinguish the fire and not to dare to light it during the night, after which he entered the tree.

Nell was not sleeping and felt better. She at once communicated this news to Stas. Saba lay close to her and warmed her with his huge body, while she stroked his head lightly, smiling when he caught with his jaws the subtile dust of the decayed wood floating in the streak of light which the last rays of the setting sun formed in the tree. She apparently was in a better frame of mind, as after a while she addressed Stas with quite a lively mien.

"And perhaps I may not die."

"You surely will not die," Stas replied; "since after the second attack you feel stronger, the third will not come at all."

But she began to blink with her eyelids as if she were meditating over something and said:

"If I had bitter powders like that which made me feel so well after the night with the lions — do you remember? — then I would not think the least bit of dying — not even so much!"

And she indicated upon her little finger just how little in that case she would be prepared to die.

"Ah!" Stas declared, "I do not know what I would not give for a pinch of quinine."

And he thought that if he had enough of it, he would at once treat Nell with two powders, even, and then he would wrap her in plaids, seat her before him on a horse, and start immediately in a direction opposite to the one in which the camp of the dervishes was located.

In the meantime the sun set and the jungle was suddenly plunged in darkness.

The little girl chattered yet for half an hour, after which she fell asleep and Stas meditated further about the dervishes and quinine. His distressed but resourceful mind began to labor and form plans, each one bolder and more audacious than the other. First he began to ponder over whether that smoke in the southern direction necessarily came from Smain's camp. It might indeed be dervishes, but it also might be Arabs from the ocean coast, who made great expeditions into the interior for ivory and slaves. These had nothing in common with the dervishes who injured their trade. The smoke might also be from a camp of Abyssinians or from some negro village at the foot-hills which the slave hunters had not yet reached. Would it not be proper for him to satisfy himself upon this point?

The Arabs from Zanzibar, from the vicinity of Bagamoyo, from Witu and from Mombasa, and in general from the

territory bordering on the ocean, were people who continuously came in contact with white men; so who knows
whether for a great reward they would not conduct them
to the nearest port? Stas knew perfectly well that he
could promise such a reward and that they would believe
his promise. There occurred to him another idea which
touched him to the depth. In Khartûm he saw that
many of the dervishes, particularly those from Nubia,
suffered fever almost as badly as the white people and that
they cured themselves with quinine which they stole
from the Europeans, and if it were hidden by renegade
Greeks or Copts they purchased it for its weight in gold.
So it might be expected that the Arabs from the coast
would be certain to have it.

"I shall go," Stas said to himself, "I shall go, for Nell."

And pondering more and more strongly upon the situation he, in the end, came to the conclusion that even if
that was Smain's division, it was incumbent for him to
go. He recollected that on account of the complete
rupture of relations between Egypt and the Sudân, Smain
in all probability knew nothing about their abduction
from Fayûm.

Fatma could not have had an understanding with him;
therefore that abduction was her individual scheme,
executed with the aid of Chamis, son of Chadigi, together
with Idris, Gebhr, and the two Bedouins. Now these men
did not concern Smain for the simple reason that among
them he knew only Chamis, and the others he never saw
in his life. He was concerned only about his own children
and Fatma. But he might long for them now, and might
be glad to return to them, particularly if in the service
of the Mahdi he apparently did not meet with great fortune, since instead of commanding powerful troops or
governing some vast region he was compelled to catch

slaves the Lord knew where — far beyond Fashoda. " I
will say to him," Stas thought, "that if you will lead us
to any seaport on the Indian Ocean and return with
us to Egypt, the government will pardon all your offenses;
you will rejoin Fatma and the children, and besides, Mr.
Rawlinson will make you rich; if not you will never again
see your children and Fatma in your life."

And he was certain that Smain would consider well
before he rejected such an arrangement.

Of course this was not altogether safe; it might even
prove disastrous, but it might become a plank of rescue
from that African whirlpool. Stas in the end began to
wonder why the possibility of meeting with Smain should
have frightened him at first and, as he was anxious for
quick relief for Nell, he determined to go, even that night.

It was easier, however, to say than to do it; it is
one thing to sit at night in the jungle near a good fire
behind a thorny zareba, and another to set forth amid
darkness, in high grass, in which at such a time the lion,
panther, and leopard, not to speak of hyenas and jackals,
are seeking their prey. The boy, however, recollected
the words of the young negro at the time when he went
during the night to search for Saba and, having returned,
said to him, "Kali feared but Kali went." And he repeated to himself, "I shall fear, but I will go."

He waited, however, until the moon rose, as the night
was extraordinarily dark, and only when the jungle was
silvered by her luster did he call Kali and say:

"Kali, take Saba into the tree, close the entrance with
thorns, and guard the little lady with Mea as the eye in
your head, while I go and see what kind of people are
in that camp."

"Great master, take Kali with you and the rifle which
kills bad animals. Kali does not want to stay."

"You shall stay!" Stas said firmly. "And I forbid you to go with me."

After which he became silent, but presently said in a somewhat hollow voice:

"Kali, you are faithful and prudent, so I am confident that you will do what I tell you. If I should not return and the little lady should die, you will leave her in the tree, but around the tree you will build a high zareba and on the bark you will carve a great sign like this."

And taking two bamboos, he formed them into a cross, after which he continued thus:

"If, however, I do not return and the 'bibi' does not die you shall honor her and serve her faithfully, and afterwards you shall conduct her to your people, and tell the Wahima warriors that they should go continually to the east until they reach the great sea. There you will find white men who will give you many rifles, much powder, beads, and wire, and as much cloth as you are able to carry. Do you understand?"

And the young negro threw himself on his knees, embraced Stas' limbs, and began to repeat mournfully:

"Bwana kubwa! You will return! You will return!"

Stas was deeply touched by the black boy's devotion, so he leaned over him, placed his hand on his head, and said:

"Go into the tree, Kali — and may God bless you!"

Remaining alone, he deliberated for a while whether to take the donkey with him. This was the safer course, for lions in Africa as well as the tigers in India, in case they meet a man riding a horse or donkey, always charge at the animal and not at the man. But he propounded to himself the question, who in such case will carry Nell's tent and on what will she herself ride? After this observation he rejected at once the idea of taking the donkey and set off on foot in the jungle.

The moon already rose higher in the heavens; it was therefore considerably lighter. Nevertheless, the difficulties began as soon as the boy plunged into the grass, which grew so high that a man on horseback could easily be concealed in it. Even in the daytime one could not see a step ahead in it, and what of the night, when the moon illuminated only the heights, and below everything was steeped in a deep shade? Under such conditions it was easy to stray and walk around in a circle instead of moving forward. Stas, nevertheless, was cheered by the thought that in the first place the camp, towards which he went, was at most three or four English miles distant from the promontory, and again that it appeared between the tops of two lofty hills; therefore, by keeping the hills in sight, one could not stray. But the grass, mimosa, and acacias veiled everything. Fortunately every few score of paces there stood white-ant hillocks, sometimes between ten and twenty feet high. Stas carefully placed the rifle at the bottom of each hillock; afterwards climbed to the top, and descrying the hills blackly outlined on the background of the sky, descended and proceeded farther.

Fear seized him only at the thought of what would happen if clouds should veil the moon and the sky, for then he would find himself as though in a subterranean cavern. But this was not the only danger. The jungle in the night time, when, amidst the stillness can be heard every sound, every step, and almost the buzz which the insects creeping over the grass make, is downright terrifying. Fear and terror hover over it. Stas had to pay heed to everything, to listen, watch, look around in every direction, have his head on screws, as it were, and have the rifle ready to fire at any second. Every moment it seemed to him that something was approaching, skulking,

hiding in ambush. From time to time he heard the grass
stir and the sudden clatter of animals running away.
He then conjectured that he had scared some antelopes
which, notwithstanding posted guards, sleep watchfully,
knowing that many yellow, terrible hunters are seeking
them at that hour in the darkness. But now something
big is darkly outlined under the umbrella-like acacia.
It may be a rock and it may be a rhinoceros or a buffalo
which, having scented a man, will wake from a nap and
rush at once to attack him. Yonder again behind a black
bush can be seen two glittering dots. Heigh! Rifle to
face! That is a lion! No! Vain alarm! Those are fireflies for one dim light rises upwards and flies above the
grass like a star shooting obliquely. Stas climbed onto
ant-hillocks, not always to ascertain whether he was
going in the right direction, but to wipe the cold perspiration from his brow, to recover his breath, and to
wait until his heart, palpitating too rapidly, calmed.
In addition he was already so fatigued that he was
barely able to stand on his feet.

But he proceeded because he felt that he must do so,
to save Nell. After two hours he got to a place, thickly
strewn with stones, where the grass was lower and it
was considerably lighter. The lofty hills appeared as
distant as before; on the other hand nearer were the
rocky ridges running transversely, beyond which the
second, higher hill arose, while both evidently enclosed
some kind of valley or ravine similar to the one in which
the King was confined.

Suddenly, about three or four hundred paces on the
right, he perceived on the rocky wall the rosy reflection
of a flame.

He stood still. His heart again beat so strongly that
he almost heard it amid the stillness of the night. Whom

would he see below? Arabs from the eastern coast?
Smain's dervishes, or savage negroes who, escaping from
their native villages, sought protection from the dervishes
in the inaccessible thickets of the hills? Would he find
death, or slavery, or salvation for Nell?

It was imperative to ascertain this. He could not
retreat now, nor did he desire to. After a while he stepped
in the direction of the fire, moving as quietly as possible and
holding the breath in his bosom. Having proceeded thus
about a hundred paces he unexpectedly heard from the
direction of the jungle the snorting of horses and again
stopped. In the moonlight he counted five horses. For
the dervishes this would not be enough, but he assumed
that the rest were concealed in the high grass. He was
only surprised that there were no guards near them nor
had these guards lighted any fires above to scare away
the wild animals. But he thanked the Lord that it was
so, as he could proceed farther without detection.

The luster on the rocks became more and more distinct.
Before a quarter of an hour passed, Stas found himself
at a place at which the opposite rock was most illuminated,
which indicated that at its base a fire must be burning.

Then, crawling slowly, he crept to the brink and glanced
below.

The first object which struck his eyes was a big white
tent; before the tent stood a canvas field bed, and on it
lay a man attired in a white European dress. A little
negro, perhaps twelve years old, was adding dry fuel to
the fire which illumined the rocky wall and a row of
negroes sleeping under it on both sides of the tent.

Stas in one moment slid down the declivity to the
bottom of the ravine.

XI

FOR some time from exhaustion and emotion he could not utter a word, and stood panting heavily before the man lying on the bed, who also was silent and stared at him with an amazement bordering almost upon unconsciousness.

Finally the latter exclaimed:

"Nasibu! Are you there?"

"Yes, master," answered the negro lad.

"Do you see any one — any one standing there before me?"

But before the boy was able to reply Stas recovered his speech.

"Sir," he said, "my name is Stanislas Tarkowski. With little Miss Rawlinson I have escaped from dervish captivity and we are hiding in the jungle. But Nell is terribly sick; and for her sake I beg for help."

The unknown continued to stare at him, blinking with his eyes, and then rubbed his brow with his hand.

"I not only see but hear!" he said to himself. "This is no illusion! What? Help? I myself am in need of help. I am wounded."

Suddenly, however, he shook himself as though out of a wild dream or torpor, gazed more consciously, and, with a gleam of joy in his eyes, said:

"A white boy! — I again see a white one! I welcome you whoever you are. Did you speak of some sick girl? What do you want of me?"

Stas repeated that the sick girl was Nell, the daughter of Mr. Rawlinson, one of the directors of the Canal; that she already had suffered from two attacks of fever and must die if he did not obtain quinine to prevent the third.

"Two attacks — that is bad!" answered the unknown. "But I can give you as much quinine as you want. I have several jars of it which are of no use to me now."

Speaking thus, he ordered little Nasibu to hand him a big tin box, which apparently was a small traveling drug store; he took out of it two rather large jars filled with a powder and gave them to Stas.

"This is half of what I have. It will last you for a year even."

Stas had a desire to shout from sheer delight, so he began to thank him with as much rapture as if his own life were involved.

The unknown nodded his head several times, and said:

"Good, good, my name is Linde; I am a Swiss from Zurich. Two days ago I met with an accident. A wart-hog wounded me severely."

Afterwards he addressed the lad:

"Nasibu, fill my pipe."

Then he said to Stas:

"In the night-time the fever is worse and my mind becomes confused. But a pipe clears my thoughts. Truly, did you say that you had escaped from dervish captivity and are hiding in the jungle? Is it so?"

"Yes, sir. I said it."

"And what do you intend to do?"

"Fly to Abyssinia."

"You will fall into the hands of the Mahdists; whose divisions are prowling all along the boundary."

"We cannot, however, undertake anything else."

"Ah, a month ago I could still have given you aid.

But now I am alone — dependent only upon Divine mercy and that black lad."

Stas gazed at him with astonishment.

"And this camp?"

"It is the camp of death."

"And those negroes?"

"Those negroes are sleeping and will not awaken any more."

"I do not understand —"

"They are suffering from the sleeping sickness.[1] Those are men from beyond the Great Lakes where this terrible disease is continually raging and all fell prey to it, excepting those who previously died of small-pox. Only that boy remains to me."

Stas, just before, was struck by the fact that at the time when he slid into the ravine not a negro stirred or even quivered, and that during the whole conversation all slept — some with heads propped on the rock, others with heads drooping upon their breasts.

"They are sleeping and will not awaken any more?" he asked, as though he had not yet realized the significance of what he had heard.

And Linde said:

"Ah! This Africa is a charnel house."

But further conversation was interrupted by the stamping of the horses, which, startled at something in the jungle, came jumping with fettered legs to the edge of the valley, desiring to be nearer to the men and the light.

"That is nothing — those are horses," the Swiss said. "I captured them from the Mahdists whom I routed a

[1] Recent investigations have demonstrated that this disease is inoculated in people by the bite of the same fly "tsetse" which kills oxen and horses. Nevertheless its bite causes the sleeping sickness only in certain localities During the time of the Mahdist rebellion the cause of the disease was unknown.

few weeks ago. There were three hundred of them; perhaps more. But they had principally spears, and my men Remingtons, which now are stacked under that wall, absolutely useless. If you need arms or ammunition take all that you want. Take a horse also; you will return sooner to your patient — how old is she?"

"Eight," Stas replied.

"Then she is still a child — Let Nasibu give you tea, rice, coffee, and wine for her. Take of the supplies whatever you want, and to-morrow come for more."

"I shall surely return to thank you once more from my whole heart and help you in whatever I can."

And Linde said:

"It is good even to gaze at a European face. If you had come earlier I would have been more conscious. Now the fever is taking hold of me, for I see double. Are there two of you above me? No, I know that you are alone and that this is only the fever. Ah! this Africa!"

And he closed his eyes.

A quarter of an hour later Stas started to return from this strange camp of sleep and death, but this time on horseback. The night was still dark, but now he paid no heed to any dangers which he might encounter in the high grass. He kept, however, more closely to the river, assuming that both ravines must lead to it. After all it was considerably easier to return, as in the stillness of the night came from a distance the roar of the waterfall; the clouds in the western sky were scattered and, besides the moon, the zodiacal light shone strongly. The boy pricked the horse on the flanks with the broad Arabian stirrups and rode at almost breakneck speed, saying in his soul: "What are lions and panthers to me? I have quinine for my little one!" And from time to time he felt the jars with his hand, as if he wanted to assure

himself that he actually possessed them and that it was
not all a dream. Various thoughts and pictures flitted
through his brain. He saw the wounded Swiss to whom
he felt immense gratitude and whom he pitied so heartily
that, at first, during their conversation, he took him for
a madman; he saw little Nasibu with skull as round
as a ball, and the row of sleeping "pagahs," and the barrels of the Remingtons stacked against the rock and
glistening in the fire. He was almost certain that the
battle which Linde mentioned was with Smain's division,
and it seemed strange to him to think that Smain might
have fallen.

With these visions mingled the constant thought of
Nell. He pictured to himself how surprised she would
be to behold on the morrow a whole jar of quinine, and
that she probably would take him for a performer of
miracles. "Ah," he said to himself, "if I had acted like
a coward and had not gone to ascertain where that smoke
came from I would not have forgiven myself during the
rest of my life."

After the lapse of a little less than an hour the roar
of the waterfall became quite distinct and, from the croaking of frogs, he conjectured that he already was near
the expansion where he had previously shot aquatic birds.
In the moon's luster he even recognized in the distance
the trees standing above it. Now it was necessary to
exercise greater caution, as that overflow formed at the
same time a watering place to which all the animals of
the locality came, for the banks of the river elsewhere
were steep and inaccessible. But it was already late and
the beasts of prey evidently hid in rocky dens after their
nocturnal quests. The horse snorted a little, scenting
the recent tracks of lions or panthers; nevertheless, Stas
rode on happily, and a moment later saw on the high

promontory the big black silhouette of "Cracow." For the first time in Africa he had a sensation as if he had arrived at home.

He reckoned that he would find all asleep, but he reckoned without Saba, who began to bark loud enough to awaken even the dead. Kali also appeared before the tree and exclaimed:

"Bwana kubwa! On horseback!"

In his voice there was, however, more joy than surprise, as he believed in Stas' powers so much that if the latter had even created a horse, the black boy would not have been very much surprised.

But as joy in negroes manifests itself in laughter, he began to slap his thighs with his palms and laugh like a madman.

"Tie this horse," Stas said. "Remove the supplies from him, build a fire, and boil water."

After this he entered the tree. Nell awoke also and began to call him. Stas, drawing aside the canvas wall, saw by the light of the fire-pot her pale face, and thin, white hands lying on the plaids with which she was covered.

"How do you feel, little one?" he asked merrily.

"Good, and I slept well until Saba awoke me. But why do you not sleep?"

"Because I rode away."

"Where?"

"To a drug store."

"To a drug store?"

"Yes, for quinine."

The little girl did not indeed relish very much the taste of the quinine powders which she had taken before, but, as she regarded them as an infallible remedy for all the diseases in the world, she sighed and said:

"I know that you have not got any quinine."

Stas raised one of the jars towards the fire-pot and asked with pride and joy:

"And what is this?"

Nell could scarcely believe her eyes, while he said hurriedly, with beaming countenance:

"Now you will be well! I shall wrap up at once a large dose in a fresh fig peel and you must swallow it. And you shall see with what you will drink it down. Why are you staring at me like at a green cat? Yes! I have a second jar. I got both from a white man, whose camp is about four miles from here. I have just returned from him. His name is Linde and he is wounded; nevertheless, he gave me a lot of good things. I went to him on foot, but I returned on horseback. You may think it is pleasant to go through the jungle at night. Brr! I would not go a second time for anything, unless I again needed quinine."

Saying this, he left the astonished little maid while he went to the "men's quarters," selected from a supply of figs the smallest one, hollowed it out, and filled the center with quinine, taking care that the dose should not be greater than those powders which he had received in Khartûm. After which he left the tree, poured tea into a utensil with water, and returned to Nell with the remedy.

And during that time she reflected upon everything which had happened. She was immensely curious as to who that white man was. From whence did Stas get the information about him? Would he come to them, and would he travel along with them? She did not doubt that since Stas had secured the quinine she would regain her health. But Stas during the night-time went through the jungle as if it were nothing. Nell, notwithstanding her admiration for him, had considered, not reflecting much over it, that everything he did for her was to be taken as a matter of course, for it is a plain thing that an older boy ought to protect a little girl. But now it occurred to her that she would have perished long ago; that he cared for her immensely; that he gratified her and defended her as no other boy of his age would have done or knew how to do. So great gratitude overflowed in her little heart, and when Stas entered again and leaned over her with the remedy she threw her thin arms around his neck and hugged him heartily.

"Stas, you are very kind to me."

While he replied:

"And to whom am I to be kind? Why, I like that! Take this medicine!"

Nevertheless he was happy; as his eyes glistened with satisfaction and again with joy and pride, he called, turning to the opening:

"Mea, serve the ' bibi ' with tea, now!"

XII

STAS did not start for Linde's camp the following day until noon, for he had to rest after the previous night's adventure. On the way, anticipating that the sick man might need fresh meat, he killed two guinea-fowl, which were really accepted with gratitude. Linde was very weak but fully conscious. Immediately after the greeting he inquired about Nell, after which he warned Stas that he should not regard quinine as an entirely sure cure for the fever and that he should guard the little one from the sun, from getting wet, from staying during the night in low and damp places, and finally from bad water. Afterwards Stas related to him, at his request, his own and Nell's history from the beginning to the arrival in Khartûm and the visit to the Mahdi; and afterwards from Fashoda to their liberation from Gebhr's hands, and their further wanderings. The Swiss gazed during the time of this narration with growing interest, often with evident admiration, and when the narrative reached an end he lit his pipe, surveyed Stas from head to foot, and said as if in a reverie:

"If in your country there are many boys like you, then they will not be able to manage you very easily."

And after a moment of silence he continued:

"The best proof of the truth of your words is this, that you are here, that you are standing before me. And believe what I tell you: your situation is terrible; the road, in any direction, is likewise terrible; who knows, however, whether such a boy as you will not save yourself and that child from this gulf."

"If Nell only will be well, then I shall do whatever I can," exclaimed Stas.

"But spare yourself, for the task which you have before you is beyond the strength of a mature person. Do you know where you are at present?"

"No, I remember that after our departure from Fashoda we crossed, near a great settlement called Deng, some kind of a river."

"Sobat," interrupted Linde.

"In Deng there were quite a number of dervishes and negroes. But beyond Sobat we entered into a region of jungles and proceeded whole weeks until we reached the ravine, in which you know what happened —"

"I know. Afterwards you went along the ravine until you reached this river. Now listen to me; it appears that after crossing the Sobat with the Sudânese you turned to the southeast, but more to the south. You are at present in a locality unknown to travelers and geographers. The river, near which we are at present, runs northwest, and in all probability falls into the Nile. I say in all probability, for I myself do not know and now cannot satisfy myself upon that point, though I turned from the Karamojo Mountains to investigate its source. After the battle, I heard from the dervish prisoners that it is called Ogeloguen, but even they were not certain, as they venture into this region only for slaves. The Shilluk tribe occupy this generally sparsely settled country, but at present the region is desolate, as the population partly died of smallpox, partly was swept away by the Mahdists, and partly sought refuge in the Karamojo Mountains. In Africa it often happens that a region thickly settled to-day becomes desolate to-morrow. According to my calculations you are a hundred and eighty-six miles, more or less, from Lado. You might escape to the south to Emin, but as Emin himself is in all probability besieged by the dervishes, that is not to be thought of."

"And to Abyssinia?" Stas asked.

"That is also about the same distance away. Yet you must bear in mind that the Mahdi is waging war against the whole world and, therefore, against Abyssinia. I know also from the prisoners that along the western and southern frontiers greater or smaller hordes of dervishes are prowling and you might therefore easily fall into their hands. Abyssinia indeed is a Christian empire, but the savage southern tribes are either pagan or profess Islam and for that reason secretly favor the Mahdi, — No, you will not get through that way."

"Well, what am I to do, and where shall I go with Nell?" Stas asked.

"I told you that your situation is extremely difficult," Linde said.

Saying this he put both hands to his head and for a long time lay in silence.

"The ocean," he finally said, "is over five hundred and sixty miles from here; you would have to cross mountains, go among savage peoples, and even pass over deserts, for it is probable that there are waterless localities. But the country nominally belongs to England. You might chance upon transports of ivory to Kismayu, to Lamu and Mombasa — perhaps upon missionary expeditions. Realizing that on account of the dervishes I would not be able to explore the course of this river because it turns to the Nile, I, too, wanted to go eastward to the ocean."

"Then we shall return together," Stas exclaimed.

"I shall never return. The wart-hog has so badly torn my

muscles and veins that an infection of the blood must set in. Only a surgeon could save me by amputating my leg. Now everything has coagulated and become numb, but during the first days I bit my hands from pain —"

"You surely will get well."

"No, my brave lad, I surely will die and you will cover me well with stones, so that the hyenas cannot dig me out. To the dead it may be all the same, but during life it is unpleasant to think of it. It is hard to die so far away from your own —"

Here his eyes were dimmed as though with a mist, after which he continued thus:

"But I already have become resigned to the idea — so let us speak about you, not about me. I will give you this advice. There remains for you only the road to the east, to the ocean. But take a good rest before starting and gain strength, otherwise your little companion will die in the course of a few weeks. Postpone the journey until the end of the rainy season, and even longer. The first summer months, when the rain ceases to fall and the water still covers the marshes, are the healthiest. Here, where we are, is a plateau lying about twenty-two hundred and eighty-nine feet above the sea. At the height of forty-two hundred and fifty feet the fever does not exist and when brought from the lower places its course is weaker. Take the little English girl up into the mountains."

Talking apparently fatigued him very much, so he again broke off and for some time impatiently brushed away the big blue flies; the same kind as those which Stas saw among the burnt débris of Fashoda.

After this he continued thus:

"Pay close attention to what I tell you. About a

day's journey towards the south there is an isolated mountain, not higher than twenty-six hundred and twenty feet; it looks like a pan turned upside down. Its sides are steep, and the only way of reaching it is by a rocky ridge so narrow that in some places two horses can barely proceed on it side by side. On its flat top, which is about thirty-five hundred feet wide, there was a negro village, but the Mahdists slaughtered and carried away the residents. It may be that this was done by that same Smain whom I defeated, but those slaves I did not capture because he had previously despatched them under an escort to the Nile. Settle on that mountain. There is a spring of excellent water, a few manioc fields, and a multitude of bananas. In the huts you will find a great many human bones, but do not fear infection from the corpses, as after the dervishes there were ants there, which drove us from the place. And now, not a living creature! Remain in that village a month or two. At such a height there is no fever. Nights are cool. There your little one will recover her health, and you will gain new strength."

"And what am I to do afterwards, and where shall I go?"

"After that it will be as God disposes. Try to get through to Abyssinia in places situated farther than where the dervishes have reached, or ride to the east — I heard that the coast Arabs are reaching some kind of lake in their search for ivory which they purchase from the Samburu and Wahima tribes."

"Wahima? Kali comes from the Wahima tribe."

Here Stas began to narrate to Linde the manner in which he inherited Kali after Gebhr's death and that Kali had told him that he was the son of the ruler of all the Wahimas.

But Linde received this information more indifferently than Stas expected.

"So much the better," he said, "as he may be helpful to you. Among the blacks there are honest souls, though as a rule you cannot depend upon their gratitude; they are children who forget what happened the day before."

"Kali will not forget that I rescued him from Gebhr's hands, I am sure of that."

"Perhaps," Linde said, and pointing at Nasibu added: "He also is a good child; take him with you after my death."

"Do not speak of death, sir."

"My dear boy," answered the Swiss, "I desire it — if it would only come without great agony; consider that now I am completely unarmed, and if any one of the Mahdists whom I routed should accidentally stray to this hollow, alone he could stab me like a sheep."

Here he pointed to the sleeping negroes.

"They will not wake any more, or rather — I speak incorrectly — all of them awake for a short time before their death and in their mental aberration fly to the jungle, from which they never more return. Of two hundred men, sixty remained to me. Many ran away, many died of smallpox, and some fell asleep in other ravines."

Stas with pity and awe began to gaze at the sleepers. Their bodies were ashen-hued, which in negroes indicates paleness. Some had their eyes closed, others half open; but these latter slept deeply, for their eyeballs were not susceptible to the light. The knees of some were swollen. All were frightfully thin, so that their ribs could be counted through their skins. Their hands and feet quivered without cessation very rapidly. The big blue flies swarmed thickly on their eyes and lips.

"Is there no help for them?" Stas asked.

"There is none. On Victoria Nyanza this disease depopulates whole villages. Sometimes more severely, sometimes less. It most frequently takes hold of the people of the villages situated in the underwood on the banks."

The sun had passed to the western sky, but still before night Linde had related to Stas his history. He was a son of a merchant of Zurich. His family came from Karlsruhe, but from the year 1848 had resided in Switzerland. His father amassed a great fortune in the silk trade. He educated his son for an engineer, but young Henry was attracted from early youth by travel. After completing his studies in a polytechnical school, having inherited his father's entire fortune, he undertook his first journey to Egypt It was before the Mahdi's time, so he reached as far as Khartûm, and hunted with Dongolese in the Sudân. After that he devoted himself to the geography of Africa and acquired such an expert knowledge of it that many geographical societies enrolled him among their members. This last journey, which was to end so disastrously for him, began in Zanzibar. He had reached as far as the Great Lakes and intended to penetrate into Abyssinia along the Karamojo Mountains, which up to that time were unknown, and from there to proceed to the ocean coast. But the natives of Zanzibar refused to go any farther. Fortunately, or unfortunately, there was a war between the kings of Uganda and Unyoro. Linde rendered important services to the king of Uganda, who in exchange for them presented him with over two hundred body-guards. This greatly facilitated the journey and the visit to the Karamojo Mountains, but afterwards smallpox appeared in the ranks, after that the dreadful sleeping sickness, and finally the wreck of the caravan.

Linde possessed considerable supplies of various kinds

of preserved food, but from fear of the scurvy he hunted
every day for fresh meat. He was an excellent shot but
not a sufficiently careful sportsman, and it happened
that when a few days before he thoughtlessly drew near
a wild boar which had fallen from his shot, the beast
started up and tore his legs frightfully, and afterwards
trampled upon his loins. This happened near the camp and
in the sight of Nasibu, who, tearing his shirt and making
bandages of it, was able to check the flow of blood and
lead the wounded man to the tent. In the foot, however,
coagulum was formed from the internal flow of blood
and gangrene threatened the patient.

Stas insisted upon dressing his wounds and announced
that he would come daily, or, so as not to leave Nell
only under the care of the two blacks, he proposed to convey him to "Cracow," on saddle-cloth, stretched between
two horses.

Linde agreed to the dressing of the wounds, but would
not agree to the removal.

"I know," he said, pointing at the negroes, "that those
men must die, but until they die, I cannot doom them
to be torn to pieces alive by hyenas, which during the
night-time are held back by the fire."

· And he began to repeat feverishly:

"I cannot! I cannot! I cannot!"

But he became calm immediately, and continued in a
strange voice:

"Come here to-morrow morning — I have a request
to make of you, and if you can perform it, God may lead
you out of this African gulf, and grant me an easy death.
I wished to postpone this request until to-morrow, but
as I may be unconscious to-morrow I make it to-day.
Take water in some utensil, stop before each one of
those poor sleeping fellows, sprinkle water over him, and

say these words: 'I baptize thee, in the name of the Father, and of the Son, and of the Holy Ghost!'"

Here emotion checked his speech and he became silent.

"I reproach myself," he said after a while, "that I did not take leave in that manner of those who died of small-pox and of those who fell into their final slumber. But now death is hovering over me, and I desire to go together with even that remnant of my caravan upon the last great journey."

Saying this he pointed with his hand at the ruddy sky, and two tears coursed slowly over his cheeks.

Stas wept like a beaver.

XIII

THE next morning's sun illuminated a strange spectacle. Stas walked along the rocky walls, stopped before each negro, moistened his forehead with water, and pronounced over him the sacramental words. And they slept with quivering hands and limbs, with heads drooping on their breasts or tilted upwards, still alive but already resembling corpses. And thus took place this baptism of the sleepers — in the morning stillness, in the luster of the sun, in the desert gloom. The sky that day was cloudless, a grayish blue, and as though sad.

Linde was still conscious, but grew weaker and weaker. After the wounds were dressed, he handed to Stas papers enclosed in a tin case, entrusted them to his care, and said nothing more. He could not eat, but thirst tormented him terribly. Before sunset he became delirious. He shouted at some imaginary children not to sail too far away on some unknown lake, and afterwards fell into chills, and clasped his head with both hands.

On the following day he did not recognize Stas at all, and at noon, three days later, he died without recovering consciousness. Stas mourned for him sincerely, and afterwards with Kali carried him to a neighboring narrow cave, the opening of which they closed with thorns and stones.

Stas took little Nasibu to "Cracow," while Kali was ordered to watch the supplies at the camp and keep a big fire burning near the sleepers. Stas bustled continually between the two ravines, conveying luggage and particularly the rifle cartridges, from which he extracted powder and made a mine for the purpose of blasting the rock which imprisoned the King. Happily Nell's health improved considerably after daily doses of quinine, and the greater variety of food increased her strength. Stas left her reluctantly and with fear, and on riding away would not permit her to leave the tree and closed the opening with thorny acacia boughs. Owing to the pressure of work which devolved upon him, he had to leave her, however, to the care of Mea, Nasibu, and Saba, upon whom after all he depended the most. Rather than to leave her alone for any length of time, he preferred to ride a score of times each day to Linde's camp for the luggage. He also overworked himself terribly, but his iron constitution endured all toil. Nevertheless, not until the tenth day were all the packs distributed; those of less value were hidden in caves, and those of more importance were brought to "Cracow"; the horses, too, were led onto the promontory and a considerable number of Remington rifles were carried by them, which rifles were to be borne later by the King.

During that time in Linde's camp, from time to time, some of the sleeping negroes would start up in an antemortem paroxysm of the disease, fly into the jungle, and return no more; there were some who died on the spot, and others, rushing blindly, crushed their heads on the rocks in the camp itself or in the neighborhood. These Kali had to bury. After two weeks only one remained, but that one soon died in his sleep from exhaustion.

Finally the time arrived for blasting the rock and the liberation of the King. He was so tame now that at Stas' order he seized him with his trunk and placed him on his

neck. He also had become accustomed to bearing things
which Kali pulled on his back over a bamboo ladder.
Nell insisted that he was too heavily burdened, but in
truth to him it was like a fly, and only the luggage inherited
from Linde could form a respectable load for him. With
Saba, at the sight of whom in the beginning he displayed
uneasiness, he became quite friendly, and played with
him in this manner: he would overturn him on the ground
with his trunk, and Saba would pretend that he was biting.
At times, however, he would unexpectedly souse the dog
with water, which act was regarded by the latter as a
joke of the poorest taste.

The children were principally pleased because the
beast, being quick of comprehension and seriously minded,
understood everything that was wanted of him and
seemed to comprehend, not only every order, but even
every nod. In this respect elephants surpass immeasurably all other domesticated animals, and the King,
beyond comparison, surpassed Saba, who wagged his
tail to all of Nell's admonitions and afterwards did whatever he pleased. The King discerned perfectly, for instance, that the person whom it was most necessary to
obey was Stas, and that the person about whom all cared
the most was Nell. So he most carefully complied with
Stas' orders, and loved Nell the most. To Kali he paid
less heed and Mea he slighted entirely.

Stas, after making the mine, inserted it in the deepest
fissure, after which he plastered it wholly with clay,
leaving only a small opening through which hung a fuse
twisted of dry palm fiber and rubbed with fine powder.
The decisive moment finally arrived. Stas personally
lit the powdered rope, after which he ran as far as his
legs could carry him to the tree in which previously he
had fastened all the others. Nell was afraid that the

King might be frightened too much, but the boy calmed
her first with the statement that he had selected a day
on which the morning was accompanied by a thunder-
storm, and then with the assurance that wild elephants
often hear the peal of thunder when the heavenly elements
are unfettered over the jungle.

They sat, however, with palpitating hearts, counting
minute after minute. A terrific roar so agitated the atmosphere that the sturdy baobab tree shook from top
to bottom and remnants of the unscraped decayed wood
poured upon their heads. Stas, at that moment, jumped
out of the tree and, avoiding the bends of the ravine,
ran to the passageway.

The results of the explosion appeared extraordinary.
One half of the lime rock was reduced to minute fragments; the other half had burst into about a score of
greater or smaller pieces, which the force of the explosion
scattered to quite a distance.

The elephant was free.

The overjoyed boy now rushed to the edge of the ravine,
where he found Nell with Mea and Kali. The King was
startled a little and, retreating to the very brink of the
ravine, stood with uplifted trunk, gazing in the direction
from which came the sound of such unusual thunder.
But when Nell began to call to him, when she came to him
through the passageway, already opened, he became
entirely quiet. More startled than the King were the
horses, of which two dashed into the jungle, and it was
not until sunset that Kali caught them.

That very same day Nell led the King "out into the
world." The colossus followed her obediently, like a
little puppy, and afterwards bathed in the river, and alone
secured his supper in this singular manner: bracing his
head against a big sycamore tree, he broke it like a

feeble reed and afterwards carefully nibbled the fruit and the leaves.

Towards evening he returned, however, to the tree, and shoving, every little while, his enormous nose through an opening, sought for Nell so zealously and persistently that Stas finally was compelled to give his trunk a sound smack.

Kali, however, was the most overjoyed with the result of that day, for upon his shoulders had fallen the work of gathering provisions for the giant, which was by no means an easy task. So then Stas and Nell heard him, while lighting the fire for supper, sing a new hymn of joy, composed of the following words:

"The great master kills men and lions. Yah! Yah! The great master crushes rocks. Yah! Yah! The elephant, himself, breaks trees and Kali can be idle and eat. Yah! Yah!"

The rainy season, or the so-called "massica," was drawing to an end. There were yet cloudy and rainy days, but there were also days entirely clear. Stas decided to remove to the mountain indicated to him by Linde, and this purpose he carried out soon after the King's liberation. Nell's health did not present any obstacles now, as she felt decidedly better.

Selecting, therefore, a clear day, they started at noon. They were not afraid now that they would stray, as the boy had inherited from Linde, among various articles, a compass and an excellent field-glass, through which it was easy to descry distant localities. Besides Saba and the donkey they were accompanied by five pack-horses and the elephant. The latter, besides the luggage on his back, on his neck bore Nell, who between his two enormous ears looked as though she were sitting in a big arm-chair. Stas without regret abandoned the promontory and the

baobab tree, for it was associated with the recollection
of Nell's illness. On the other hand, the little girl gazed
with sad eyes at the rocks, at the trees, at the waterfall, and announced that she would return there when
she should be "big."

Sadder still was little Nasibu, who had loved sincerely
his former master, and, at present riding on the donkey
in the rear, he turned around every little while and looked
with tears in his eyes towards the place where poor Linde
would remain until the day of the great judgment.

The wind blew from the north and the day was unusually cool. Thanks to this they did not have to stop and
wait from ten to three, until the greatest heat was over,
and they could travel a longer distance than is customary
with caravans. The road was not long, and a few hours
before sunset Stas espied the mountain towards which
they were bound. In the distance on the background
of the sky was outlined a long chain of other peaks,
and this mountain rose nearer and lonely, like an island in a
jungle sea. When they rode closer it appeared that its
steep sides were washed by a loop of the river near which
they previously had settled. The top was perfectly flat,
and seen from below appeared to be covered by one dense
forest. Stas computed that since the promontory, on
which their baobab tree grew, was about twenty-three
hundred feet high and the mountain about twenty-six
hundred feet, they would dwell at an elevation of about
forty-nine hundred feet and in a climate not much
warmer, therefore, than that of Egypt. This thought encouraged him and urged him to take possession of this
natural fortress as quickly as possible.

They easily found the only rocky ridge which led to
it and began the ascent. After the lapse of half an hour
they stood on the summit. That forest seen from below

was really a forest — but of bananas. The sight of them
delighted all exceedingly, not excepting the King, and
Stas was particularly pleased, for he knew that there is not
in Africa a more nourishing and healthy food nor a better
preventative of all ailments than the flour of dried banana
fruit. There were so many of them that they would
suffice even for a year.

Amidst the immense leaves of these plants was hidden
the negro village; most of the huts had been burned or
ruined at the time of the attack, but some were still whole.
In the center stood the largest, belonging at one time to
the king of the village; it was prettily made of clay, with
a wide roof forming around the walls a sort of veranda.
Before the huts lay here and there human bones and
skeletons, white as chalk, for they had been cleaned by
the ants of whose invasion Linde spoke. From the time
of the invasion many weeks had already elapsed; nevertheless, in the huts could be smelt the leaven of ants,
and one could find in them neither the big black cock-
roaches, which usually swarm in all negro hovels, nor
spiders nor scorpions nor the smallest of insects.

Everything had been cleaned out by the terrible "siafu."
It was also a certainty that there was not on the whole
mountain-top a single snake, as even boas fall prey to
these invincible little warriors.

After conducting Nell and Mea into the chief's hut,
Stas ordered Kali and Nasibu to remove the human bones.
The black boys carried out this order by flinging them
into the river, which carried them farther. While thus
employed, however, they found that Linde was mistaken
in declaring that they would not find a living creature on
the mountain. The silence which reigned after the seizure
of the people by the dervishes and the sight of the bananas
had allured a great number of chimpanzees which built

for themselves, on the loftier trees, something like um-
brellas or roofs, for protection against rain. Stas did
not want to kill them, but decided to drive them away,
and with this object in view he fired a shot into the air.
This produced a general panic, which increased still
more when after the shot Saba's furious bass barking resounded, and the King, incited by the noise, trumpeted
threateningly. But the apes, to make a retreat, did not
need to seek the rocky ridge; they dashed over the broken
rocks towards the river and the trees growing near it with
such rapidity that Saba's fangs could not reach any of them.

The sun had set. Kali and Nasibu built a fire to prepare for supper. Stas, after unpacking the necessary
articles for the night, repaired to the king's hut, which
was occupied by Nell. It was light and cheerful in the
hut, for Mea had lit, not the fire-pot which had illuminated
the interior of the baobab tree, but a large traveling lamp
inherited from Linde. Nell did not at all feel fatigued
from the journey in a day so cool, and fell into perfect
good humor, especially when Stas announced that the
human bones, which she feared, had been taken away.

"How nice it is here!" she exclaimed. "Look, even
the floor is covered with resin. It will be fine here."

"To-morrow I shall fully examine our possessions,"
he answered; "judging, however, by what I have seen
to-day, one could dwell here all his life."

"If our papas were here, then we could. But how will
you name this possession?"

"The mountain ought to be called Mount Linde in geographies; and let this village be named after you, Nell."

"Then I shall be in the geographies?" asked she with
great glee.

"You will, you will," Stas replied in all seriousness.

XIV

THE next day it rained a little, but there were hours when the weather was clear, so Stas early in the morning started to visit his possessions and at noon had viewed thoroughly all the nooks. The inspection on the whole created a favorable impression. First, in respect to safety, Mount Linde was as though the chosen spot of all Africa. Its sides were accessible only to chimpanzees. Neither lions nor panthers could climb over its precipitous sides. As to the rocky ridge, it was sufficient to place the King at its entrances to be able to sleep safely on both ears. Stas came to the conclusion that there he could repulse even a small division of dervishes, as the road leading to the mountain was so narrow that the King could barely pass on it and a man armed with a good weapon need not permit a living soul to reach the top. In the middle of the "island" gushed a spring, cool and pure as crystal, which changed into a stream and, running sinuously amid the banana groves, finally fell over the steep hanging rocks to the river, forming a narrow waterfall resembling a white tape. On the southern side of the "island" lay a field, covered abundantly with manioc, the roots of which supply the negroes with their favorite food, and beyond the fields towered immeasurably high cocoa palms with crowns in the shape of magnificent plumes of feathers.

The "island" was surrounded by a sea of jungle and the view from it extended over an immense expanse.

From the east loomed lividly the Karamojo Mountain chain. On the south could also be seen considerable elevations, which, to judge from their dark hue, were covered with forests. On the other hand, on the western side the view ran as far as the horizon's boundary, at which the jungle met the sky. Stas descried, however, with the help of the field-glass, numerous hollows and, scattered sparsely, mighty trees rising above the grass like churches. In places, where the grasses had not yet shot up too high, could be perceived even with the naked eye whole herds of antelopes and zebras or groups of elephants and buffaloes. Here and there giraffes cut through the dark green surface of the sea of grass. Close by the river a dozen or more water-bucks disported and others every little while thrust their horny heads out of the depths. In one place where the water was calm, fishes like those which Kali had caught leaped every little while out of the water, and, twinkling in the air like silvery stars, fell again into the river. Stas promised to himself to bring Nell there when the weather had settled and show her this whole menagerie.

On the "island," on the other hand, there were none of the larger animals; instead there were a great number of butterflies and birds. Big parrots, white as snow, with black beaks and yellow crests flew above the bushes of the grove; tiny, wonderfully plumaged widow-birds swung on the thin manioc stalks, changing color and glittering like jewels, and from the high cocoa trees came the sounds of the African cuckoos and the gentle cooing of the turtle-dove.

Stas returned from his inspection trip with joy in his soul. "The climate," he said, "is healthy; the security is perfect, the provisions are abundant, and the place is as beautiful as Paradise." Returning to Nell's hut he learned to his surprise that there were larger animals on the "island"; two, in fact, for little Nasibu had discovered in a banana thicket while Stas was absent a goat with a kid, which the dervishes had overlooked. The goat was a little wild, but the kid at once became friendly with Nasibu, who was immeasurably proud of his discovery and of the fact that through his instrumentality "bibi" would now have excellent fresh milk daily.

"What shall we do now, Stas?" Nell asked one day, when she had settled down for good to her housekeeping on the "island."

"There is plenty of work to do," the boy answered, after which, spreading out the fingers of one hand, he began to count on them all the work awaiting them.

"In the first place Kali and Mea are pagans, and Nasibu, as a native of Zanzibar, is a Mohammedan. It is necessary to enlighten them, teach them the faith, and baptize them. Then, it is necessary to smoke meat for our future journey and therefore I must go hunting; thirdly, having a good supply of rifles and cartridges, I want to teach Kali to shoot in order that there shall be two of us to defend you; and fourthly — you probably forgot about the kites?"

"About the kites?"

"Yes, those which you will glue, or better still, you will sew. That shall be your work."

"I don't want to play only."

"That won't be all play, but work most useful for all. Don't think that it will end with one kite for you must be ready for fifty or more."

"But why so many?" asked the girl, whose curiosity was aroused.

So Stas began to explain his plans and hopes. He would write on each kite their names, how they had escaped from the hands of the dervishes, where they were, and whither they were bound. He would also inscribe a request for help and that a message be despatched to Port Said. After that he would fly these kites every time the wind was blowing from the west to the east.

"Many of them," he said, "will fall not far off; many will be stopped by the mountains, but let only one of them fly to the coast and fall into European hands — then we are saved."

Nell was enchanted with the idea and announced that in comparison with the wisdom of Stas not even that of the King could be mentioned. She also was quite certain that a multitude of the kites would fly even to their papas, and she promised to glue them from morning until night. Her joy was so great that Stas, from fear that she might get a fever, was compelled to restrain her ardor.

And from that time the work that Stas spoke of began in earnest. Kali, who was ordered to catch as many leaping fish as possible, ceased to catch them on a line and instead made a high fence of thin bamboo, or rather something in the nature of a trellis, and this sluice he pulled across the river. In the middle of the trellis was a big opening through which the fishes had to swim in order to get into the free water. In this opening Kali placed a strong net plaited of tough palm ropes, and in this manner was assured of a bountiful catch.

He drove fish into the treacherous net with the help of the King, who, led into the water, muddied and stirred it so that not only those silvery leapers but all other creatures vanished as far as they could to an unmuddied depth. On account of this, some damage also occurred, as several times escaping crocodiles overturned the trellis, or at times the King did this himself; cherishing for crocodiles some sort of inbred hatred, he pursued them, and when they were in shallow waters he seized them with his trunk, tossed them onto the bank, and trampled upon them furiously. They found also in the nets tortoises, from which the young exiles made an excellent broth. Kali dressed the fish and dried them in the sun, while the bladders were taken to Nell, who cut them open, stretched them upon a board, and changed them into sheets as large as the palms of two hands.

She was assisted at this by Stas and Mea, as the work was not at all easy. The membranes were thicker, indeed, than that of the bladders of our river fish, but after drying up they became very frail. Stas after some time discovered that they ought to be dried in the shade. At times, however, he lost patience, and if he did not abandon the design of making kites from the membranes it was because he regarded them as lighter than paper and of better proof against rain.

The dry season of the year was already approaching, but he was uncertain whether rain did not fall during the summer — particularly in the mountains.

However, he glued kites with paper, of which a large amount was found among Linde's effects. The first one, big and light, was let go in a western wind; it shot up at once very high, and when Stas cut the string, flew, carried by a powerful current of air, to the Karamojo mountain chain. Stas watched its flight with the aid of the field-glass until it became as small as a butterfly, a little speck, and until finally it dissolved in the pale azure of the sky. The following day he let go others made of fish bladder, which shot up still higher, but on account of the transparency of the membranes soon disappeared entirely from view.

Nell worked, however, with extraordinary zeal, and

in the end her little fingers acquired such skill that neither
Stas nor Mea could keep up with her work. She did
not lack strength now. The salubrious climate of Mount
Linde simply regenerated her. The period during which
the fatal third attack could come, had definitely passed.
That day Stas hid himself in a banana thicket and wept
from joy. After a fortnight's stay on the mountain he
observed that the "Good Mzimu" looked entirely different from what she did below in the jungle. Her cheeks
were plumper, her complexion from yellow and transparent
became rosy again, and from under the abundant tufts
of hair, merry eyes full of luster gazed upon the world.
The boy blessed the cool nights, the translucent spring-
water, the flour of dried bananas, and, above all, Linde.

He himself became lean and swarthy, which was
evidence that the fever would not take hold of him, as
sufferers from that disease do not tan from the sun —
and he was growing up and becoming manly. Activity
and physical labor intensified his bravery and strength.
The muscles of his hands and limbs became like steel.
Indeed, he was already a hardened African traveler.
Hunting daily and shooting only with bullets, he became
also a matchless shot.

He did not at all fear the wild animals, for he understood that it was more dangerous for the shaggy-haired and
the spotted hunters of the jungle to meet him than for
him to meet them. Once he killed with a single shot a
big rhinoceros, which, aroused from a light nap under an
acacia, charged at him unexpectedly. He treated with
indifference the aggressive African buffaloes, which at
times disperse whole caravans.

Aside from the gluing of kites and other daily engagements, he and Nell also began the work of converting
Kali, Mea, and Nasibu. But it was harder than they

expected. The black trio listened most willingly to the instructions, but received them in their own negro way. When Stas told them of the creation of the world, about paradise and about the snake, the teaching proceeded fairly well, but when he related how Cain killed Abel, Kali involuntarily stroked his stomach and asked quite calmly:

"Did he eat him afterwards?"

The black boy always claimed, indeed, that the Wahimas never ate people, but evidently memory of that custom still lingered among them as a national tradition.

He likewise could not understand why God did not kill the wicked "Mzimu," and many similar things. His conception of good and evil was too African; in consequence of which there once occurred between the teacher and pupil this colloquy:

"Tell me," asked Stas, "what is a wicked deed?"

"If any one takes away Kali's cow," he answered after a brief reflection, "that then is a wicked deed."

"Excellent!" exclaimed Stas, "and what is a good one?"

This time the answer came without any reflection:

"If Kali takes away the cow of somebody else, that is a good deed."

Stas was too young to perceive that similar views of evil and good deeds were enunciated in Europe not only by politicians but by whole nations.

Nevertheless, slowly, very slowly, the light dawned in their benighted minds, and that which they could not comprehend with their heads they understood with their warm hearts. After a time they were fitted for the baptismal rites, which were performed with great solemnity. The god-parents gave to each child sixteen yards of white percale and a string of blue beads. Mea, nevertheless, felt somewhat disappointed, for in the simplicity of her soul she thought that after the baptism her skin would at once turn white, and great was her astonishment when she observed that she remained as black as before. Nell comforted her, however, with the assurance that now she possessed a white soul.

XV

STAS instructed Kali also how to shoot from a Remington rifle, and this instruction proceeded more easily than the teaching of the catechism. After ten days' shooting at a mark and at crocodiles which slept on the sandy river banks, the young negro killed a big antelope cob; after that a few ariels and finally a wart-hog. The encounter with the latter, however, almost resulted in the same kind of accident which befell Linde, for the wart-hog, which Kali approached carelessly after the shot, started up suddenly and charged at him with tail upraised. Kali, flinging away the rifle, sought refuge in a tree, where he sat until his cries brought Stas, who, however, found the wild boar already dead. Stas did not yet permit the boy to hunt for buffaloes, lions, and rhinoceroses. He himself did not shoot at the elephants which came to the watering place, because he had promised Nell that he would never kill one.

When, however, in the morning or during the afternoon hours, from above he espied, through the field-glass, herds of zebras, hartbeests, ariels, or springboks grazing in the jungle, he took Kali with him. During these excursions he often questioned the boy about the Wahima and Samburu nations, with which, desiring to go eastward, to the ocean coast, they necessarily must come in contact.

"Do you know, Kali," he asked a certain day, "that after twenty days on horseback we could reach your country?"

"Kali does not know where the Wahimas live," the young negro answered, sadly shaking his head.

"But I know that they live in the direction in which the sun rises in the morning, near some great water."

"Yes! Yes!" exclaimed the boy with amazement and joy; "Basso-Narok! That in our language means, great and black water. The great master knows everything."

"No, for I do not know how the Wahimas would receive us if we came to them."

"Kali would command them to fall on their faces before the great master and before the 'Good Mzimu.'"

"And would they obey?"

"Kali's father wears a leopard's hide — and Kali, too." Stas understood this to mean that Kali's father was a king, and that Kali was his oldest son and the future ruler of the Wahimas.

So he continued to ask further:

"You told me that white travelers visited you and that the older people remember them."

"Yes, and Kali has heard that they had a great deal of percale on their heads."

"Ah!" thought Stas, "so those were not Europeans, but Arabs, whom the negroes on account of their lighter complexion and white dress mistook for white men."

Inasmuch, however, as Kali did not remember them and could not give any more specific details about them, Stas propounded to him other questions.

"Have not the Wahimas killed any of these men dressed in white?"

"No! Neither the Wahimas nor the Samburus can do that."

"Why?"

"For they said that if their blood should soak into the ground the rain would cease to fall."

"I am glad to hear that they believe so."

Stas thought for a while, after which he asked:

"Would the Wahimas go with us to the sea, if I promised them a big quantity of percale, beads, and rifles?"

"Kali goes and the Wahimas also, but the great master would first have to subdue the Samburus, who are settled on the other side of the water."

"And who lives beyond the Samburus?"

"Beyond the Samburus there are no mountains, and there is a jungle, and in it lions."

With this the conversation ended. Stas more and more frequently thought of the great journey towards the east, remembering that Linde had said that they might meet coast Arabs trading in ivory, and perhaps a missionary expedition. He knew that such a journey would be a series of terrible hardships for Nell and full of new dangers, but he realized that they could not remain all their lives on Mount Linde and it was necessary to start soon on the journey. The time, after the rainy season, when water covers the pestilential swamps, and is to be found everywhere, was the most suitable for the purpose. The heat could not yet be felt on the high table-land; the nights were so cool still that it was necessary to be well covered. But in the jungle below it was considerably hotter, and he knew well that intense heat would soon come. The rain now seldom bedewed the earth and the water level in the river lowered daily. Stas assumed that in summer the river would change into one of those "khors," of which he saw many in the Libyan Desert, and that only in the very middle of it would flow a narrow stream of water.

Nevertheless, he postponed the departure from day

to day. On Mount Linde it was so well with all, themselves as well as the animals! Nell not only was rid of the fever but of anæmia also; Stas' head never ached; Kali's and Mea's skins began to shine like black satin; Nasibu looked like a melon walking on thin legs, and the King, no less than the horses and the donkey, grew fat. Stas well knew that they would not until the end of the journey find another island like this amidst the jungle sea. And he viewed the future with fear; moreover, they had in the King great assistance and in case of necessity a defense.

Thus a week more elapsed before they commenced preparations for the journey. In moments free from packing their effects they did not cease, however, to send out kites with the announcement that they were going eastward towards some lake, and towards the ocean. They continued to fly them because they were favored by a strong western wind, resembling at times a hurricane, which seized and carried them to the mountains and far beyond the mountains. In order to protect Nell from the scorching heat, Stas constructed from pieces of a tent a palanquin in which the little maid was to ride on the elephant. The King, after a few trials, became accustomed to this not great burden, as well as to the fastening of the palanquin on his back with strong palm ropes. This load after all was a feather in comparison to others with which it was intended to burden him and upon the distribution and tying of which Kali and Mea were engaged.

Little Nasibu was commissioned to dry bananas and grind them into flour between two flat stones. At the plucking of the heavy bunches of fruit he was assisted by the King, at which work they overfed themselves to such an extent that, in the neighborhood of the huts, bananas were soon entirely gone, and they had to go to another plantation lying on the opposite extremity of the table-land. Saba, who had nothing to do, most frequently accompanied them on these excursions.

But Nasibu, for his zeal, almost paid with his life, or at least with captivity of a singular kind. For it happened that once when he was plucking bananas above the brink of a steep hanging rock he suddenly beheld in the rocky gap a hideous face, covered with black hair, blinking at him with its eyes, and displaying white fangs as though smiling. The boy was stupefied from terror at first and then began to scurry away as fast as his legs could carry him. He ran between ten and twenty paces when a hairy arm wound around him, he was lifted off his feet, and the monster, black as night, began to fly with him to the precipice.

Fortunately the gigantic ape, having seized the boy, could run only on two feet, in consequence of which Saba, who was in the vicinity, easily overtook it and buried his fangs in its back. A horrible fight began, in which the dog, notwithstanding his powerful stature and strength, would surely have had to succumb, for a gorilla vanquishes even a lion. Simians as a rule, however, do not relinquish their quarry even though their lives and liberty are in danger. The gorilla, being caught from behind, could not easily reach Saba; nevertheless, having grabbed him by the neck with its left hand it had already raised him, when the ground gave a dull sound under heavy steps and the King appeared.

One light thwack with the trunk sufficed to prostrate with a shattered skull and neck the terrible "forest demon," as the negroes call the gorilla. The King, however, for greater certainty or through inborn fury, pinned the gorilla with his tusks to the ground and afterwards did not cease to wreak his vengeance upon it until Stas, disquieted by the roar and howling, came running up with a rifle and ordered him to stop.

The huge gorilla, with the whites of the eyes rolled up and fangs displayed, terrible still, though not alive, lay in a puddle of blood which Saba lapped and which crimsoned the King's tusks. The elephant trumpeted triumphantly and Nasibu, ashen from terror, related to Stas what had happened. The latter pondered for a while whether or not to bring Nell and show her this monstrous ape, but abandoned the intention, for suddenly he was seized by fear. Of course, Nell often strolled alone over the island. So something similar might befall her.

It appeared, therefore, that Mount Linde was not so safe a shelter as it seemed in the first instance.

Stas returned to the hut and related the incident to Nell, while she listened with curiosity and fear, opening wide her eyes and repeating every little while:

"You see what would have happened without the King."

"True! With such a nurse one need not fear about a child. So then, until we leave, do not move a step without him."

"When shall we leave?"

"The supplies are ready; the packs distributed; so it is necessary only to load the animals and we can start even to-morrow."

"To our papas!"

"If God permits," Stas answered gravely.

XVI

NEVERTHELESS, they did not start until several days
after this conversation. The departure, after a short
prayer in which they warmly commended themselves
to God, took place at daybreak, six o'clock in the morning.
Stas rode at the head, on horseback, preceded by Saba.
After him the King ambled gravely, moving his ears and
bearing on his powerful back a canvas palanquin and in
the palanquin Nell with Mea; they were followed by
Linde's horses one after another, tied together with a
long palm rope and carrying numerous packs; and the
procession closed with little Nasibu on the donkey, as
fat as himself.

On account of the early hour, the heat was not at first
oppressive, though the day was clear and from beyond
the Karamojo Mountains the sun rolled magnificently,
not shaded by a cloudlet. But an eastern breeze molli-
fied the intense heat of its rays. At moments there rose
quite a strong wind, under whose breath the grass lay
low and the whole jungle became wavy like the sea. After
the copious rains all vegetation grew so exuberantly that,
in lower places especially, not only the horses were hidden
in the grass, but even the King; so that above the waving
green surface could be seen only the white palanquin,
which moved forward like a launch on a lake. After an
hour's journey, on a dry, not high elevation, they chanced
upon gigantic thistles having stems as thick as the trunk

of a tree and flowers the size of a man's head. On the
sides of some mountains which from a distance appeared
barren they saw furze-bushes about twenty-six feet
high. Other plants which in Europe belong to the smallest
varieties assumed here proportions corresponding to the
thistles and furze-bushes; and gigantic, isolated trees
rose above the jungle, looking like churches. Particularly prominent were fig-trees, called "daro," whose
weeping boughs, touching the ground and changing into
new trunks, covered immense spaces, so that each tree
formed as it were a separate grove.

This region, from a distance, seemed like one forest;
nearer, however, it appeared that the great trees grew a
dozen or even some score paces apart. In the northern
direction very few of them could be seen and the region
assumed the character of a mountainous steppe, covered
with an even jungle over which rose only umbrella-like
acacias. The grass there was more greenish, shorter,
and evidently better for pasturage, for Nell from the King's
back and Stas from heights on which he rode, saw far
greater herds of antelopes than up to that time they had
met elsewhere. The animals sometimes grazed alone
and at times mingled together; gnus, cobs, ariels, antelope-
cows, hartbeests, springboks, and great kudus. Zebras
and giraffes also were not lacking. The herds, at the
sight of the caravan, stopped feeding, raised their heads,
and pricking their ears, gazed at the white palanquin with
extraordinary amazement, after which in a moment
they scampered away, and having run between ten and
twenty paces they again stood still, staring at this object
unknown to them, until, having gratified their curiosity,
they began to graze calmly. From time to time a rhinoceros started up suddenly before the caravan with a
crash and in a rage, but in spite of its impetuous nature

and its readiness to attack everything which comes within range of its vision, it ran away shamefully at the sight of the King, whom only the commands of Stas restrained from pursuit.

An African elephant detests a rhinoceros, and if he finds its fresh tracks, trusting to superior strength, he follows until he finds his adversary and commences a combat in which the rhinoceros is almost always the victim. It was not easy for the King, who undoubtedly was already responsible for the death of many, to renounce this habit, but now he was so tame and was so accustomed to regard Stas as his master, that hearing his voice and observing the threatening look in his eyes, he dropped his uplifted trunk and walked ahead quietly. Stas did not lack a desire to witness a fight between giants, but he feared for Nell. If the elephant started on a full run, the palanquin might be wrecked, and what is worse, the huge beast might bump it against a bough, and then Nell's life would be in terrible danger. Stas knew from descriptions of hunts which he had read in Port Said that the tiger-hunters in India fear, more than the tigers, that the elephant in a panic or in pursuit may dash the howdah against a tree. Finally, the full run of the giant is so heavy that no one without impairment of his health could long endure such rides.

On the other hand, the presence of the King removed a multitude of dangers. The malignant and bold buffaloes, which they met that day bound for the little lake at which all the animals of the vicinity gathered at evening, also scampered away at sight of him and, making a circuit of the whole lake, drank on the other side. At night the King, with one hind leg tied to a tree, guarded the tent in which Nell slept. This was a watch so secure that though Stas ordered a fire to be built, he regarded

the erection of a zareba as a superfluous precaution,
though he knew that the lions would not be missing in
a region abounding with such numerous herds of antelopes.   In fact, it happened that very night that some
lions began to roar among the gigantic junipers [1] growing
on the hillsides.   Notwithstanding the blazing fire the
lions, allured by the odor of horses, drew nearer to the
camp; but, when the King became tired of hearing their
voices and suddenly, amid the stillness, his threatening,
thunder-like clarion tones resounded, they hushed as
though abashed, apparently understanding that with
such an individual it was best not to have any direct
dealings.   The children slept excellently the balance of
the night, and only at daybreak did they proceed upon
their further journey.

But for Stas anxiety and worry again began.   In the
first place, he perceived that they were traveling slowly
and that they could not make more than six miles a day.
Proceeding in this manner they would be able indeed to
reach the Abyssinian frontier after a month, but as Stas
was determined to follow Linde's advice in every respect,
and Linde had positively claimed that they would not be
able to go through to Abyssinia, there remained only the
road to the ocean.   But according to the calculation of
the Swiss they were over six hundred and twenty miles
from the ocean, and that in a direct line; then Mombasa
being situated farther south, the goal was still further;
therefore, the entire journey would require over three
months.   With alarm Stas thought that it would be three
months of excessive heat, toil, and dangers from negro
tribes which they might encounter.   They were still in a
desolate country from which the population had been

[1] Junipers in the Karamojo Mountains in Abyssinia attain the
height of one hundred and sixty feet.   See Elisée Reclus.

driven by the smallpox and news of the dervish raids; but Africa, on the whole, is quite populous, so sooner or later they must reach localities inhabited by unknown races, ruled usually by savage and cruel petty kings. It was an uncommon task to extricate one's self with life and liberty from such difficulties.

Stas relied simply upon this: that if he chanced upon the Wahima people, he would drill a few tens of warriors in shooting, and afterwards induce them by great promises to accompany him to the ocean. But Kali had no idea where the Wahimas lived; neither could Linde, who had heard something of the tribe, indicate the way to them, nor could he designate specifically the locality occupied by them. Linde had mentioned some great lake, of which he knew only from narratives, and Kali contended with positiveness that one side of that lake, which he called Basso-Narok, was occupied by the Wahimas, and the other by the Samburus. Now Stas was troubled by this: that in the geography of Africa, which in the school in Port Said was taught very thoroughly, there was no mention made of such a lake. If Kali only had spoken of it, he would have assumed that it was Victoria Nyanza, but Linde could not err for he had just come from Victoria, northward, along the Karamojo Mountains, and, from reports of natives of those mountains, he had come to the conclusion that this mysterious lake was situated further east and north. Stas did not know what to think of it all; he feared, however, that he might not chance upon the Wahimas at the lake; he feared also the savage tribes, the waterless jungle, the insurmountable mountains, the tsetse flies which destroy animals; he feared the sleeping sickness, the fever for Nell, the heat, and that immeasurable expanse which still separated them from the ocean.

But after leaving Mount Linde, naught else remained to do than to go ahead continually eastward. Linde indeed had said that this journey was beyond the strength of an experienced and energetic traveler, but Stas had already acquired a great deal of experience, and as to energy, why, as Nell was concerned, he determined to use as much of it as might be necessary. In the meantime it was essential to spare the strength of the little girl; so he decided to travel only from six until ten o'clock in the forenoon, and to make the second march from three to six in the afternoon only in case that at the first stopping place there was no water.

But in the meantime, as the rain fell during the massica quite copiously, they found water everywhere. The little lakes, formed by the downpours in the valleys, were still well filled, and from the mountains flowed here and there streams, pouring crystalline, cool water in which bathing was excellent and at the same time absolutely safe, for crocodiles live only in the greater waters in which fish, which form their usual food, are to be found.

Stas, however, did not permit the little girl to drink crude water as he had inherited from Linde a filter whose action always filled Kali and Mea with amazement. Both seeing how the filter, immerged in a turbid, whitish liquid, admitted to the reservoir only pure and translucent water, lay down with laughter and slapped their knees with the palms of their hands in sign of surprise and joy.

On the whole, the journey at the beginning progressed easily. They had from Linde considerable supplies of coffee, tea, sugar, bouillon, various preserves, and all kinds of medicine. Stas did not have to save his packs for there were more of them than they could take along; they did not lack also various implements, weapons of all calibers, and sky-rockets, which on encountering negroes might prove very useful. The country was fertile; game, therefore fresh meat, was everywhere in abundance, likewise fruit. Here and there in the low lands they chanced upon marshes, but still covered with water, therefore not infecting the air with their noxious exhalations. On the table-land there were none of the mosquitoes which inoculate the blood with fever. The heat from ten o'clock in the morning became unbearable but the little travelers stopped during the so-called "white hours" in the deep shade of great trees, through the dense foliage of which not a ray of the sun could penetrate. Perfect health also favored Nell, Stas, and the negroes.

XVII

On the fifth day Stas rode with Nell on the King, for they had chanced upon a wide belt of acacias, growing so densely that the horses could move only on a path beaten down by the elephant. The hour was early, the morning radiant and dewy. The children conversed about the journey and the fact that each day brought them nearer to the ocean and to their fathers, for whom both continually longed. This, from the moment of their abduction from Fayûm, was the inexhaustible subject of all their conversations, which always moved them to tears. And they incessantly repeated in a circle that their papas thought that they already were dead and both were grieving and in spite of hope were despatching Arabs to Khartûm for news while they were now far away, not only from Khartûm but from Fashoda, and after five days would be still farther until finally they would reach the ocean, or perhaps before that time, some kind of place from which they could send despatches. The only person in the whole caravan who knew what still awaited them was Stas; — Nell, on the other hand, was most profoundly convinced that there was nothing in the world which "Stes" could not accomplish and she was quite certain that he would conduct her to the coast. So many times, anticipating events, she pictured to herself in her little head what would happen when the first news of them arrived and, chirping like a little bird, related it to Stas.

"Our papas are sitting," she said, "in Port Said and weeping, when in comes a boy with a despatch. What is it? My papa or your papa opens it and looks at the signatures and reads 'Stas and Nell.' Then they will rejoice! Then they will start up to prepare to meet us! Then there will be joy in the whole house and our papas will rejoice and everybody will rejoice and they will praise you and they will come and I shall hug tightly papa's neck, and after that we shall always be together — and — "

And it ended in this: that her chin commenced to quiver, the beautiful eyes changed into two fountains, and in the end she leaned her head on Stas' arm and wept from sorrow, longing, and joy at the thought of the future meeting. And Stas, allowing his imagination to roam into the future, divined that his father would be proud of him; that he would say to him: "You behaved as became a Pole;" and intense emotion possessed him and in his heart was bred a longing, ardor, and courage as inflexible as steel. "I must," he said to himself, "rescue Nell. I must live to see that moment." And at such moments it seemed to him that there were no dangers which he was not able to overcome nor obstacles which he could not surmount.

But it was yet far to the final victory. In the meantime they were making their way through the acacia grove. The long thorns of these trees even made white marks upon the King's hide. Finally the grove became thinner and across the branches of the scattered trees could be seen in the distance a green jungle. Stas, notwithstanding that the heat was very oppressive, slipped out of the palanquin and sat on the elephant's neck to see whether there were any herds of antelopes or zebras within view, for he wished to replenish his supply of meat.

In fact, on the right side he espied a herd of ariels,

composed of a few head, and among them two ostriches, but when they passed the last clump of trees and the elephant turned to the left, a different sight struck the eyes of the boy. At the distance of about a third of a mile he observed a large manioc field and at the border of the field between ten and twenty black forms apparently engaged at work in the field.

"Negroes!" he exclaimed, turning to Nell.

And his heart began to beat violently. For a while, he hesitated as to whether he should turn back and hide again in the acacias, but it occurred to him that, sooner or later, he would have to meet the natives in populated districts and enter into relations with them, and that the fate of the whole traveling party might depend upon how those relations were formed; so, after brief reflection, he guided the elephant towards the field.

At the same moment Kali approached and, pointing his hand at a clump of trees, said:

"Great master! That is a negro village and there are women working at the manioc. Shall I ride to them?"

"We will ride together," Stas answered, "and then you shall tell them that we come as friends."

"I know what to tell them, master," exclaimed the young negro with great self-assurance.

And turning the horses towards the workers, he placed the palms of his hands around his lips and began to shout:

"Yambo, he yambo sana!"

At this sound, the women engaged in hoeing the manioc field started up suddenly and stood as if thunderstruck, but this lasted only the twinkling of an eye, for afterwards, flinging away in alarm the hoes and baskets, they began to run away, screaming, to the trees amidst which the village was concealed.

The little travelers approached slowly and calmly. In

the thicket resounded the yelling of some hundred voices, after which silence fell. It was interrupted finally by the hollow but loud rumble of a drum, which did not cease even for a moment.

It was evidently a signal of the warriors for battle, for three hundred of them suddenly emerged from the thicket. All stood in a long row before the village. Stas stopped the King at the distance of one hundred paces and began to gaze at them. The sun illuminated their well-shaped forms, wide breasts, and powerful arms. They were armed with bows and spears. Around their thighs some had short skirts of heath, and some of monkey skin. Their heads were adorned with ostrich and parrot feathers, or great scalps torn off baboons' skulls. They appeared warlike and threatening, but they stood motionless and in silence, for their amazement was simply unbounded and subdued the desire for fighting. All eyes were fastened upon the King, on the white palanquin, and the white man sitting on his neck.

Nevertheless, an elephant was not an unknown animal to them. On the contrary, they continually live in dread of elephants, whole herds of which destroy at night their manioc fields as well as banana and doom-palm plantations. As the spears and arrows do not pierce the elephant's hide, the poor negroes fight the depredators with the help of fire, with the aid of cries imitating a cockerel's crow, by digging pits, and constructing traps made of the trunks of trees. But that an elephant should become slave of man and permit one to sit on his neck was something which none of them ever saw before, and it never entered into the mind of any of them that anything like that was possible. So the spectacle which was presented to them passed so far beyond their understanding and imagination that they did not know what to do: whether to fight or to run where their eyes should lead them, though it would result in leaving them to the caprice of fate.

So in uncertainty, alarm, and amazement they only whispered to each other:

"Oh, mother! What creatures are these which have come to us, and what awaits us at their hands?"

But at this Kali, having ridden within a spear's throw of them, stood up in the stirrups and began to shout:

"People! people! Listen to the voice of Kali, the son of Fumba, the mighty king of the Wahimas on the shores of Bassa-Narok. Oh listen, listen, and if you understand his speech, pay heed to each word that he utters."

"We understand," rang the answer of three hundred mouths.

"Let your king stand forth; let him tell his name and let him open his ears and lips that he may hear better."

"M'Rua! M'Rua!" numerous voices began to cry.

M'Rua stepped in front of the ranks, but not more than three paces. He was a negro, already old, tall and powerfully built, but evidently did not suffer from too much courage, as the calves of his legs quivered so that he had to implant the edge of a spear in the ground and support himself on the shaft in order to stand on his legs.

After his example, the other warriors also drove the spears into the ground in sign that they wanted to hear peaceably the words of the arrival.

And Kali again raised his voice.

"M'Rua, and you, M'Rua's men, you heard that to you speaks the son of the king of the Wahimas, whose cows cover as thickly the mountains around the Bassa-Narok as the ants cover the body of a slain giraffe. And what says Kali, the son of the king of Wahima? Lo, he announces to you the great and happy tidings that there comes to your village the 'Good Mzimu.'"

After which he yelled still louder:

"That is so! The Good Mzimu! Ooo!"

In the stillness which ensued could be perceived the great sensation which Kali's words created. The wave of warriors surged back and forth, for some, impelled by curiosity, advanced a few paces, while others retreated in fear. M'Rua supported himself with both hands on the spear — and for some time the hollow silence continued. Only after a while a murmur passed through the ranks and individual voices began to repeat "Mzimu! Mzimu!" and here and there resounded shouts of "Yancig! Yancig!" expressive at the same time of homage and welcome.

But Kali's voice again predominated over the murmurs and shouts:

"Look and rejoice! Lo, the 'Good Mzimu' sits there in that white hut on the back of the great elephant and the great elephant obeys her as a slave obeys a master and like a child its mother! Oh, neither your fathers nor you have seen anything like that."

"We have not seen! Yancig! Yancig!"

And the eyes of all warriors were directed at the "hut," or rather at the palanquin.

And Kali, who during the religious instructions on Mount Linde had learned that faith moves mountains, was deeply convinced that the prayer of the little white "bibi" could procure everything from God; so he spoke thus further and in perfect sincerity:

"Listen! Listen! The 'Good Mzimu' is riding on an elephant in the direction in which the sun rises, beyond the mountains out of the waters; there the 'Good Mzimu' will tell the Great Spirit to send you clouds, and those clouds during a drought will water with rain your millet, your manioc, your bananas, and the grass in the jungle, in order that you may have plenty to eat and that your cows shall have good fodder and shall give thick and fat milk. Do you want to have plenty of food and milk — oh, men?"

"He! We do, we do!"

"And the 'Good Mzimu' will tell the Great Spirit to send to you the wind, which will blow away from your village that sickness which changes the body into a honeycomb. Do you want him to blow it away — oh, men?"

"He! Let him blow it away!"

"And the Great Spirit at the prayer of the 'Good Mzimu' will protect you from attacks and slavery and from depredations in your fields and from the lion and from the panther and from the snake and from the locust —"

"Let her do that."

"So, listen yet and look who sits before the hut between the ears of the terrible elephant. Lo, there sits bwana kubwa, the great and mighty white master, whom the elephant fears!"

"He!"

"Who has thunder-bolts in his hand and kills with it bad men —"

"He!"

"Who kills lions —"

"He!"

"Who lets loose fiery snakes —"

"He!"

"Who crushes rocks —"

"He!"

"Who, however, will do you no harm, if you will honor the 'Good Mzimu.'"

"Yancig! Yancig!"

"And if you will bring to him an abundance of dry flour from bananas, eggs of chickens, fresh milk, and honey."

"Yancig! Yancig!"

"So approach and fall on your faces before the 'Good Mzimu!'"

M'Rua and his warriors started and, not ceasing to "yancig" for a moment, advanced between ten and twenty paces, but they approached cautiously, for a superstitious fear of the "Mzimu" and downright terror before the elephant impeded their steps. The sight of Saba startled them anew as they mistook him for a "wobo," that is, a big, yellowish-brown leopard, which lives in that region as well as in Southern Abyssinia, and whom the natives fear more than a lion, for it prefers human flesh above all other, and with unheard-of daring attacks even armed men. They quieted, however, seeing that the little obese negro held the terrible "wobo" on a rope. But they were acquiring a still greater idea of the power of the "Good Mzimu," as well as of the white master, and, staring now at the elephant then at Saba, they whispered to each other: "If they bewitched even the 'wobo,' who in the world can oppose them?" But the most solemn moment did not come until Stas, turning to Nell, first bowed profoundly and afterwards drew aside the curtain-like walls of the palanquin and exhibited to the eyes of the crowd the "Good Mzimu." M'Rua and all the warriors fell on their faces so that their bodies formed a long, living deck. Not one of them dared to move, and fear prevailed in all hearts all the more when the King, either at Stas' order or of his own volition, raised his trunk and began to trumpet strongly; and after his example Saba emitted the deepest bass of which he was capable. Then from all breasts issued, resembling entreating groans, "Aka! Aka! Aka!" and this continued until Kali again addressed them.

"Oh, M'Rua, and you, children of M'Rua! You have

paid homage to the 'Good Mzimu'; therefore rise, gaze, and fill your eyes, for whoever does that gains the blessing of the Great Spirit. Drive away, also, fear from your breasts and bellies and know that wherever the 'Good Mzimu' sojourns, human blood cannot be shed."

At these words, and particularly as a result of the announcement that in the presence of the "Good Mzimu" no one can meet death, M'Rua rose, and after him the other warriors, and began to gaze, bashfully but eagerly at the kind divinity. Indeed, they would have to acknowledge, if Kali again should ask them about it, that neither their fathers nor they ever had beheld anything like it. For their eyes were accustomed to monstrous figures of idols, made of wood and shaggy cocoanuts, and now there appeared before them on an elephant's back a bright divinity, gentle, sweet, and smiling, resembling a white bird, and at the same time a white flower. So, too, their fears passed away, their breasts breathed freely; their thick lips began to grin and their hands were involuntarily stretched out towards the charming phenomenon.

"Oh! Yancig! Yancig! Yancig!"

Nevertheless, Stas, who was watching everything with the closest possible attention, observed that one of the negroes, wearing a pointed cap of rats' skin, slunk away from the ranks immediately after Kali's last words and, crawling like a snake in the grass, turned to an isolated hut standing apart, beyond the enclosure, but surrounded likewise by a high stockade bound by climbing plants.

In the meantime the "Good Mzimu," though greatly embarrassed by the rôle of a divinity, at Stas' request stretched out her little hand and began to greet the negroes. The black warriors watched with joy in their eyes each movement of that little hand, firmly believing it

possessed powerful "charms," which would protect them
and secure them against a multitude of disasters. Some,
striking their breasts and hips, said: "Oh, mother, now it
will be well — for us and our cows." M'Rua, now entirely emboldened, drew near the elephant and prostrated
himself once more before the "Good Mzimu" and after
that, bowing to Stas, spoke in the following manner:

"Would the great master, who leads the white divinity
on the elephant, be pleased to eat a small piece of M'Rua,
and would he consent that M'Rua should eat a small
piece of him, in order that they should become brothers,
among whom there is no falsehood and treachery?"

Kali at once translated these words, but perceiving
from Stas' countenance that he did not have the slightest
desire to eat a small piece of M'Rua, turned to the old
negro and said:

"Oh, M'Rua! Do you really think that the white
master, whom the elephant fears, who holds thunderbolts in his hands, who kills lions, to whom the 'wobo'
wags its tail, who lets loose fiery snakes and crushes rocks,
could form a blood brotherhood with a mere king?
Reflect, oh, M'Rua, whether the Great Spirit would not
punish you for your audacity, and whether it is not enough
of glory for you if you eat a small piece of Kali, the son of
Fumba, the ruler of the Wahimas, and if Kali, the son of
Fumba, eats a small piece of you?"

"Are you not a slave?" M'Rua asked.

"The great master did not seize Kali, neither did he buy
him; he only saved his life; therefore Kali is conducting
the 'Good Mzimu' and the master to the country of the
Wahimas in order that the Wahimas and Fumba should
pay honors to them and give them great gifts."

"Let it be as you say and let M'Rua eat a small piece
of Kali and Kali a small piece of M'Rua."

"Let it be so," repeated the warriors.

"Where is the fetish-man?" the king asked.

"Where is the fetish-man? Where is the fetish-man? Where is Kamba?" numerous voices began to call.

Then something occurred which might change entirely the state of affairs, embroil the friendly relations, and make the negroes enemies of the newly arrived guests. From the hut standing apart and surrounded by a separate stockade, there suddenly resounded an infernal din. It was like the roar of a lion, like thunder, like the rumbling of a drum, like the laughter of a hyena, the howling of a wolf, and like the shrill creaking of rusty iron hinges. The King hearing these dreadful sounds, began to trumpet, Saba barked, the donkey, on which Nasibu sat, brayed. The warriors leaped as if scalded, and pulled the spears out of the ground. Confusion ensued. Stas' ears were assailed by the uneasy shouts of: "Our Mzimu! Our Mzimu!" The esteem and favor, with which they looked at the arrivals, vanished in one moment. The eyes of the savages began to cast suspicious and hostile glances. Threatening murmurs began to rise among the crowd and the horrible noise in the isolated hut increased more and more.

Kali was terrified and, approaching Stas quickly, said in a voice broken with emotion:

"Master! the fetish-man has awakened the wicked Mzimu, who fears that he will lose gifts and is roaring in a rage. Master, quiet the fetish-man and the wicked Mzimu with great gifts, for otherwise these men will turn against us."

"Quiet them?" Stas asked.

And suddenly he was possessed by anger at the perversity and greed of the fetish-man; and the unexpected danger roused him to the bottom of his soul. His swarthy face assumed the same expression which it had when he shot Gebhr, Chamis, and the Bedouins. His eyes glittered ominously; his lips were compressed and his cheeks paled.

"Ah! I'll quiet them!" he said.

And without any reflection he drove the elephant towards the hut.

Kali, not desiring to remain alone among the negroes, ran after him. From the breasts of the savage warriors there came a shout — it was not known whether of alarm or of rage, but, before they recovered their wits, the stockade under the pressure of the elephant's head crashed and tumbled; after that the clay walls of the hut crumbled and amid dust the roof flew up in the air; and after a while M'Rua and his men saw the black trunk raised high and at the end of the trunk the fetish-man, Kamba.

And Stas, observing on the floor a big drum made of the hollowed trunk of a tree with monkey skin stretched over it, ordered Kali to hand it to him and, returning, stopped directly among the amazed warriors.

"Men!" he said in a loud voice, "it is not your Mzimu who roars; it is this rogue who makes the noise on the drum to wheedle gifts out of you, and whom you fear like children!"

Saying this, he seized the rope drawn through the dried-up skin of the drum and began to twirl it around with all his strength. The same sounds which had previously so startled the negroes resounded now, and even more shrilly, as they were not muffled by the walls of the hut.

"Oh, how stupid are M'Rua and his children!" shouted Kali.

Stas gave the drum back to Kali while the latter began to make a noise with it with such zeal that for a while a word could not be heard. When finally he had enough, he flung the drum at M'Rua's feet.

"This is your Mzimu," he exclaimed, with great laughter.

After which he began with the usual negro exuberance of words to address the warriors; at which he was not at all sparing of jeers at them and at M'Rua. He declared to them, pointing at Kamba, that "that thief in the cap made of rat's skin" cheated them through many rainy and dry seasons and they fed him on beans, flesh of kids, and honey. Is there another king and nation as stupid in the world? They believed in the power of the old deceiver and in his charms, and look now, how that great fetish-man hangs from the elephant's trunk and is crying " Aka!" to arouse the pity of the white master. Where is his power? Where are his charms? Why does not any wicked Mzimu roar in his defense? Ah! What is this, their Mzimu? A clout of monkey skin and piece of wood hollowed through decay which the elephant will tread to pieces. Among the Wahimas, neither the women nor the children would be afraid of such a Mzimu, and M'Rua and his men fear him. There is only one genuine Mzimu and one really great and powerful master. Let them pay honors to them; let them bring as many gifts as they possibly can, as otherwise calamities, of which they hitherto have not heard, will befall them.

For the negroes even these words were unnecessary as the fetish-man, together with his wicked Mzimu, appeared so vastly weaker than the new divinity and the white master, that it sufficed most fully to make them desert him and load him with contempt. So they commenced anew to " yancig" with even greater humility and haste. But as they were angry at themselves because they had allowed Kamba to cheat them for so many years, they wanted, by all means, to kill him. M'Rua himself begged Stas to allow him to bind and keep him until he could devise a sufficiently cruel death. Nell, however, was determined to spare his life, and as Kali had announced that wherever the "Good Mzimu" sojourns human blood cannot be shed, Stas consented only to the expulsion of the hapless fetish-man from the village.

Kamba, who expected that he would die in the most ingeniously devised tortures, fell on his face before the "Good Mzimu" and, blubbering, thanked her for saving his life. From beyond the stockade women and children poured, for the news of the arrival of the extraordinary guests had already spread over the whole village, and the desire to see the white Mzimu overcame their terror. Stas and Nell for the first time saw a settlement of real savages, which even the Arabs had not succeeded in reaching. The dress of these negroes consisted only of heath or skins tied around their hips; all were tattooed. Men as well as women had perforated ears, and in the opening, chunks of wood or bone so big that the expanded lobes reached the shoulders. In the lower lips they carried "peleles," that is, wooden or bony rings as large as saucers. The more distinguished warriors and their wives had around their throats collars of iron or brass wire so high and stiff that they could barely move their heads.

They apparently belonged to the Shilluk tribe, which extends far into the east, for Kali and Mea understood their speech excellently and Stas partly. They did not have, however, limbs as long as their kindred living on the overflowing banks of the Nile; they were broader in the shoulders, not so tall, and generally less like wading birds. The children looked like fleas and, not being yet disfigured by "peleles," were, without comparison, better looking than the older people.

The women, having first from a distance sated their eyes with looking at the "Good Mzimu," began to vie with the warriors in bringing gifts to her, consisting of kids, chickens, eggs, black beans, and beer brewed of millet. This continued until Stas stopped the afflux of supplies; as he paid for them liberally with beads and colored percale, and Nell distributed between ten and twenty looking-glasses inherited from Linde, immense joy reigned in the whole village; and around the tent, in which the little travelers sought shelter, shouts, happy and full of enthusiasm, continually resounded. After that, the warriors performed a war-dance in honor of the guests and fought a sham battle, and finally they proceeded to form a blood brotherhood between Kali and M'Rua.

Owing to the absence of Kamba, who for this ceremony was usually indispensable, his place was taken by an old negro sufficiently conversant with the adjuration. The latter, having killed a kid and extracted its liver, divided it into fair-sized morsels; after which he began to turn a kind of spinning-wheel with his hand and foot and, gazing now at Kali and then at M'Rua, addressed them in a solemn voice:

"Kali, son of Fumba, do you desire to eat a piece of M'Rua, the son of M'Kuli, and you, M'Rua, son of M'Kuli, do you desire to eat a piece of Kali, the son of Fumba?"

"We do," announced the future brethren.

"Do you desire that the heart of Kali should be the heart of M'Rua and the heart of M'Rua the heart of Kali?"

"We do."

"And the hands and the spears and the cows?"

"And the cows!"

"And everything which each one possesses and will possess?"

"And what he possesses and will possess."

"And that there should not be between you falsehood, nor treachery, nor hatred?"

"Nor hatred!"

"And that one shall not pilfer from the other?"

"Never!"

"And that you shall be brethren?"

"Yes!"

The wheel turned more and more rapidly. The warriors, gathered around, watched its revolutions with ever-increasing interest.

"Ao!" exclaimed the aged negro, "if one of you deceives the other by lies, if he betrays him, if he steals from him, if he poisons him, may he be accursed!"

"May he be accursed!" repeated all the warriors.

"And if he is a liar and is plotting treason, let him not swallow the blood of his brother, and let him spit it out before our eyes."

"Oh, before our eyes!"

"And let him die!"

"Let him die!"

"Let him be torn to pieces by a wobo!"

"Wobo!"

"Or a lion!"

"Or a lion!"

"May he be trampled upon by an elephant and a rhinoceros and a buffalo!"

"Oh — and a buffalo!" repeated the chorus.

"May he be bit by a snake!"

"Snake!"

"And may his tongue become black!"

"Black!"

"And his eyes sink to the back of his head!"

"To the back of his head!"

"And may he walk on his heels upward!"

"Ha! on his heels upward!"

Not only Stas but Kali bit his lips in order not to burst out laughing. In the meantime adjurations were repeated, more and more horrible, and the wheel kept spinning so quickly that the eyes could not keep pace with its whirl. This continued until the old negro entirely lost his strength and breath.

Then he squatted on the ground, and for some time nodded his head in both directions in silence. After a while, however, he rose and taking a knife, cut with it the skin at Kali's shoulder and smearing a piece of kid's liver with his blood, shoved it into M'Rua's mouth; the other piece smeared in the king's blood he shoved into Kali's mouth. Both swallowed so quickly that their wind-pipes began to play, and their eyes bulged out; after which they grabbed hold of hands in sign of loyal and everlasting friendship.

The warriors on the other hand began to shout with glee:

"Both swallowed; neither spat it out, therefore they are sincere and there is no treachery between them."

And Stas in his soul thanked Kali that he had acted as his proxy at this ceremony, for he felt that at the swallowing of "a piece" of M'Rua he undoubtedly would have given proof of insincerity and treachery.

From that moment, however, the little travelers were not threatened on the part of the savages with deceit or any unexpected attacks; on the contrary they were treated with a hospitality and an esteem almost god-like. This esteem increased when Stas, after making an observation on a barometer, a great heritage from Linde, predicted rain, and when rain fell that very same day quite copiously, as though the massica [1] desired to shake off the rest of

[1] The spring rainy season, which had just passed.

its supplies upon the earth, the negroes were convinced
that this downpour was the gift of the "Good Mzimu" and
their gratitude to Nell was unbounded. Stas joked with
her about this, saying that since she had become a negro
divinity he would proceed alone on his further journey
and leave her in M'Rua's village, where the negroes would
erect for her a chapel of ivory, and would bring beans
and bananas to her.

But Nell had no uncertainty, and, standing on her
little toes, whispered in his ear, according to her custom,
only four words: "You won't leave me!" After which
she began to leap from joy, saying that since the negroes
were so kind, the whole journey to the ocean would be
easy and quick. This happened in front of the tent and
in the presence of the crowd, so old M'Rua, seeing a
jumping Mzimu, began at once to leap as high as he could
with his crooked shanks in the conviction that through
that act he gave proof of his piety. In emulation of their
superior "the ministers" started to leap, and after them
the warriors, and later the women and children; in a
word, the whole village for some time was jumping as
if all had lost their wits.

This example given by the divinity amused Stas so
much that he lay down and roared with laughter. Nevertheless, during the night-time he rendered to the pious
king and his subjects a real and enduring service, for when
the elephants made depredations upon their banana
field he drove towards them on the King and shot a few
rockets among the herd. The panic caused by the "fiery
snakes" surpassed even his expectation. The huge
beasts, seized by a frenzy of terror, filled the jungle with
a roar and the noise of hoofs, and, escaping blindly,
tumbled down and trampled upon one another. The
mighty King chased after his flying companions with

extraordinary alacrity, not sparing blows of his trunk and tusks. After such a night one could be certain that not an elephant would appear in the banana and doom-palm plantations belonging to the village of old M'Rua.

In the village great joy also reigned, and the negroes passed the whole night in dancing and drinking beer of millet and palm wine. Kali learned from them, however, many important things; it appeared that some of them had heard of some great water lying east and surrounded by mountains. For Stas this was proof that the lake, of which no mention was made in the geography which he had studied, actually existed; also, that going in the direction which they had selected, they would finally encounter the Wahima people. Inferring from the fact that Mea's and Kali's speech differed very little from M'Rua's speech, he came to the conclusion that the name of "Wahima" was in all probability the designation of a locality, and that the peoples living on the shores of "Bassa-Narok" belonged to the great Shilluk tribe, which begins on the Nile and extends, it is not known how far, to the east.

XVIII

THE population of the whole village escorted afar the
"Good Mzimu" and took leave of her with tears, begging
vehemently that she would deign to come sometime
to M'Rua, and to remember his people. Stas for some
time hesitated whether he should point out to the negroes
the ravine in which he had hidden the wares and supplies
left by Linde, which owing to want of porters he could
not take with him, but reflecting that the possession of
such treasures might evoke envy and discord among
them, awaken covetousness, and embroil the peace of
their lives, he abandoned this design, and, instead, shot
a big buffalo and left its meat for a farewell feast. The
sight of such a large amount of "niama" also really
delighted them.

For the following three days the caravan again proceeded through a desolate country. The days were scorching, but, owing to the high altitude of the region, the nights
were so cold that Stas ordered Mea to cover Nell with
two shaggy coverlets. They now often crossed mountainous ravines, sometimes barren and rocky, sometimes
covered with vegetation so compact that they could force
their way through it only with the greatest difficulty.
At the brinks of these ravines they saw big apes and
sometimes lions and panthers. Stas killed one of them at
the entreaty of Kali, who afterwards dressed himself in
its hide in order that the negroes might at once know
that they had to do with a person of royal blood.

Beyond the ravines, on high table-lands, negro villages again began to appear. Some lay near together, some at the distance of a day or two. All were surrounded by high stockades for protection against lions, and these were so entwined with creepers that even close at hand they looked like clumps of a virgin forest. Only from the smoke rising from the middle of the village could one perceive that people dwelt there. The caravan was everywhere received more or less as at M'Rua's village; that is, at first with alarm and distrust and afterwards with admiration, amazement, and esteem. Once only did it happen that the whole village, at the sight of the elephant, Saba, the horses, and the white people, ran away to an adjacent forest, so that there was no one to converse with. Nevertheless, not a spear was aimed against the travelers, for negroes, until Mohammedanism fills their souls with cruelties and hatred against infidels, are rather timid and gentle. So it most frequently happened that Kali ate a "piece" of the local king and the local king a "piece" of Kali, after which the relations were of the most friendly character. To the "Good Mzimu," the negroes furnished evidence of homage and piety in the shape of chickens, eggs, and honey, extracted from wooden logs suspended from the boughs of great trees with the aid of palm ropes. The "great master," the ruler of the elephant, thunder, and fiery snakes, aroused mainly fear, which soon, however, changed into gratitude when they became convinced that his generosity equaled his might. Where the villages were closer to one another the arrival of the extraordinary travelers was announced from one village to the other by the beating of drums, for the negroes give notice of everything with the aid of drumming. It happened also that the entire populace would come out to meet them, being well disposed in advance.

In one village, numbering one thousand heads, the local ruler, who was fetish-man and king in the same person, consented to show them "the great fetish," which was surrounded by such extraordinary veneration and fear that the people did not dare to approach the ebony chapel, covered with a rhinoceros hide, and make offerings any nearer than fifty paces. The king stated that this fetish not long before fell from the moon, that it was white and had a tail. Stas declared that he himself at the command of the " Good Mzimu " sent it, and in saying that he did not deviate from the truth, for it appeared that the "great fetish" was plainly one of the kites, despatched from Mount Linde. Both children were pleased with the thought that other kites in a suitable wind might fly still further. They determined to fly others from heights in the farther course of time. Stas made and sent out one that very same night, which convinced the negroes that the " Good Mzimu " and the white master also came to earth from the moon, and that they were divinities who could not be served with sufficient humility.

But more delightful to Stas than these marks of humility and homage was the news that Bassa-Narok lay only about thirteen days' distance and that the denizens of the village in which they stopped at times received from that direction salt in exchange for doom-palm wine. The local king had even heard of Fumba, as the ruler of the people called "Doko." Kali confirmed this by saying that more distant neighbors so called the Wahimas and Samburus. Less consoling was the news that on the shores of the great water a war was raging, and to go to Bassa-Narok it was necessary to cross immense, wild mountains and steep ravines, full of rapacious beasts. But Stas now did not much heed rapacious beasts, and

he preferred mountains, though the wildest, to the low
plain country where fever lay in wait for travelers.

In high spirits they started. Beyond that populous
village they came to only one settlement, very wretched
and hanging like a nest on the edge of a chasm. After
that the foot-hills began, cut rarely by deep fissures. On
the east rose a hazy chain of peaks, which from a distance
appeared entirely black. This was an unknown region
to which they were bound, not knowing what might befall them before they reached Fumba's domains. In the
highlands which they passed trees were not lacking, but
with the exception of dragon-trees and acacias standing
alone they stood in clusters, forming small groves. The
travelers stopped amid these clumps for refreshment and
rest as well as for the abundant shade.

Amid the trees birds swarmed. Various kinds of pigeons,
big birds with beaks, which Stas called toucans, starlings,
turtle-doves, and countless beautiful "bingales" flitted
in the foliage or flew from one clump to another, singly
and in flocks, changing color like the rainbow. Some trees
appeared from a distance to be covered with many-colored
flowers. Nell was particularly charmed by the sight of
paradisaical fly-catchers and rather large, black birds,
with a crimson lining to the wings, which emitted sounds
like a pastoral fife. Charming woodpeckers, rosy on
top and bright blue beneath, sped in the sun's luster,
catching in their flight bees and grasshoppers. On the
treetops resounded the screams of the green parrot, and
at times there reached them sounds as though of silvery
bells, with which the small green-gray birds hidden under
Adansonia leaves greeted one another.

Before sunrise and after sunset flocks of native spar-
rows flew by, so countless that were it not for their twitter
and the rustle of their little wings they would be mis-

taken for clouds. Stas assumed that it was their pretty little bills which rang so, while in daytime they were scattered on single clumps.

But other birds flying in little flocks, which gave real concerts, filled both children with the greatest surprise and ecstasy. Every little flock consisted of five or six females and one male, with glittering metallic feathers. They sat on a single acacia in this particular manner: the male was perched on the top of the tree and the others lower, and after the first notes, which seemed like the tuning of their little throats, the male began a song and the others listened in silence. Only when he had finished did they repeat together in a chorus the last refrain of his song. After a brief pause, he resumed and finished, and they again repeated; after this the whole flock flew in a light wavy flight to the nearest acacia and the concert, composed of the soloist and chorus, again resounded in the southern stillness. The children could not listen enough to this. Nell, catching the leading tune of the concert, joined with the chorus and warbled in her thin little voice the notes resembling the quickly repeated sound of "tui, tui, tui, twiling-ting! ting!"

Once the children, following the winged musicians from tree to tree, went away over half a mile from the camp, leaving in it the three negroes, the King, and Saba. Stas was about to start on a hunting trip and did not want to take Saba with him, for fear that his barking might scare away the game. When the little flock finally flew to the last acacia on the other side of a wide ravine, the boy stopped Nell and said:

"Now I will escort you to the King and after that I shall see whether there are any antelopes or zebras in the high jungle, for Kali says that the smoked meats will not last longer than two days."

"Why, I am big now," answered Nell, who was always anxious to make it appear that she was not a little child, "so I will return alone. We can see the camp perfectly from here, and the smoke also."

"I am afraid that you may stray."

"I won't stray. In a high jungle we might stray, but here, see how low the grass is!"

"Still, something may happen to you."

"You yourself said that lions and panthers do not hunt in the daytime. Besides, you hear how the King is trumpeting from longing after us. What lion would dare to hunt there where the sound of the King reaches?"

And she began to importune:

"Stas, dear, I will go alone, like a grown-up."

Stas hesitated for a while but finally assented. The camp and smoke really could be seen. The King, who longed for Nell, trumpeted every little while. In the low grass there was no danger of going astray, and as to lions, panthers, and hyenas, there plainly could be no talk of them as these animals seek prey during the night. The boy after all knew that nothing would afford the little maid greater pleasure than if he acted as though he did not regard her as a little child.

"Very well," he said, "go alone, but go directly, and do not tarry on the way."

"And may I pluck just those flowers?" she asked, pointing at a cusso bush, covered with an immense number of rosy flowers.

"You may."

Saying this, he turned her about, pointed out to her once more for greater certainty the clump of trees from which the smoke of the camp issued and from which resounded the King's trumpeting, after which he plunged into the high jungle growing on the brink of the ravine.

But he had not gone a hundred paces when he was seized by uneasiness. "Why, it was stupid on my part," he thought, "to permit Nell to walk alone in Africa. Stupid, stupid. She is such a child! I ought not to leave her for a step unless the King is with her. Who knows what may happen! Who knows whether under that rosy bush some kind of snake is not lying! Big apes can leap out of the ravine and carry her away from me or bite her. God forbid! I committed a terrible folly."

And his uneasiness changed into anger at himself, and at the same time into a terrible fear. Not reflecting any longer, he turned around as if stung by a sudden evil presentiment. Walking hurriedly, he held the rifle ready to fire, with that great dexterity which he had acquired through daily hunting, and advanced amid the thorny mimosas without any rustle, exactly like a panther when stealing to a herd of antelopes at night. After a while he shoved his head out of the high underwood, glanced about and was stupefied.

Nell stood under a cusso bush with her little hand outstretched; the rosy flowers, which she had dropped in terror, lay at her feet, and from the distance of about twenty paces a big tawny-gray beast was creeping towards her amid the low grass.

Stas distinctly saw his green eyes fastened upon the little maid's face, which was as white as chalk, his narrow head with flattened ears, his shoulder-blades raised upward on account of his lurking and creeping posture, his long body and yet longer tail, the end of which he moved with a light, cat-like motion. One moment more — one spring and it would be all over with Nell.

At this sight the boy, hardened and inured to danger, in the twinkling of an eye understood that if he did not regain self-command, if he did not muster courage, if he shot badly and only wounded the assailant, even though heavily, the little maid must perish. But he could master himself to that degree that under the influence of these thoughts his hands and limbs suddenly became calm like steel springs. With one glance of the eye he detected a dark spot in the neighborhood of the beast's ear, — with one light motion he directed the barrel of the rifle at it and fired.

The report of the shot, Nell's scream, and a short, shrill bleat resounded at the same moment. Stas jumped towards Nell, and covering her with his own body, he aimed again at the assailant.

But the second shot was entirely unnecessary, for the dreadful cat lay like a rag, flattened out, with nose close to the ground and claws wedged in the grass — almost without a quiver. The bursting bullet had torn out the back of its head and the nape of its neck. Above its eyes, gory, torn, white convolutions of its brain oozed out.

And the little hunter and Nell stood for some time, gazing now at the slain beast, then at each other, not being able to utter a word. But after that something strange happened. Now this same Stas, who a moment before would have astonished the most experienced hunter in the whole world by his calmness and coolness, suddenly became pale; his limbs began to tremble, tears flowed from his eyes, and afterwards he seized his head with the palms of his hands and began to repeat:

"Oh, Nell! Nell! If I had not returned!"

And he was swayed by such consternation, such belated despair, that every fiber within him quivered as if he had a fever. After an unheard-of exertion of his will and all the powers of his soul and body a moment of weakness and relaxation had come. Before his eyes was the picture of the dreadful beast, resting with blood-stained muzzle in some dark cave and tearing Nell's body to pieces. And of course, this could have happened and would have happened if he had not returned. One minute, one second more and it would have been too late. This thought he plainly could not banish.

Finally it ended in this, that Nell, recovering from her fear and alarm, had to comfort him. The little upright soul threw both her little arms around his neck and, weeping also, began to call to him loudly, as if she wanted to arouse him from slumber.

"Stas! Stas! Nothing is the matter with me. See, nothing is the matter with me. Stas! Stas!"

But he came to himself and grew calm only after a long time. Immediately after that Kali, who heard the shot not far from the camp and knew that the "Bwana kubwa" never fired in vain, came leading a horse to carry away the game. The young negro, glancing at the slain beast, suddenly retreated, and his face at once became ashen.

"Wobo!" he shouted.

The children now approached the carcass, already growing rigid. Up to that time Stas did not have an accurate idea as to what kind of beast of prey had fallen from his shot. At the first glance of the eye it seemed to the boy that it was an exceptionally large serval; nevertheless, after closer examination he saw that it was not, for the slain beast exceeded the dimensions of even a leopard. His tawny skin was strewn with chestnut-hued spots, but his head was narrower than that of a leopard, which made him resemble somewhat a wolf; his legs were higher, paws wider, and his eyes were enormous. One of them was driven to the surface by a bullet, the other still stared at the children, fathomless, motionless, and awful.

Stas came to the conclusion that this was a species of panther unknown to zoölogy, just as Lake Bassa-Narok was unknown to geography.

Kali gazed continually with great terror at the beast stretched upon the ground, repeating in a low voice, as if he feared to awaken it:

"Wobo! The great master killed a wobo!"

But Stas turned to the little maid, placed his hand on her head, as though he desired definitely to assure himself that the wobo had not carried her away, and then said:

"You see, Nell. You see that even if you are full-grown, you cannot walk alone through the jungle."

"True, Stas," answered Nell with a penitent mien, "but I can go with you or the King."

"Tell me how it was? Did you hear him draw near?"

"No — Only a golden fly flew out of those flowers. So I turned around after it and saw how he crept out of the ravine."

"And what then?"

"He stood still and began to look at me."

"Did he look long?"

"Long, Stas. Only when I dropped the flowers and guarded myself from him with my hands did he creep towards me."

It occurred to Stas that if Nell were a negress she would have been pounced upon at once, and that in part she owed her preservation to the astonishment of the beast, which seeing before it for the first time a being unknown to it, for a while was uncertain what to do.

A chill passed through the boy's bones.

"Thank God! Thank God that I returned!"

After which he asked further:

"What were you thinking of at that moment?"

"I wanted to call you, and — I could not — but —"

"But what?"

"But I thought that you would protect me — I myself do not know —"

Saying this she again threw her little arms around his neck, and he began to stroke her tufts of hair.

"You are not afraid, now?"

"No."

"My little Mzimu! My Mzimu! You see what Africa is."

"Yes, but you will kill every ugly beast?"

"I will."

Both again began to examine closely the rapacious beast. Stas, desiring to preserve its skin as a trophy ordered Kali to strip it off, but the latter from fear that another wobo might creep out of the ravine begged him not to leave him alone, and to the question whether he feared a wobo more than a lion, said:

"A lion roars at night and does not leap over stockades, but a wobo in the white day can leap over a stockade and kill a great many negroes in the middle of the village, and after that he seizes one of them and eats him. Against a wobo a spear is no protection, nor a bow, only charms, for a wobo cannot be killed."

"Nonsense," said Stas, "look at this one; is he not well slain?"

"The white master kills wobo; the black man cannot kill him," Kali replied.

It ended in this, that the gigantic cat was tied by a rope to the horse and the horse dragged him to the camp. Stas, however, did not succeed in preserving his hide, for the King, who evidently surmised that the wobo wanted to carry off his little lady, fell into such a frenzy of rage that even Stas' orders were unable to restrain him. Seizing the slain beast with his trunk he tossed it twice into the air; after which he began to strike it against a tree and in the end trampled upon it with his legs and changed it into a shapeless, jelly-like mass. Stas succeeded in saving the jaws, which with the remnants of the head he placed on an ant-column on the road, and the ants cleaned the bones in the course of an hour so thoroughly that not an atom of flesh or blood remained.

XIX

FOUR days later Stas stopped for a longer rest on a hill somewhat similar to Mount Linde, but smaller and narrower. That same night Saba after a hard battle killed a big male baboon, whom he attacked at a time when the baboon was playing with the remnants of a kite, the second in order of those which they had sent before starting for the ocean. Stas and Nell, taking advantage of the stay, determined to glue new ones continually, but to fly them only when the monsoon blew from the west to the east. Stas placed great reliance upon this, that even if but one of them should fall into European or Arabian hands it would undoubtedly attract extraordinary attention and would cause an expedition to be despatched expressly for their rescue. For greater certainty, besides English and French inscriptions he added Arabian, which was not difficult for him, as he knew the Arabian language perfectly.

Soon after starting from the resting-place, Kali announced that in the mountain chain, which he saw in the east, he recognized some of the peaks which surrounded Bassa-Narok; nevertheless, he was not always certain, as the mountains assumed different shapes, according to the place from which they were viewed. After crossing a small valley overgrown with cusso bushes and looking like a lake of roses, they chanced upon a hut of lone hunters. There were two negroes in it and one of them

was sick, having been bitten by a thread-like worm.[1] But
both were so savage and stupid and in addition so terrified
by the arrival of the unexpected guests, so certain that
they would be murdered, that at first it was impossible
to ascertain anything from them. But a few slices of
smoked meat unloosened the tongue of the one who was
not only sick, but famished, as his companion doled out
food to him very stingily. From him, therefore, they
learned that about a day's journey away there lay strag-
gling villages, governed by petty kings, who were independent of one another; and afterwards, beyond a steep
mountain, the domain of Fumba began, extending on
the west and south of the great water. When Stas heard
this, a great load fell off his heart and new courage entered his soul. At any rate, they now were almost on the
threshold of the land of the Wahimas.

It was difficult to foresee how their further journey
would progress; nevertheless, the boy in any event could
expect that it would not be harder or even longer than
that terrible journey from the banks of the Nile which
they had undergone, thanks to his exceptional resourcefulness, and during which he had saved Nell from destruction.
He did not doubt that, thanks to Kali, the Wahimas
would receive them with the greatest hospitality and
would give every assistance to them. After all, he already
well understood the negroes, knew how to act towards
them, and was almost certain that, even without Kali, he
would have been able somehow to take care of himself
among them.

"Do you know," he said to Nell, "that we have passed
more than one-half of the way from Fashoda, and that
during the journey which is still before us we may meet

[1] Filandria medineusis, a worm as thin as thread, and a yard
long. Its bite sometimes causes gangrene.

very savage negroes, but now will not encounter any dervishes."

"I prefer negroes," the little maid replied.

"Yes, while you pass as a goddess. I was kidnapped from Fayûm with a little lady whose name was Nell, and now am conducting some kind of Mzimu. I shall tell my father and Mr. Rawlinson that they never should call you anything else."

Her eyes began to sparkle and smile:

"Perhaps we may see our papas in Mombasa."

"Perhaps. If it were not for that war on the shores of Bassa-Narok, we would be there sooner. Too bad that Fumba should be engaged in one at this time!"

Saying this, he nodded at Kali.

"Kali, did the sick negro hear of the war?"

"He heard. It is a big war, very big — Fumba with Samburus."

"Well, what will happen? How shall we get through the Samburu country?"

"The Samburus will run away before the great master, before the King and before Kali."

"And before you?"

"And before Kali, because Kali has a rifle which thunders and kills."

Stas began to meditate upon the part which would devolve upon him in the conflict between the Wahima and Samburu tribes and determined to conduct his affairs in such a manner as not to retard his journey. He understood that their arrival would be an entirely unexpected event which would at once assure Fumba of a superiority. Accordingly it was necessary only to make the most of a victory.

In the villages, of which the sick hunter spoke, they derived new information about the war. The reports

were more and more accurate, but unfavorable for Fumba.
The little travelers learned that he was conducting a
defensive campaign, and that the Samburus under the
command of their king, named Mamba, occupied a considerable expanse of the Wahima country and had captured a multitude of cows. The villagers said that the
war was raging principally on the southern border of the
great water where on a wide and high rock King Fumba's
great "boma" [1] was situated.

This intelligence greatly grieved Kali, who begged
Stas to cross the mountain separating them from the
seat of the war as quickly as possible, assuring him, at
the same time, that he would be able to find the road
on which he could lead not only the horses but the King.
He was already in a region which he knew well and now
distinguished with great certainty peaks which were
familiar to him from childhood.

Nevertheless, the passage was not easy, and if it were
not for the aid of the inhabitants of the last village, won
by gifts, it would have been necessary to seek another
road for the King. These negroes knew better than Kali
the passes leading from that side of the mountain, and
after two days' arduous travel, during which great cold
incommoded them during the nights, they successfully
led the caravan to a depression in a crest of a mountain
and from the mountain to a valley lying in the Wahima
country.

Stas halted in the morning for a rest in this desolate valley, surrounded by underwood, while Kali, who begged
to be allowed to scout on horseback in the direction of
his father's "boma," which was about a day's distance,
started that very night. Stas and Nell waited for him

---

[1] The same as a zareba in the Sudân. A great boma may also
be a sort of fortress or fortified camp.

the whole day with the greatest uneasiness and feared that he had perished or fallen into the hands of the enemy, and when finally he appeared on a lean and panting horse, he himself was equally fatigued and so dejected that the sight of him excited pity.

He fell at once at Stas' feet and began to implore for help.

"Oh, great master," he said, "the Samburus have defeated Fumba's warriors; they killed a multitude of them and dispersed those they did not kill. They besiege Fumba in a boma on Boko Mountain. Fumba and his warriors have nothing to eat in the boma and will perish if the great master does not kill Mamba and all the Samburus with Mamba."

Begging thus, he embraced Stas' knees, while the latter knitted his brow and meditated deeply as to what was to be done, for in everything he was particularly concerned about Nell.

"Where," he finally asked, "are Fumba's warriors whom the Samburus dispersed?"

"Kali found them and they will be here at once."

"How many are there?"

The young negro moved the fingers of both hands and the toes of both his feet about a score of times, but it was evident that he could not indicate the exact number for the simple reason that he could not count above ten and every greater amount appeared to him as "wengi," that is, a multitude.

"Well, if they come here, place yourself at their head and go to your father's relief."

"They fear the Samburus and will not go with Kali, but with the great master they will go and kill 'wengi, wengi,' of Samburu."

Stas pondered again.

"No," he finally said, "I can neither take the 'bibi' to a battle nor leave her alone, and I will not do it for anything in the world."

At this Kali rose and folding his hands began to repeat incessantly:

"Luela! Luela! Luela!"

"What is 'Luela'?" Stas asked.

"A great boma for Wahima and Samburu women," the young negro replied.

And he began to relate extraordinary things. Now Fumba and Mamba had been engaged in continual warfare with each other for a great many years. They laid waste to the plantations of each other and carried away cattle. But there was a locality on the southern shore of the lake, called Luela, at which even during the fiercest war the women of both nations assembled in the market-place with perfect safety. It was a sacred place. The war raged only between men; no defeats or victories affected the fate of the women, who in Luela, behind a clay enclosure surrounding a spacious market-place, found an absolutely safe asylum. Many of them sought shelter there during the time of hostilities, with their children and goods. Others came from even distant villages with smoked meat, beans, millet, manioc, and various other supplies. The warriors were not allowed to fight a battle within a distance of Luela which could be reached by the crowing of a rooster. They were likewise not permitted to cross the clay rampart with which the market-place was surrounded. They could only stand before the rampart and then the women would give them supplies of food attached to long bamboo poles. This was a very ancient custom and it never happened that either side violated it. The victors also were always concerned that the way of the defeated to Luela should be cut off and they did not permit them to approach the sacred place within a distance which could be reached by a rooster's crow.

"Oh, great master!" Kali begged, again embracing Stas' knees, "great master, lead 'the bibi' to Luela, and you yourself take the King, take Kali, take the rifle, take fiery snakes and rout the wicked Samburus."

Stas believed the young negro's narrative, for he had heard that in many localities in Africa war does not include women. He remembered how at one time in Port Said a certain young German missionary related that in the vicinity of the gigantic mountain, Kilima-Njaro, the immensely warlike Massai tribe sacredly observed this custom, by virtue of which the women of the contending parties walked with perfect freedom in certain market-places and were never subject to attack. The existence of this custom on the shores of Bassa-Narok greatly de-lighted Stas, for he could be certain that no danger threat-ened Nell on account of the war. He determined also to start with the little maid without delay for Luela, all the more because before the termination of the war they could not think of a further journey for which not only the aid of the Wahimas but that of the Samburus was necessary.

Accustomed to quick decisions, he already knew how he should act. To free Fumba, to rout the Samburus but not to permit a too bloody revenge, and afterwards to command peace and reconcile the belligerents, appeared to him an imperative matter not only for himself but also most beneficial for the negroes. "Thus it should be and thus it shall be!" he said to himself in his soul, and in the meantime, desiring to comfort the young negro for whom he felt sorry, he announced that he did not refuse aid.

"How far is Luela from here?" he asked.

"A half day's journey."

"Listen, then! we will convey the 'bibi' there at once,

after which I shall ride on the King and drive away the
Samburus from your father's boma. You shall ride with
me and shall fight with them."

"Kali will kill them with the rifle!"

And passing at once from despair to joy, he began to
leap, laugh, and thank Stas with as much ardor as though
the victory was already achieved. But further outbursts
of gratitude and mirth were interrupted by the arrival of
the warriors, whom he had gathered together during his
scouting expedition and whom he commanded to appear
before the white master. They numbered about three
hundred; they were armed with shields of hippopotamus
leather, with javelins and knives. Their heads were
dressed with feathers, baboon manes, and ferns. At the
sight of an elephant in the service of a man, at the sight
of the white faces, Saba, and the horses, they were seized
by the same fear and the same amazement which had possessed the negroes in those villages through which the
children previously passed. But Kali warned them in
advance that they would behold the "Good Mzimu" and
the mighty master "who kills lions, who killed a wobo,
whom the elephant fears, who crushes rocks, lets loose
fiery snakes," etc. So, instead of running away, they stood
in a long row in silence, full of admiration, with the whites
of their eyes glistening, uncertain whether they should
kneel or fall on their faces. But at the same time they were
full of faith that if these extraordinary beings would help
them then the victories of the Samburus would soon end.
Stas rode along the file on the elephant, just like a commander who is reviewing his army, after which he ordered
Kali to repeat his promise that he would liberate Fumba,
and issued an order that they should start for Luela.

Kali rode with a few warriors in advance to announce
to the women of both tribes that they would have the

inexpressible and unheard-of pleasure of seeing the "Good Mzimu," who would arrive on an elephant. The matter was so extraordinary that even those women who, being members of the Wahima tribe, recognized Kali as the lost heir to the throne, thought that he was jesting with them and were surprised that he wanted to jest at a time that was so heavy for the whole tribe and Fumba. When, however, after the lapse of a few hours they saw a gigantic elephant approaching the ramparts and on it a white palanquin, they fell into a frenzy of joy and received the "Good Mzimu," with such shouts and such yells that Stas at first mistook their voices for an outburst of hatred, and the more so as the unheard-of ugliness of the negresses made them look like witches.

But these were manifestations of extraordinary honor. When Nell's tent was set in a corner of the market-place under the shade of two thick trees, the Wahima and Samburu women decorated it with garlands and wreaths of flowers, after which they brought supplies of food that would have sufficed a month, not only for the divinity herself but for her retinue. The enraptured women even prostrated themselves before Mea, who, attired in rosy percale and a few strings of blue beads, as a humble servant of the Mzimu, appeared to them as a being far superior to the common negresses.

Nasibu, out of regard for his childish age, was admitted behind the rampart and at once took advantage of the gifts brought for Nell so conscientiously that after an hour his little abdomen resembled an African war drum.

XX

Stas, after a brief rest under the ramparts of Luela, started with Kali before sunset at the head of three hundred warriors for Fumba's boma, for he wanted to attack the Samburus during the night, relying upon the fact that in the darkness the fiery snakes would create a greater sensation. The march from Luela to Mount Boko, on which Fumba was defending himself, counting the rests, required nine hours, so that they appeared before the fortress at about three o'clock in the morning. Stas halted the warriors and, having ordered them to preserve the deepest silence, began to survey the situation. The summit of the mountain on which the defenders had sought refuge was dark; on the other hand the Samburus burnt a multitude of camp-fires. Their glare illuminated the steep walls of the rock and the gigantic trees growing at its foot. From a distance came the hollow sounds of drums and the shouts and songs of warriors who evidently were not sparing in their indulgence of pombe,[1] desiring already to celebrate a near and decisive victory. Stas advanced at the head of his division still farther, so that finally not more than a hundred paces separated him from the last camp-fires. There were no signs of camp sentinels and the moonless night did not permit the savages to catch sight of the King who, be-

[1] A beer of millet with which the negroes intoxicate themselves.

sides, was screened by the underwood. Stas, sitting on
his neck, quietly issued the final orders, after which he
gave Kali the signal to light one of the sky-rockets. A
red ribbon flew up, hissing, high in the dark sky, after
which, with an explosive sound, it scattered into a bouquet
of red, blue, and golden stars. All voices became hushed
and a moment of gloomy silence ensued. A few seconds
later two more fiery snakes flew out, as though with an
infernal hiss, but this time they were aimed horizontally
directly at the Samburu camp; simultaneously resounded
the King's roar and the loud cries of the three hundred
Wahimas who, armed with assagais,[1] maces, and knives,
rushed ahead with irrepressible speed. A battle began,
which was the more terrible because it took place in the
darkness, as all the camp-fires in the confusion were at
once trampled out. But, at the very beginning, blind
terror at the sight of the fiery snakes seized the Samburus. What was happening passed entirely beyond
their understanding. They only knew that they were
attacked by some terrible beings and that horrible and
unavoidable destruction threatened them. A greater
part of them ran away before they could be reached by
the spears and maces of the Wahimas. A hundred and
a few tens of warriors, whom Mamba succeeded in rallying
about him, offered stubborn resistance; when, however,
in the flashes of the shots, they saw a gigantic beast and
on him a person dressed in white, and when their ears
were dinned with the reports of the weapon which Kali
from time to time discharged, their hearts sank. Fumba
on the mountain, seeing the first sky-rocket, which burst
in the heights, fell on the ground from fright and lay as
though dead for a few minutes. But, regaining consciousness, he imagined from the desperate yells of the

[1] Negro spears.

warriors one thing, namely, that some kind of spirits were exterminating the Samburus below. Then the thought flashed through his mind that if he did not come to the aid of those spirits, he might incur their wrath, and as the extermination of the Samburus was his salvation, he mustered all his warriors about him and sallied forth from a secret side exit of the boma and cut off the road of a greater part of the fugitives. The battle now changed into a massacre. The Samburu drums ceased to beat. In the darkness, which was rent only by the red flashes cast by Kali's rifle, resounded the howls of the men being killed, the hollow blows of the maces against shields and the groans of the wounded. Nobody begged for mercy, for mercy is unknown to negroes. Kali, from a fear that in the darkness and confusion he might wound his own people, finally ceased to fire, and seizing Gebhr's sword rushed with it into the midst of the enemies. The Samburus could now flee from the mountains towards their frontiers only by way of one wide pass, but as Fumba blocked this pass with his warriors, out of the whole host only those were safe who, throwing themselves upon the ground, permitted themselves to be taken alive, though they knew that a cruel slavery awaited them, or even immediate death at the hands of the victors. Mamba defended himself heroically until a blow of a mace crushed his skull. His son, young Faru, fell into Fumba's hand, who ordered him bound, as a future sacrifice of gratitude to the spirits which had come to his assistance.

Stas did not drive the terrible King into the battle; he permitted him only to trumpet to increase the terror of the enemies. He himself did not fire a single shot from his rifle at the Samburus, for in the first place he had promised little Nell on leaving Luela that he would not kill any one, and again he actually had no desire to kill people who had done no harm to him or Nell. It was enough that he assured the Wahimas a victory and freed Fumba, who was besieged in a great boma. Soon, also, when Kali came running with news of a definite victory, he issued an order for the cessation of the battle, which raged yet in the underwood and rocky recesses and which was prolonged by the implacable hatred of old Fumba.

However, before Kali succeeded in quelling it, it was daylight. The sun, as is usual under the equator, rolled quickly from beyond the mountains, and flooded with a bright light the battle-field on which lay over two hundred Samburu corpses pierced by spears or crushed by maces. After a certain time, when the battle finally ceased and only the joyful yells of the Wahimas disturbed the morning's quiet, Kali again appeared, but with a face so dejected and sad that it could be perceived even from a distance that some kind of misfortune had overtaken him.

In fact, when he stood before Stas, he began to strike his head with his fists and exclaim sorrowfully:

"Oh, great master! — Fumba kufa! Fumba kufa!" (is slain).

"Slain?" Stas repeated.

Kali related what had happened, and from his words it appeared that the cause of the occurrence was only the inveterate hatred of Fumba, for after the battle had ceased, he still wanted to give the last blow to two Samburus, and from one of them he received the stroke of a spear.

The news spread among all the Wahimas in the twinkling of an eye and around Kali a mob gathered. A few moments later six warriors bore on spears the old king, who was not killed but fatally wounded. Before his

death he desired to see the mighty master, the real conqueror of the Samburus, sitting on an elephant.

Accordingly uncommon admiration struggled in his
eyes with the dusk with which death was dimming them,
and his pale lips, stretched by "pelele," whispered lowly:
"Yancig! Yancig!"

But immediately after that his head reclined backward,
his mouth opened wide — and he died.

Kali, who loved him, with tears threw himself upon
his breast. Among the warriors some began to strike
their heads, others to proclaim Kali king and to "yancig"
in his honor. Some fell before the young ruler on their
faces. No one raised a voice in opposition, as the right
to rule belonged to Kali not only by law, as the oldest
son of Fumba, but also as a conqueror.

In the meantime, in the huts of the fetish-men in the
boma on the mountain-top, resounded the savage din
of the wicked Mzimu, the same as Stas had heard in the
first negro village, but this time it was not directed against
him but was demanding the death of the prisoners for
killing Fumba. The drums began to rumble. The warriors
formed in a long host of three men in a row and commenced
a war dance around Stas, Kali, and Fumba's corpse.

"Oa, Oa! Yach, yach!" all voices repeated; all heads
nodded right and left in unison, the whites of their eyes
glistened, and the sharp points of the spears twinkled
in the morning sun.

Kali rose and turning to Stas, said:

"Great master, bring the 'bibi' to the boma and let her
dwell in Fumba's hut. Kali is king of the Wahimas and
the great master is Kali's king."

Stas nodded his head in sign of assent but remained
a few hours, for he and the King were entitled to a rest.

He did not leave until towards the evening. During

his absence the bodies of the slain Samburus were removed
and thrown into a neighboring deep abyss, over which at
once a swarm of vultures flocked; the fetish-men made
preparations for Fumba's funeral and Kali assumed
authority as the only master of the life and death of all
his subjects.

"Do you know what Kali is?" Stas asked the little
maid on the return journey from Luela.

Nell gazed at him with surprise.

"He is your boy."

"Aha! A boy! Kali is now king of all the Wahimas."

This news delighted Nell immensely. This sudden
change, thanks to which the former slave of the cruel
Gebhr, and later the humble servant of Stas, became a
king, seemed to her something extraordinary and at the
same time exceedingly amusing.

Nevertheless, Linde's remark that negroes were like
children who were incapable of remembering what transpired the day before, did not appear just in its application
to Kali, for as soon as Stas and Nell stopped at the foot
of Mount Boko the young monarch hurried to meet them;
he greeted them with the usual marks of humility and
joy and repeated the words which he had previously
uttered:

"Kali is the king of the Wahimas, and the great master
is Kali's king."

And he surrounded both with an adoration almost
divine and prostrated himself, particularly before Nell,
in the presence of all the people, for he knew from experience, acquired during the journey, that the great master
cared more for the little "bibi" than for himself.

Leading them solemnly to the capital boma on the summit he surrendered to them Fumba's hut, which resembled a great shed divided into several rooms. He ordered

the Wahima women, who came with them from Luela, and who could not look enough at the "Good Mzimu," to place a utensil with honey and sour milk in the first room, and when he learned that the "bibi," tired by the journey, had fallen asleep, he commanded all the inhabitants to observe the deepest silence under the penalty of cutting out their tongues. But he decided to honor them still more solemnly, and with this in view, when Stas, after a brief rest, came out of the shed, he approached him and, prostrating himself, said:

"To-morrow Kali shall order Fumba to be buried and shall cause as many slaves to be cut down for Fumba and for Kali as both have fingers on their hands, but for the 'bibi' and for the great master, Kali shall order Faru, the son of Mamba, to be cut to pieces and 'wengi, wengi' of other Samburus who were captured by the Wahimas."

And Stas knitted his brows and began to gaze with his steely eyes into Kali's eyes; after which he answered:

"I forbid you to do that."

"Master," the young negro said in an uncertain voice, "the Wahimas always cut down slaves. The old king dies — cut them down; the young succeeds — cut them down. If Kali did not command them to be cut down, the Wahimas would think that Kali is not king."

Stas looked more and more sternly:

"What of it?" he asked. "Did you not learn anything on Mount Linde, and are you not a Christian?"

"I am, oh, great master!"

"Listen, then! The Wahimas have black brains, but your brains ought to be white. You, as soon as you became their king, should enlighten them and teach them what you learned from me and from the 'bibi.' They are like jackals and like hyenas—make men of them. Tell them it is not allowable to cut down captives, for the Great Spirit

to whom I and the 'bibi' pray avenges the blood of the
defenseless. The white people do not murder slaves, and
you want to be worse to them than Gebhr was to you
— you, a Christian! Shame on you, Kali. Change the
ancient and abominable customs of the Wahimas for good
ones and God will bless you for this and the 'bibi' will not
say that Kali is a savage, stupid, bad negro."

A horrible din in the huts of the fetish-men deafened
his words. Stas waved his hand and continued:

"I hear! That is your wicked Mzimu, which wants
the blood and heads of the captives. But you, of course,
know what that means and it will not frighten you.
Well, I say this to you· take a bamboo stick, go to each
hut and thrash the hides of the fetish-men until they
begin to roar louder than their drums. Cast out the
drums into the middle of the boma, in order that all the
Wahimas may see and understand how these knaves
have deceived them. Tell your foolish Wahimas, at
the same time, that which you yourself announced to
M'Rua's people, that wherever the 'Good Mzimu' sojourns
no human blood can be shed."

Stas' words evidently persuaded the young king, as he
glanced at him boldly and said:

"Kali will beat, oh, beat the fetish-men; throw out
the drums and tell the Wahimas that there where the
'Good Mzimu' is it is not allowable to kill any one. But
what shall Kali do with Faru and with the Samburus
who killed Fumba?"

Stas, who already had formed his plans for everything
and who only waited for this question, answered at once:

"Your father perished and his father perished, therefore it is a head for a head. You shall conclude a blood
alliance with Faru, after which the Wahimas and Samburus shall dwell in harmony; they shall peacefully culti-

vate manioc, and hunt. You shall tell Faru of the Great
Spirit, who is the Father of all white and black people,
and Faru shall love you like a brother."

"Kali now has a white brain," answered the young
negro.

And with this the conversation ended. A while later
again resounded wild roars; this time they were not the
roars of the wicked Mzimu but only of both fetish-men,
whom Kali cudgelled with all his might and main. The
warriors, who below continually surrounded the King
in a compact circle, came running up as fast as their legs
could carry them to see what was happening, and soon
became convinced with their own eyes and from the con-
fessions of the fetish-men that the bad Mzimu before
which heretofore they trembled was only a hollowed-out
trunk with monkey skin stretched over it.

And young Faru, when he was informed that in honor
of the "Good Mzimu" and the great master his head
would not be dashed to pieces, but that Kali was to eat a
piece of him and he a piece of Kali, could hardly believe
his ears, and on learning to whom he was indebted for
his life, lay on his face on the ground before the entrance
to Fumba's hut, and remained there until Nell came out
and ordered him to rise. Then he embraced with his black
hands her little foot and placed it on his head in sign that
through his entire life he desired to remain her slave.

The Wahimas were greatly astonished at the commands
of the young king, but the presence of the unknown guests
whom they regarded as the most powerful sorcerers in
the world had the effect of disarming all opposition.
The older people, however, were displeased with the new
customs, and both fetish-men, understanding that their
prosperous days were forever over, swore in their souls a
terrible revenge against the king and the new arrivals.

In the meantime they buried Fumba with great solemnity at the foot of the rock below the boma. Kali placed
above his grave a cross made of bamboo, while the negroes
left a few utensils with pombe and smoked meat "in order
that he should not annoy and haunt them during the
night-time."

Mamba's body, after the conclusion of the blood
brotherhood between Kali and Faru, was surrendered
to the Samburus.

XXI

"NELL, can you enumerate our journeys from Fayûm?"
Stas asked.

"I can."

Saying this the little maid raised her eyebrows and
began to count on her little fingers.

"At once. From Fayûm to Khartûm — that is one;
from Khartûm to Fashoda — that is the second; from
Fashoda to that ravine in which we found the King —
that is the third; and from Mount Linde to the lake — that
is the fourth."

"Yes. There probably is not another fly in the world
which has flown over such a piece of Africa."

"That fly would look queer without you."

Stas began to laugh.

"A fly on an elephant! A fly on an elephant!"

"But not a tsetse! Honestly, Stas — not a tsetse."

"No," he answered, "a very agreeable fly."

Nell, pleased with the praise, propped her little nose on
his arm; after which she asked:

"When shall we start on our fifth journey?"

"As soon as you have rested thoroughly, and I can
instruct those men whom Kali has promised to me how
to shoot a little."

"And shall we ride long?"

"Long, Nell — long! Who knows whether it will not
be the longest journey?"

"And you, as usual, will be equal to it."

"I must be."

Somehow Stas had managed to shift for himself as best he could, but this fifth journey required great preparations. They were to venture into unknown regions in which they were threatened with manifold dangers, so the boy desired to be protected against them better than he previously had been. With this in view he gave instructions in shooting from Remington rifles to forty young Wahimas who were to form the principal armed force and in a measure Nell's body-guard. More rifle-men he could not have, as the King carried only twenty-five rifles and the horses bore only fifteen. The rest of the army was to consist of one hundred Wahimas and a hundred Samburus, armed with spears and bows, whom Faru promised to furnish, and whose presence removed many difficulties of travel through the wide and wild country inhabited by the Samburu tribe. Stas, not without a certain pride, thought that having escaped during his journey from Fashoda with only Nell and the two negroes, without any means, he might come to the ocean coast at the head of two hundred armed men with an elephant and horses. He pictured to himself what would be said by the English people who prized resourcefulness highly, but above all he thought of what his father and Mr. Rawlinson would say. The thought of this sweetened all his toils.

Nevertheless, he was not at all at ease as to his own and Nell's fate, for he surely would pass through the possessions of the Wahimas and the Samburus without any difficulties, but after that, what? Upon what tribes would he yet chance, into what regions would he enter, and how much travel still remained? Linde's directions were too vague. Stas was greatly worried because he actually did not know where he was, as that part of Africa appeared on the maps from which he studied geography

entirely like a blank page. He also had no idea what this
Lake Bassa-Narok was and how great it was. He was
on its southern border, at which the width of the overflow
might amount to ten miles. But neither the Wahimas
nor the Samburus could tell him how far the lake extended to the north. Kali, who knew the Kiswahili
language passably well, answered all questions with,
"Bali! bali!" which meant "far! far!" but this was all
that Stas could elicit from him.

As the mountains on the north, shutting off the view,
appeared quite near, he assumed that it was a small,
brackish lake, like many others in Africa. A few years later
it appeared how great an error he committed.[1] For the
time being, however, he was not concerned so much about
ascertaining the exact dimensions of Bassa-Narok as
whether some river did not flow out of it, which afterwards coursed to the ocean. The Samburus — subjects
of Faru — claimed that east of their country lay a waterless
desert which no one had yet traversed. Stas, who knew
negroes from the narratives of travelers, from Linde's
adventures, and partly from his own experience, was
aware that when the dangers and the hardships began,
many of his men would desert to return home, and perhaps not one would remain. In such case he would find
himself in the wilds and desert with only Nell, Mea, and
little Nasibu. Above all he understood that a lack of
water would disperse the caravan at once, and for that
reason he inquired so eagerly about the river. Going
along its course, they really might avoid those horrors to
which travelers in waterless regions are exposed.

But the Samburus could not tell him anything definite;
he himself could not make any longer explorations of the

[1] It was the great lake which was discovered in 1888 by the
celebrated traveler Teleki and which he named Lake Rudolf.

eastern shore of the lake, for other employment kept him
at Boko. He reckoned that in all probability none of
the kites that he flew from Mount Linde and from the
negro villages had crossed the chain of mountains surrounding Bassa-Narok. For this reason it was necessary
to make and fly new ones, for these the wind could now
carry across the flat desert far away — perhaps as far
as the ocean. Now this work he had to supervise personally. For though Nell could glue them perfectly,
and Kali had learned how to fly them, neither of them
were able to inscribe on them all that it was necessary to
write. Stas regarded this as a matter of great importance
which it was not allowable to neglect.

So this labor occupied so much of his time that the
caravan was not ready for the journey until three weeks
had elapsed. But on the eve of the day on which they
were to start at daybreak the young King of the Wahimas
appeared before Stas and, bowing profoundly, said:

"Kali goes with the master and the 'bibi' as far as the
water on which great pirogues of the white people float."

Stas was touched by this proof of attachment; nevertheless, he thought that he had no right to take the boy
with him upon such an immense journey, a return from
which might be uncertain.

"Why do you want to go with us?" he asked.

"Kali loves the great master and the 'bibi.'"

Stas placed the palm of his hand on Kali's woolly head.

"I know, Kali, that you are an honest and good boy.
But what will become of your kingdom and who will
govern the Wahimas in your place?"

"M'Tana, brother of Kali's mother."

Stas knew that strife for rulership raged among the
negroes and power lured them the same as the white
people; so he pondered for a while and said:

"No, Kali. I cannot take you with me. You must remain with the Wahimas in order to make good people of them."

"Kali will return to them."

"M'Tana has many sons — Well, what will happen if he himself should desire to become king and leave the kingdom to his sons, and should induce the Wahimas to expel you?"

"M'Tana is good. He would not do that."

"But if he should do it?"

"Then Kali will again go to the great water — to the great master and the 'bibi.'"

"We shall not be there then."

"Then Kali will sit beside the water and weep from grief."

Speaking thus he crossed his hands above his head; after a while he whispered:

"Kali loves the great master and the 'bibi' very much — very much!"

And two big tears glistened in his eyes.

Stas hesitated how to act. He was sorry for Kali, nevertheless, he did not assent to his entreaty. He understood — not to speak of the dangers of return — that if M'Tana or the fetish-men stirred up the negroes, then the boy was threatened not only with expulsion from the country but with death.

"It is better for you to remain," he said, "better without question."

But while he was saying this, Nell entered. Through the thin mat which separated the rooms she had heard perfectly the whole conversation, and now seeing tears in Kali's eyes she began to wipe his eyelids with her little fingers, and afterward turned to Stas:

"Kali is going with us," she said with great firmness.

"Oho!" answered Stas, somewhat ruffled, "that does not depend upon you."

"Kali is going with us," she repeated.

"No, he will not go."

Suddenly she stamped her little foot.

"I want it."

And she burst into a genuine flood of tears.

Stas stared at her with the greatest amazement, as though he did not understand what had happened to the little maid who was always so good and gentle, but seeing that she stuck both of her little fists in her eyes and, like a little bird, caught the air with her opened mouth, he began to exclaim with great haste:

"Kali is going with us! He is going! He is going! Why are you crying? How unbearable you are! He is going! My, how pale you are! He is going! Do you hear?"

And thus it happened. Stas was ashamed until the evening of his weakness for the "Good Mzimu," and the "Good Mzimu" having carried her point, was as quiet, gentle, and obedient as ever.

XXII

THE caravan started at daybreak on the following day. The young negro was happy, the little female despot was now gentle and obedient, and Stas was full of energy and hope. They were accompanied by one hundred Samburus and one hundred Wahimas — forty of the latter were armed with Remingtons from which they could shoot passably well. The white commander who drilled them during three weeks knew, indeed, that in a given case they would create more noise than harm, but thought that in meeting savages noise plays no less a part than bullets, and he was pleased with his guards. They took with them a great supply of manioc, cakes baked of big, fat white ants and ground into flour, as well as a great quantity of smoked meats. Between ten and twenty women went with the caravan. They carried various good things for Nell and water-bags made of antelope skin. Stas, from the King's back, kept order, issued commands — perhaps not so much because they were necessary, but because he was intoxicated by the rôle of a commander — and with pride viewed his little army.

"If I wanted to," he said to himself, "I could remain the king of all the people of Doko, like Beniowsky in Madagascar."

And a thought flitted through his head whether it would not be well to return here sometime, conquer a great tract of country, civilize the negroes, found in that locality

a new Poland, or even start at the head of a drilled black
host for the old. As he felt, however, that there was
something ludicrous in the idea and as he doubted whether
his father would permit him to play the rôle of the Mace-
donian Alexander in Africa, he did not confide his plans to
Nell, who certainly would be the only person in the world
ready to applaud them.

And besides, before subjugating that region of Africa,
it was necessary above all things to get out of it, so he
occupied himself with nearer matters. The caravan
stretched out in a long string. Stas, sitting on the King's
neck, decided to ride at the end in order to have everything and everybody in sight.

Now when the people passed by him, one after another,
he observed, not without surprise, that the two fetish-
men, M'Kunje and M'Pua — the same who had received
a drubbing at Kali's hands — belonged to the caravan
and that they set out with packs on their heads together
with the others on the road.

So he stopped them and asked:

"Who ordered you to go?"

"The king," they answered, bowing humbly.

But under the mask of humility their eyes glittered
savagely and their faces reflected such malice that Stas
at once wanted to drive them away, and if he did not
do it, it was only because he did not want to undermine
Kali's authority.

Nevertheless, he summoned him at once.

"Did you order the fetish-men to go with us?" he asked.

"Kali ordered it, for Kali is wise."

"Then I shall ask you why your wisdom did not leave
them at home?"

"Because if M'Kunje and M'Pua remain they would
instigate the Wahimas to kill Kali upon his return, but

if we take them with us Kali will be able to watch
them."

Stas meditated for a while and said:

"Perhaps you are right; nevertheless, do not lose
sight of them, day or night, for they have a wicked look."

"Kali will have bamboo sticks," the young negro
replied.

The caravan proceeded. Stas at the last moment
ordered the guard, armed with Remingtons, to close the
procession, as they were men chosen by him, and most
reliable. During the drills, which lasted quite long, they
had become attached in a certain degree to this young
commander, and at the same time, as the nearest to his
august person, they regarded themselves as something
better than the others. At present they were to watch
over the whole caravan and seize those who should take
a fancy to desert. It was to be foreseen that when the
hardships and dangers began deserters would not be
lacking.

But the first day everything proceeded in the best
possible manner. The negroes with the burdens on their
heads, each one armed with a bow and a few smaller
javelins or so-called assagais, extended in a long serpentine
column amidst the jungle. For some time they skirted
along the southern shore of the lake over the level ground,
but as the lake was surrounded on all sides by high peaks
they had to climb mountains when they turned to the
east. The old Samburus, who knew that locality, claimed
that the caravan would have to cross high passes between the mountains which they called Kullal and Inro,
after which they would enter into the Ebene country,
lying south of Borani. Stas understood that they could
not go directly east for he remembered that Mombasa
was situated a few degrees beyond the equator and there-

fore considerably south of that unknown lake. Possessing
a few compasses which Linde left, he did not fear that he
would stray from the proper road.

The first night they lodged upon a wooded hill. With
the coming of darkness a few scores of camp-fires blazed,
at which the negroes roasted dried meat and ate a dough
of manioc roots, picking it out of the utensils with their
fingers. After appeasing their hunger and thirst they
were gossiping among themselves as to where the "Bwana
kubwa" would lead them and what they would receive
from him for it. Some sang, squatting and stirring up
the fire, while all talked so long and so loudly that Stas
finally had to command silence in order that Nell should
sleep.

The night was very cold, but the next day, when the
first rays of the sun illuminated the locality, it became warm
at once. About sunrise the little travelers saw a strange
sight. They were just approaching a little lake over
a mile wide, or rather a great slough formed by the rains
in the mountain valley, when suddenly Stas, sitting
with Nell on the King, and looking about the region
through a field-glass, exclaimed:

"Look, Nell! Elephants are going to the water."

In fact, at a distance of about five hundred yards could
be seen a small herd composed of five heads, approaching
the little lake slowly one after the other.

"These are some kind of strange elephants," Stas
said, gazing at them with keen attention; "they are
smaller than the King, their ears are far smaller, and I
do not see any tusks at all."

In the meantime the elephants entered the water but
did not stop at the shore, as the King usually did, and
did not begin to splash with their trunks, but going
continually ahead they plunged deeper and deeper until

finally only their backs protruded above the water like boulders of stone.

"What is this? They are diving!" Stas exclaimed.

The caravan approached considerably towards the shore and finally was close by it. Stas halted it and began to stare with extraordinary astonishment now at Nell, then at the lake.

The elephants could not be seen at all; in the smooth watery pane even with the naked eye could be distinguished five spots like round red flowers, jutting above the surface and rocking with a light motion.

"They are standing on the bottom and those are the tips of their trunks," Stas said, not believing his own eyes. Then he shouted to Kali.

"Kali, did you see them?"

"Yes, master, Kali sees. Those are water-elephants,"[1] answered the young negro quietly.

"Water-elephants?"

"Kali has seen them often."

"And do they live in water?"

"During the night they go to the jungle and feed and during the day they live in the lake the same as a kiboko (hippopotamus). They do not come out until after sunset."

Stas for a long time could not recover from his surprise, and were it not that it was urgent for him to proceed on his way he would have halted the caravan until night in order to view better these singular animals. But it occurred to him that the elephants might emerge from

[1] Africa contains many uninvestigated secrets Rumors of water-elephants reached the ears of travelers but were given no credence Recently M. Le Petit, sent to Africa by the Museum of Natural History, Paris, saw water-elephants on the shores of Lake Leopold in Congo. An account of this can be found in the German periodical "Kosmos," No 6.

the water on the opposite side, and even if they came out nearer it would be difficult to observe them closely in the dusk.

He gave the signal for the departure, but on the road said to Nell:

"Well! We have seen something which the eyes of no European have ever seen. And do you know what I think? — that if we reach the ocean safely nobody will believe us when I tell them that there are water-elephants in Africa."

"But if you caught one and took him along with us to the ocean?" Nell said, in the conviction that Stas as usual would be able to accomplish everything.

XXIII

AFTER ten days' journey the caravan finally crossed the depressions in the crests of mountains and entered into a different country. It was an immense plain, broken here and there by small hills, but was mainly level. The vegetation changed entirely. There were no big trees, rising singly or in clumps over the wavy surface of the grass. Here and there projected at a considerable distance from each other acacias yielding gum, with coral-hued trunks, umbrella-like, but with scant foliage and affording but little shade. Among the white-ant hillocks shot upwards here and there euphorbias, with boughs like the arms of a candle-stick. In the sky vultures soared, and lower there flew from acacia to acacia birds of the raven species with black and white plumage. The grass was yellow and, in spike, looked like ripe rye. But, nevertheless, that dry jungle obviously supplied food for a great number of animals, for several times each day the travelers met considerable herds of antelopes, hartbeests, and particularly zebras. The heat on the open and treeless plain became unbearable. The sky was cloudless, the days were excessively hot, and the night did not bring any rest.

The journey became each day more and more burdensome. In the villages which the caravan encountered, the extremely savage populace received it with fear, but principally with reluctance, and if it were not for the large number of armed guards as well as the sight of the white faces, the King, and Saba, great danger would have threatened the travelers.

With Kali's assistance Stas was able to ascertain that farther on there were no villages and that the country was waterless. This was hard to believe, for the numerous herds which they encountered must have drunk somewhere. Nevertheless, the account of the desert, in which there were no rivers nor sloughs, frightened the negroes and desertions began. The first example was set by M'Kunje and M'Pua. Fortunately their escape was detected early, and pursuers on horseback caught them not far from the camp; when they were brought back Kali, with the aid of the bamboo sticks, impressed upon them the impropriety of their conduct. Stas, assembling all the guards, delivered a speech to them, which the young negro interpreted into the native language. Taking advantage of the fact that at the last stopping place lions roared all night about the camp, Stas endeavored to convince his men that whoever ran away would unavoidably become their prey, and even if he passed the night on acacia boughs the still more terrible "wobo" would find him there. He said afterwards that wherever the antelopes live there must be water, and if in the further course of their journey they should chance upon a region entirely destitute of water, they could take enough of it with them in bags of antelope skin for two or three days' journey. The negroes, hearing his words, repeated every little while, one after another: "Oh, mother, how true that is, how true!" but the following night five Samburus and two Wahimas ran away, and after that every night somebody was missing.

M'Kunje and M'Pua did not, however, try their fortune a second time for the simple reason that Kali at sunset ordered them to be bound.

Nevertheless, the country became drier and drier, and the sun scorched the jungle unmercifully. Even acacias could not be seen. Herds of antelopes appeared continually but in smaller numbers. The donkey and the horses yet found sufficient food, as under the high, dry grass was hidden in many places lower grass, greener and less dry. But the King, though he was not fastidious, grew lean. When they chanced upon an acacia he broke it with his head, and nibbled diligently its leaves and even the pods of the previous year. The caravan indeed came upon water every day, but frequently it was so bad that it had to be filtered or else it was unfit even for the elephant to drink. Afterwards it happened several times that the men, sent in advance, returned under Kali's command, not finding a slough nor a stream hidden in the earth's fissures, and Kali with troubled face would announce: "Madi apana" (no water).

Stas understood that this last journey would not be any easier than the previous ones and began to worry about Nell, as changes were taking place in her. Her little face, instead of tanning from the sun and wind, became each day paler and her eyes lost their usual luster. On the dry plain, free from mosquitoes, she was not threatened with fever, but it was apparent that the terrible heat was wasting the little maid's strength. The boy, with compassion and with fear, now gazed at her little hands, which became as white as paper, and bitterly reproached himself because, having lost so much time in the preparation and in drilling the negroes to shoot, he had exposed her to a journey in a season of the year so parching.

Amid these fears day after day passed. The sun drank up the moisture and the life out of the soil more and more greedily and unmercifully. The grass shriveled and dried

up to such a degree that it crumbled under the hoofs of
the antelopes, and herds, rushing by, though not numerous,
raised clouds of dust.   Nevertheless, the travelers chanced
once more upon a little river, which they recognized by
a long row of trees growing on its banks.   The negroes
ran in a race towards the trees and, reaching the bank, lay
flat on it, dipping their heads and drinking so greedily
that they stopped only when a crocodile seized the hand
of one of their number.   Others rushed to their companion's rescue and in one moment they pulled out of the
water the loathsome lizard, which, however, did not let
go of the man's hand though his jaws were opened with
spears and knives.   The matter was only terminated by
the King who, placing his foot on him, crushed him as
easily as if he were a mouldy mushroom.

When the men finally quenched their thirst, Stas
ordered the erection in the shallow water of a round
enclosure of high bamboos with only one entrance from
the bank, in order that Nell might bathe with perfect
safety.   And at the entrance he stationed the King.
The bath greatly refreshed the little maid and a rest
restored her strength somewhat.

To the great joy of the whole caravan and Nell, "Bwana
kubwa" decided to stop two days near this water.   At
this news the men fell into excellent humor and at once
forgot the toils they had endured.   After taking a nap
and refreshments the negroes began to wander among
the trees above the river, looking for palms bearing wild
dates and so-called "Job's tears," from which necklaces
are made.   A few of them returned to the camp before
sunset, carrying some square objects which Stas recognized as his own kites.

One of these kites bore the number 7, which was evidence that it was sent out from Mount Linde, as the

children flew from that place a few score. Stas was hugely overjoyed at this sight and it gave him renewed courage.

"I did not expect," he said to Nell, "that kites could fly such a distance. I was certain that they would remain on the summits of Karamojo and I only let them fly prepared for any accident. But now I see that the wind can carry them where it wants to and I have a hope that those which we sent from the mountains surrounding Bassa-Narok, and now on the road, will fly as far as the ocean."

"They surely will," Nell answered.

"God grant," the boy acquiesced, thinking of the dangers and hardships of the further journey.

The caravan started from the river on the third day, taking with them a great supply of water in leather bags. Before nightfall they again entered upon a region grilled by the sun, in which not even acacias grew, and the ground in some places was as bare as a threshing-floor. Sometimes they met passion-flowers with trunks imbedded in the ground and resembling monstrous pumpkins two yards in diameter. In these huge globes there shot out lianas as thin as string, which, creeping over the ground, covered immense distances, forming a thicket so impenetrable that it would be difficult even for mice to penetrate it. But notwithstanding the beautiful color of these plants, resembling the European acanthus, there were so many thorns in them that neither the King nor the horses could find any nourishment in them. Only the donkey nibbled them cautiously.

Sometimes in the course of several English miles they did not see anything except coarse, short grass and low plants, like immortelles, which crumbled upon being touched. After a night's bivouac, during the whole of the following day a living fire descended from heaven. The air quivered as on the Libyan Desert. In the sky there was not even a cloudlet. The earth was so flooded with light that everything appeared white, and not a sound, not even the buzz of insects, interrupted this deadly stillness surfeited with an ill-omened luster.

The men were dripping with sweat. At times they deposited their packs of dried meats and shields in one pile to find a little shade under them. Stas issued orders to save the water, but the negroes are like children, who have no thought of the morrow. Finally it was necessary to surround with a guard those who carried the supplies of water and to apportion the water to each one separately. Kali attended to this very conscientiously, but this consumed a great deal of time and delayed the march, and therefore the finding of some kind of watering-place. The Samburus complained in addition that the Wahimas got more than their share to drink, and the Wahimas that the Samburus were favored. These latter began to threaten to return, but Stas declared to them that Faru would cut off their heads. He himself ordered the men armed with Remingtons to go on guard and not let any one leave.

The next night was passed upon a level plain. They did not build a boma, or, as the Sudânese say, a zareba, for there was nothing to build one with. The duties of sentinel were performed by the King and Saba. This was sufficient, but the King, who received only a tenth of the water he needed, trumpeted for it until sunrise, and Saba, with hanging tongue, turned his eyes towards Stas and Nell in mute appeal for even one drop. The little maid wanted Stas to give him a mouthful from a rubber flask left by Linde, which Stas carried with a string across his shoulder, but he was saving this remnant for the little one in the dark hour; therefore he declined.

On the fourth day towards evening only five bags with water remained, or not quite half a cupful for each member of the party. As the nights, however, at any rate were cooler than the days, and the thirst at such times vexed them less than under the burning rays of the sun, and as the people had received in the morning a small quantity of water, Stas ordered those bags saved for the following day. The negroes grumbled at this order, but fear of Stas was still great; so they did not dare to rush at this last supply, especially as near it stood a guard of two men armed with Remingtons, the guard being changed every hour.

The Wahimas and Samburus cheated their thirst by pulling out blades of poor grass and chewing its roots. Nevertheless, there was almost no moisture in it, as the inexorable sun burnt it, even below the earth's surface.[1]

Sleep, though it did not quench their thirst, at least permitted them to forget it; so when night followed, the men, weary and exhausted with the whole day's march, dropped as though lifeless, wherever they stopped, and fell into deep slumber. Stas also fell asleep, but in his soul he had too many worries and was disturbed too much to sleep peacefully and long. After a few hours he awoke and began to meditate on what was to come, and where he could secure water for Nell, and for the whole caravan, together with the people and the animals. His situation was hard and perhaps horrible, but the resourceful boy did not yet yield to despair. He began to recall all the incidents, from the time of their abduction from Fayûm until that moment: the great journey across the Sahara, the hurricane in the desert, the attempts to escape,

[1] About the waterless plains in this region see the excellent book, entitled "Kilima-Njaro," by the Rev. Mr. Le Roy, at present Bishop of Gabon.

Khartûm, the Mahdi, Fashoda, their liberation from Gebhr's hands; afterwards the further journey after Linde's death until reaching Lake Bassa-Narok and that place at which they were passing the night. "So much did we undergo, so much have we suffered," he soliloquized, "so often did it seem that all was lost and that there was no help; nevertheless, God aided me and I always found help. Why, it is impossible that, after having passed over such roads and gone through so many terrible dangers, we should perish upon this the last journey. Now we have yet a little water and this region — why, it is not a Sahara, for if it were the people would know about it."

But hope was mainly sustained in him by this, that on the southeast he espied through the field-glass some kind of misty outlines as though of mountains. Perhaps they were hundreds of English miles away, perhaps more. But if they succeeded in reaching them, they would be saved, as mountains are seldom waterless. How much time that would consume was something he could not compute for it all depended upon the height of the mountains. Lofty peaks in such transparent atmosphere as that of Africa can be seen at an immeasurable distance; so it was necessary to find water before that time. Otherwise destruction threatened them.

"It is necessary," Stas repeated to himself.

The harsh breathing of the elephant, who exhaled from his lungs as best he could the burning heat, interrupted every little while the boy's meditations. But after a certain time it seemed to him that he heard some kind of sound, resembling groans, coming from the direction in which the water-bags lay covered in the grass for the night. As the groans were repeated several times, he rose to see what was happening and, walking towards the grass plot a few score paces distant from the tent, he perceived two dark bodies lying near each other and two Remington barrels glistening in the moonlight.

"The negroes are always the same," he thought; "they were to watch over the water, more precious now to us than anything in the world, and both went to sleep as though in their own huts. Ah! Kali's bamboo will have some work to do to-morrow."

Under this impression he approached and shook the foot of one of the sentinels, but at once drew back in horror.

The apparently sleeping negro lay on his back with a knife sticking in his throat up to the handle and beside him was the other, likewise cut so terribly that his head was almost severed from the trunk.

Two bags with water had disappeared; the other three lay in the littered grass, slashed and sunken.

Stas felt that his hair stood on end.

XXIV

In response to his shout Kali was the first to come rushing; after him came the two guardsmen who were to relieve the previous watch, and a few moments later all the Wahimas and Samburus assembled at the scene of the crime, shouting and yelling. A commotion, full of cries and terror, ensued. The people were concerned not so much about the slain and the murderers as about the water which soaked into the parched jungle soil. Some negroes threw themselves upon the ground and, clawing out with their fingers lumps of earth, sucked out the remnants of moisture. Others shouted that evil spirits had murdered the guards and slashed the bags. But Stas and Kali knew what it all meant. M'Kunje and M'Pua were missing from those men howling above that grass patch. In that which had happened there was something more than the murder of two guards and the theft of water. The remaining slashed bags were evidence that it was an act of revenge and at the same time a sentence of death for the whole caravan. The priests of the wicked Mzimu revenged themselves upon the good one. The fetish-men revenged themselves upon the young king who exposed their frauds and did not permit them to deceive the ignorant Wahimas. Now the wings of death stretched over the entire caravan like a hawk over a flock of doves.

Kali recollected too late that, having his mind troubled and engrossed with something else, he forgot to have the fetish-men bound, as from the time of their flight he had ordered them to be each evening. It was apparent that both sentinels, watching the water, through inbred negro carelessness, lay down and fell asleep. This facilitated the work of the rogues and permitted them to escape unpunished.

Before the confusion subsided somewhat and the people recovered from their consternation, considerable time elapsed; nevertheless, the assassins could not be far away, as the ground under the cut bags was moist and the blood which flowed from both of the slain did not yet coagulate. Stas issued an order to pursue the runaways not only for the purpose of punishing them, but also to recover the last two bags of water. Kali, mounting a horse and taking with him about thirteen guardsmen, started in pursuit. Stas at first wanted to take part in it, but it occurred to him that he could not leave Nell alone among the excited and enraged negroes; so he remained. He only directed Kali to take Saba along with him.

He himself remained, for he feared a downright mutiny, particularly among the Samburus. But in this he was mistaken. The negroes as a rule break out easily, and sometimes for trivial causes, but when crushed by a great calamity and particularly when the inexorable hand of death weighs upon them, they submit passively; not only those whom Islam teaches that a struggle with destiny is vain, but all others. Then neither terror nor the moments of torture can arouse them from their torpor. It happened thus at this time. The Wahimas, as well as the Samburus, when the first excitement passed away and the idea that they must die definitely found lodgment in their minds, lay down quietly on the ground waiting for death; in view of which not a mutiny was to be feared, but rather that on the morrow they would not want to rise and start upon their further journey. Stas, when he observed this, was seized by a great pity for them.

Kali returned before daybreak and at once placed before Stas two bags torn to pieces, in which there was not a drop of water.

"Great Master," he said, "madi apana!"

Stas rubbed his perspiring forehead with his hand; after which he said:

"And M'Kunje and M'Pua?"

"M'Kunje and M'Pua are dead," Kali replied.

"Did you order them to be killed?"

"A lion or 'wobo' killed them."

And he began to relate what happened. The bodies of the two murderers were found quite far from the camp at the place where they met death. Both lay close to each other, both had skulls crushed from behind, lacerated shoulders, and gnawed spines. Kali assumed that when the "wobo" or lion appeared before them in the moonlight they fell on their faces before it and began to entreat it that it should spare their lives. But the terrible beast killed both, and afterwards, having appeased its hunger, scented water and tore the bags to pieces.

"God punished them," Stas said, "and the Wahimas should be convinced that the wicked Mzimu is incapable of rescuing any one."

And Kali added:

"God punished them, but we have no water."

"Far ahead of us in the east I saw mountains. There must be water there."

"Kali sees them also, but it is many, many days to them."

A moment of silence followed.

"Master," spoke out Kali, "let the 'Good Mzimu' — let the 'bibi' beg the Great Spirit for rain or for a river."

Stas left him, making no reply. But before the tent he saw Nell's little figure; the shouts and yells had awakened her some time before.

"What has happened, Stas?" she asked, running up to him.

And he placed his hand on her little head and solemnly said:

"Nell, pray to God for water; otherwise we all shall perish."

So the little maiden upraised her pale little face and, fastening her eyes on the moon's silvery shield, began to implore for succor Him who in heaven causes the stars to revolve and on earth tempers the wind for the shorn lamb.

After a sleepless, noisy, and anxious night the sun rolled upon the horizon suddenly, as it always does under the equator, and a bright day followed. On the grass there was not a drop of dew; on the sky not a cloudlet. Stas ordered the guards to assemble the men and delivered a short speech to them. He declared to them that it was impossible to return to the river now, for they of course well knew that they were separated from it by five days' and nights' journey. But on the other hand no one knew whether there was not water in the opposite direction. Perhaps even not far away they would find some stream, some rivulet or slough. Trees, indeed, could not be seen, but it often happens upon open plains where the strong gale carries away the seeds, trees do not grow even at the water-side. Yesterday they saw some big antelopes and a few ostriches running towards the east, which was a sign that yonder there must be some watering place, and in view of this whoever is not a fool and whoever has in his bosom a heart, not of a hare but of a lion or buffalo, will prefer to move forward, though in thirst and pain, rather than to lie down and wait there for vultures or hyenas.

And saying this, he pointed with his hand at the vultures, a few of which coursed already in an ill-omened circle above the caravan. After these words the Wahimas, whom Stas commanded to rise, stood up almost as one man, for, accustomed to the dreadful power of kings, they did not dare to resist. But many of the Samburus, in view of the fact that their king Faru remained at the lake, did not want to rise, and these said among themselves: "Why should we go to meet death when she herself will come to us?" In this manner the caravan proceeded, reduced almost one-half, and it started from the outset in torture. For twenty-four hours the people had not had a drop of water or any other fluid in their mouths. Even in a cooler climate this, at labor, would have been an unendurable suffering; and how much more so in this blazing African furnace in which even those who drink copiously perspire the water so quickly that almost at the same moment they can wipe it off their skin with their hands. It was also to be foreseen that many of the men would drop on the way from exhaustion and sunstroke. Stas protected Nell as best he could from the sun and did not permit her to lean for even a moment out of the palanquin, whose little roof he covered with a piece of white percale in order to make it double. With the rest of the water, which he still had in the rubber bottle, he prepared a strong tea for her and handed it to her when cooled off, without any sugar, for sweets increase thirst. The little girl urged him with tears to drink also; so he placed to his lips the bottle in which there remained scarcely a few thimblefuls of water, and, moving his throat, pretended that he drank it. At the moment when he felt the moisture on his lips it seemed to him that his breast and stomach were aflame and that if he did not quench that flame he would drop dead. Before his eyes red spots began to flit, and in his jaws he felt a terrible pain, as if some one stuck a thousand pins in them. His hands shook so that he almost spilt these last drops. Nevertheless, he caught only two or three in his mouth with his tongue; the rest he saved for Nell.

A day of torture and toil again passed, after which, fortunately, a cooler night came. But the following morning the intense heat became terrible. There was not a breath of air. The sun, like an evil spirit, ravaged with living flame the parched earth. The borders of the horizon whitened. As far as the eyes reached not even euphorbias could be seen. Nothing — only a burnt, desolate plain, covered with tufts of blackened grass and heather. From time to time there resounded in the immeasurable distance light thunder, but this in fair skies proclaims not storms but a drought.

About noon, when the heat became the greatest, it was necessary to halt. The caravan broke ranks in gloomy silence. It appeared that one horse fell and about thirteen of the guards remained on the road. During the rest nobody thought of eating. The people had sunken eyes and cracked lips and on them dried clots of blood. Nell panted like a bird, so Stas surrendered to her the rubber bottle, and exclaiming: "I drank! I drank!" he ran to the other side of the camp, for he feared that if he remained he would snatch that water from her or would demand that she should share it with him. This perhaps was his most heroic act during the course of the journey. He himself, however, began to suffer horribly. Before his eyes there flew continually the red patches. He felt a tightening of his jaws so strongly that he opened and closed them with difficulty. His throat was dry, burning; there was no saliva in his mouth; the tongue was as though wooden. And of course this was but the beginning of the torture for him and for the caravan.

The thunder announcing the drought resounded incessantly on the horizon's border. About three o'clock, when the sun passed to the western side of the heavens, Stas ordered the caravan to rise and started at its head towards the east. But now hardly seventy men followed him, and every little while some one of them lay down beside his pack to rise nevermore. The heat decreased a few degrees but was still terrible. The still air was permeated as though with the gas of burning charcoal. The people had nothing to breathe and the animals began to suffer no less. In an hour after the start again one of the horses fell. Saba panted and his flanks heaved; from his blackened tongue not a drop of froth fell. The King, accustomed to the dry African jungle, apparently suffered the least, but he began to be vicious. His little eyes glittered with a kind of strange light. To Stas, and particularly to Nell, who from time to time talked to him, he answered still with a gurgle, but when Kali carelessly came near him he grunted menacingly and waved his trunk so that he would have killed the boy if he had not jumped aside in time.

Kali's eyes were bloodshot, the veins in his neck were inflated, and his lips cracked the same as the other negroes. About five o'clock he approached Stas and, in a hollow voice which with difficulty issued out of his throat, said:

"Great master, Kali can go no further. Let the night come here."

Stas overcame the pain in his jaws and answered with an effort:

"Very well. We will stop. The night will bring relief."

"It will bring death," the young negro whispered.

The men threw the loads off their heads, but as the fever in their thickened blood already reached the highest degree, on this occasion they did not immediately lie down on the ground. Their hearts and the arteries in their temples, hands, and limbs pulsated as if in a moment they would burst. The skin of their bodies, drying up and shrinking, began to itch; in their bones they were sensible of an excessive disquiet and in their entrails and throats a fire. Some walked uneasily among the packets; others could be seen farther away in ruddy rays of the setting sun as they strolled one after another among the dried tufts as though seeking something, and this continued until their strength was entirely exhausted. Then they fell in turn on the ground and lay in convulsions. Kali sat, squatting near Stas and Nell, catching the air with open mouth, and began to repeat entreatingly between one breath and the other:

"Bwana kubwa, water."

Stas gazed at him with a glassy stare and remained silent.

"Bwana kubwa, water!"

And after a while:

"Kali is dying."

At this, Mea, who for an unknown reason endured thirst the easiest and suffered the least of all, approached, sat close to him, and, embracing his neck with her arms, said in her quiet, melodious voice.

"Mea wants to die together with Kali."

A long silence followed.

In the meantime the sun set and night covered the region. The sky became dark-blue. On its southern side the Cross glistened. Above the plain a myriad of stars twinkled. The moon came out from under the earth and began to satiate the darkness with light, and on the west with the waning and pale twilight extended the zodiacal luminosity. The air was transformed into a great luminous gulf. The ever-increasing luster submerged the region. The palanquin, which remained forgotten on the King's back, and the tents glistened, just as whitewashed houses glisten in a bright night. The world sank into silence and sleep encompassed the earth.

And in the presence of this stillness and this quiet of nature the people howled from pain and waited for death. On the silvery background of the darkness the gigantic black form of the elephant was strongly outlined. The moon's beams illuminated besides the tents, Stas' and Nell's dresses and, amid tufts of heather, the dark, shriveled bodies of the negroes and, scattered here and there, piles of packages. Before the children sat, propped on his fore legs, Saba, and, raising his head towards the moon's shield, he howled mournfully.

In Stas' soul oscillated only the remnants of thought, changed into a gloomy and despairing feeling that this time there was no help and that all those prodigious toils and efforts, those sufferings, those acts of will and courage, which he had performed during the terrible journey — from Medinet to Khartûm, from Khartûm to Fashoda, and from Fashoda to the unknown lake — would avail naught, and that an inexorable end of the struggle and of life was approaching. And this appeared to him all the more horrible because this end came during the time of the final journey, at the termination of which lay the ocean. Ah! He would not now conduct little Nell to the coast; he would not convey her by a steamer to Port Said, would not surrender her to Mr. Rawlinson; he himself would not fall into his father's arms and would not hear from his lips that he had acted like a brave boy and like a true Pole! The end, the end! In a few days the sun would shine only upon the lifeless bodies and afterwards would dry them up into a semblance of those mummies which slumber in an eternal sleep in the museums in Egypt.

From torture and fever his mind began to get confused. Ante-mortem visions and delusions of hearing crowded upon him. He heard distinctly the voices of the Sudânese and Bedouins yelling "Yalla! Yalla!" at the speeding camels. He saw Idris and Gebhr. The Mahdi smiled at him with his thick lips, asking: "Do you want to drink at the spring of truth?" — Afterwards the lion gazed at him from the rock; later Linde gave him a gallipot of quinine and said: "Hurry, hurry, for the little one will die." And in the end he beheld only the pale, very dear little face and two little hands stretched out towards him.

Suddenly he trembled and consciousness returned to him for a moment, for hard by murmured the quiet whisper of Nell, resembling a moan:

"Stas — water!"

And she, like Kali previously, looked to him only for help.

But as twelve hours before he had given her the last drop, he now started up suddenly, and exclaimed in a voice in which vibrated an outburst of pain, despair, and affliction.

"Oh, Nell, I only pretended that I was drinking! For three days I have had nothing in my mouth!"

And clasping his head with both hands he ran away in order not to look at her sufferings. He rushed blindly among tufts of grass and heather until he fell upon one of the tufts. He was unarmed. A leopard, lion, or even a big hyena would find in him an easy prey. But only

Saba came running to him. Having smelt at him on all sides, he again began to howl, as if summoning aid for him.

Nobody, however, hurried with aid. Only from above, the moon, quiet and indifferent, looked on him. For a long time the boy lay like dead. He was revived only by a cooler breath of wind, which unexpectedly blew from the east. Stas sat up and after a while attempted to rise to return to Nell.

The cooler wind blew a second time. Saba ceased howling and, turning towards the east, began to dilate his nostrils. Suddenly he barked once or twice a short, broken bass and dashed ahead. For some time he could not be heard, but soon his barking again resounded. Stas rose and, staggering on his numb legs, began to look after him. Long journeys, long stays in the jungle, the necessity of holding all his senses in continual restraint, and continual dangers had taught the boy to pay careful heed to everything which was taking place about him. So, notwithstanding the tortures he felt at that moment, notwithstanding his half-conscious mind, through instinct and habit he watched the behavior of the dog. And Saba, after the lapse of a certain time, again appeared near him, but was somewhat strangely agitated and uneasy. A few times he raised his eyes at Stas, ran around, again rushed ahead, scenting and barking in the heather; again he came back and finally, seizing the boy's clothes, began to pull him in a direction opposite to the camp.

Stas completely recovered his senses.

"What is this?" he thought. "Either the dog's mind, from thirst, is disordered or he has scented water. But no! If water was near he would have run to it to drink and would have wet jaws. If it was far away, he would not have scented it — water has no smell. He is not pulling me to antelopes, for he did not want to eat during the evening. Nor to beasts of prey. Well, what is it?"

And suddenly his heart began to beat in his bosom yet more strongly.

"Perhaps the wind brought him the odor of men? — Perhaps — in the distance there is some negro village? — Perhaps one of the kites has flown as far — Oh, merciful Christ! Oh, Christ! — "

And under the influence of a gleam of hope he regained his strength and began to run towards the camp, notwithstanding the obstinacy of the dog, who incessantly barred his way. In the camp Nell's form loomed white before him and her weak voice reached him: after a while he stumbled over Kali lying on the ground, but he paid no heed to anything. Reaching the pack in which the sky-rockets were, he tore it open and drew out one of them. With trembling hands he tied it to a bamboo stick, planted it in a crack in the ground, struck a match and lit the string of the tube hanging at the bottom.

After a while a red snake flew upwards with a sputter and a sizzle. Stas seized a bamboo pole with both hands in order not to fall and fixed his eyes on the distance. His pulse and his temples beat like sledge hammers; his lips moved in fervent prayer. His last breath, and in it his whole soul, he sent to God.

One minute passed, another, a third, and a fourth. Nothing! Nothing! The boy's hand dropped, his head bowed to the ground, and immense grief flooded his tortured breast.

"In vain! In vain!" he whispered. "I will go and sit beside Nell and we will die together."

At this moment far, far away on the silvery background of the moonlit night, a fiery ribbon suddenly soared upward and scattered into golden stars, which fell slowly, like great tears, upon the earth.

"Succor!" Stas shouted.

And immediately these people, who were half-dead a short time before, dashed pell-mell in a race across tufts of shrubs and grass. After the first sky-rocket, a second and third appeared. After that the breeze brought a report as though of tapping, in which it was easy to divine distant shots. Stas ordered all the Remingtons to be fired, and from that time the colloquy of rifles was not interrupted at all and became more and more distinct. The boy, sitting on a horse, which also as though by a miracle recovered its strength, and keeping Nell before him, dashed across the plain towards the saving sounds. Beside him rushed Saba and after him trumpeted the gigantic King. The two camps were separated by a space of a few miles, but as from both sides they drew to each other simultaneously, the whole trip did not last long. Soon the rifle shots could not only be heard but seen. Yet one last sky-rocket flew out in the air not farther than a few hundred paces. After that numerous lights glistened. The slight elevation of the ground hid them for a while, but when Stas passed it he found himself almost in front of a row of negroes holding in their hands burning torches.

At the head of the row were two Europeans, in English helmets and with rifles in their hands.

With one glance of the eye Stas recognized them as being Captain Glenn and Doctor Clary.

XXV

THE object of the Captain Glenn and Doctor Clary expedition was not at all to find Stas and Nell. It was a large and abundantly equipped government expedition despatched to explore the eastern and northern slopes of the gigantic mountain Kilima-Njaro, as well as the little-known vast regions lying north of that mountain. The captain as well as the doctor knew indeed about the abduction of the children from Medinet el-Fayûm, as intelligence of it was published in the English and Arabian papers, but they thought that both were dead or were groaning in slavery under the Mahdi, from whom thus far not a European had been rescued. Clary, whose sister married Rawlinson in Bombay and who was very much charmed by little Nell during the trip to Cairo, felt keenly her loss. But with Glenn, he mourned also for the brave boy. Several times they sent despatches from Mombasa to Mr. Rawlinson asking whether the children were found, and not until the last unfavorable reply, which came a considerable time before the starting of the caravan, did they finally lose all hope.

And it never even occurred to them that the children imprisoned in distant Khartûm could appear in that locality. Often, however, they conversed about them in the evening after finishing their daily labors, for the doctor could by no means forget the beautiful little girl.

In the meantime the expedition advanced farther and farther. After a long stay on the eastern slope of Kilima-

Njaro, after exploring the upper courses of the Sabak and Tany rivers, as well as Kenia Mountain, the captain and doctor turned in a northerly direction, and after crossing the marshy Guasso-Nijiro they entered upon a vast plain, uninhabited and frequented by countless herds of antelopes. After three months of travel the men were entitled to a long rest, so Captain Glenn, discovering a small lake of wholesome brown water, ordered tents to be pitched near it and announced a ten days' stop.

During the stop the white men were occupied with hunting and arranging their geographical and scientific notes, and the negroes devoted themselves to idleness, which is always so sweet to them. Now it happened one day that Doctor Clary, shortly after he arose, when approaching the shore, observed between ten and twenty natives of Zanzibar, belonging to the caravan, gazing with upturned faces at the top of a high tree and repeating in a circle:

"Ndege? Akuna ndege? Ndege?" (A bird? Not a bird? A bird?)

The doctor was short-sighted, so he sent to his tent for a field-glass; afterwards he looked through it at the object pointed out by the negroes and great astonishment was reflected upon his countenance.

"Ask the captain to come here," he said.

Before the negroes reached him the captain appeared in front of the tent, for he was starting on an antelope-hunt.

"Look, Glenn," the doctor said, pointing with his hand upwards.

The captain, in turn, turned his face upwards, shaded his eyes with his hand, and was astonished no less than the doctor.

"A kite," he exclaimed.

"Yes, but the negroes do not fly kites. So where did it come from?"

"Perhaps some kind of white settlement is located in the vicinity or some kind of mission."

"For three days the wind has blown from the west, or from a region unknown and in all probability as uninhabited as this jungle. You know that here there are no settlements or missions."

"This is really curious."

"We had better get that kite."

"It is necessary. Perhaps we may ascertain where it came from."

The captain gave the order. The tree was a few tens of yards high, but the negroes climbed at once to the top, removed carefully the imprisoned kite, and handed it to the doctor who, glancing at it, said:

"There is some kind of inscription on it. We 'll see."
And blinking with his eyes he began to read.

Suddenly his face changed, his hands trembled.

"Glenn," he said, "take this, read it, and assure me that I did not get a sunstroke and that I am in my sound mind."

The captain took the bamboo frame to which a sheet was fastened and read as follows:

"Nelly Rawlinson and Stanislas Tarkowski, sent from Khartûm to Fashoda and conducted from Fashoda east from the Nile, escaped from the dervishes. After long months' travel they arrived at a lake lying south of Abyssinia. They are going to the ocean. They beg for speedy help."

At the side of the sheet they found the following addition written in smaller letters:

"This kite, the 54th in order, was flown from the mountains surrounding a lake unknown to geography. Whoever finds it should notify the Directory of the Canal at Port Said or Captain Glenn in Mombasa.

Stanislas Tarkowski."

When the captain's voice died away, the two friends gazed at each other in silence.

"What is this?" Doctor Clary finally asked.

"I do not believe my own eyes!" the captain answered.

"This, of course, is no illusion."

"No."

"It is plainly written, 'Nelly Rawlinson and Stanislas Tarkowski.'"

"Most plainly."

"And they may be somewhere in this region."

"God rescued them, so it is probable."

"Thank Him for that," exclaimed the doctor fervently. "But where shall we seek them?"

"Is there no more on the kite?"

"There are a few other words but in the place torn by the bough. It is hard to read them."

Both leaned their heads over the sheet and only after a long time were they able to decipher:

"The rainy season passed long ago."

"What does that mean?"

"That the boy lost the computation of time."

"And in this manner he endeavored to indicate the date, therefore this kite may have been sent up not very long ago."

"If that is so, they may not be very far from here."

The feverish, broken conversation lasted for a while, after which both began to scrutinize the document and discuss every word inscribed upon it. The thing appeared, however, so improbable that if it were not for the fact that this occurred in a region in which there were no Europeans at all — about three hundred and seventy-five miles from the nearest coast — the doctor and the captain would have assumed that it was an ill-timed joke, which had been perpetrated by some European children who had read the newspapers describing the abduction, or by wards of missions. But it was difficult not to believe their eyes; they had the kite in hand and the little rubbed inscriptions were plainly in black before them.

Nevertheless, there were many things which they could not comprehend. Where did the children get the paper for the kite? If it had been furnished to them by a caravan, then they would have joined it and would not have appealed for help. For what reason did the boy not attempt to fly with his little companion to Abyssinia? Why did the dervishes send them east of the Nile into an unknown region? In what manner did they succeed in escaping from the hands of the guards? Where did they hide? By what miracle through long months of journey did they not die from starvation, or become the prey of wild animals? Why were they not killed by savages? To all these questions there was no reply.

"I do not understand it, I do not understand it," repeated Doctor Clary; "this is perhaps a miracle of God."

"Undoubtedly," the captain answered.

After which he added:

"But that boy! For that, of course, was his work."

"And he did not abandon the little one. May the blessings of God flow upon his head!"

"Stanley — even Stanley would not have survived three days under these circumstances."

"And nevertheless they live."

"But appeal for help. The stop is ended. We start at once."

And so it happened. On the road both friends scrutinized the document continually in the conviction that they might obtain from it an inkling of the direction in which it was necessary for them to go with help. But directions were lacking. The captain led the caravan in a zigzag way, hoping that he might chance upon some trace, some extinct fire, or a tree with a sign carved on the bark. In this manner they advanced for a few days. Unfortunately they entered afterwards upon a plain, entirely treeless, covered with high heather and tufts of dried grass. Uneasiness began to possess both friends. How easy it was to miss each other in that immeasurable expanse, even with a whole caravan; and how much more so two children, who, as they imagined, crept like two little worms somewhere amid heather higher than themselves! Another day passed. Neither fires at night nor tin boxes, with notes in them, fastened on the tufts helped them any. The captain and the doctor at times began to lose hope of ever succeeding in finding the children and, particularly, of finding them alive.

They sought for them zealously, however, during the following days. The patrols, which Glenn sent right and left, finally reported to him that farther on began a desert entirely waterless; so when they accidentally discovered cool water in a cleft it was necessary to halt in order to replenish their supplies for the further journey.

The cleft was rather a fissure, a score of yards deep and comparatively narrow. At its bottom flowed a warm spring, seething like boiling water, for it was saturated with carbonic acid. Nevertheless, it appeared that the water, after cooling, was good and wholesome. The spring was so abundant that the three hundred men of the caravan could not exhaust it. On the contrary the more water they drew from it the more it flowed, and filled the fissure higher.

"Perhaps sometime," Doctor Clary said, "this place will be a resort for the health-seeker, but at present this water is inaccessible for animals because the walls of the fissure are too steep."

"Could the children chance upon a similar spring? "

"I do not know. It may be that more of them can be found in this locality. But if not, then without water they must perish."

Night fell. Fires were lit. Nevertheless, a boma was not erected, for there was nothing to build one with. After the evening refreshments, the doctor and the captain sat upon folding chairs, and lighting their pipes, began to converse of that which lay most upon their hearts.

"Not a trace," declared Clary.

"It had occurred to me," Glenn replied, "to send ten of our men to the ocean coast with a despatch that there is news of the children. But I am glad that I did not do that, as the men would perish on the way, and, even if they reached the coast, why should we awaken vain hopes?"

" And revive the pain —"

The doctor removed the white helmet from his head and wiped his perspiring forehead.

"Listen," he said; "if we should return to that lake and order the men to hew down trees and at night light a gigantic bonfire, perhaps the children might descry it."

"If they were near we would find them anyway, and if they are far off the rolling ground would hide the fire. Here the plain is seemingly level, but in reality is in knobs, wavy as the ocean. Besides, by retreating we would definitely lose the possibility of finding even traces of them."

"Speak candidly. You have no hope?"

"My dear sir, we are grown-up, strong, and resourceful men, and think of what would become of us if we two were here alone, even with weapons — but without supplies and men —"

"Yes! alas — yes! I picture to myself the two children going in such a night across the desert."

"Hunger, thirst, and wild animals."

"And nevertheless the boy writes that under such conditions they proceeded for long months."

"There is also something in that which passes my comprehension."

For a long time could be heard amid the stillness only the sizzling of the tobacco in the pipes. The doctor gazed into the depth of the night, after which he said in a subdued voice:

"It is already late, but sleep has deserted me. And to think that they, if alive, are straying somewhere in the moonlight amid these dry heathers — alone — such children! Do you remember, Glenn, the little one's angelic countenance?"

"I remember it, and cannot forget."

"Ah, I would allow my hand to be cut off, if —"

And he did not finish, for Glenn started up suddenly as if scalded.

"A sky-rocket in the distance!" he shouted.

"A sky-rocket!" repeated the doctor.

"Some kind of caravan is ahead of us."

"Which might have found the children."

"Perhaps. Let us hurry to them."

"Forward!"

The captain's orders resounded in one moment throughout the camp. The Zanzibarians sprang up suddenly on their feet. Soon torches were lit. Glenn in reply to the distant signal directed that a few rockets, one after the other, be sent up; and afterwards that the salvo of rifle shots be continued. Before a quarter of an hour elapsed the whole camp was on the way.

From the distance shots replied. There was no doubt

that this was some kind of European caravan, appealing, from unknown reasons, for help.

The captain and the doctor raced forward, swept alternately by fear and hope. Would they find the children or would they not? The doctor said in his soul that, if not, they in the further journey could seek only for their remains amid those terrible heather-bushes.

After a half-hour one of those knobs, of which they had spoken before, obstructed the further view of the friends. But they were already so near that they heard distinctly the clatter of a horse's hoofs. In a few minutes, and on the top of the elevation, appeared a rider, holding before him a white object.

"Torches up," commanded Glenn.

In the same moment the rider brought his horse into the circle of light.

"Water! Water!"

"The children!" Doctor Clary cried.

"Water!" Stas repeated.

And he almost hurled Nell into the captain's arms and leaped out of the saddle.

But immediately he staggered, and fell like a corpse upon the ground.

CONCLUSION

Joy in the camp of Captain Glenn and Doctor Clary was boundless, but the curiosity of both Englishmen was subjected to a severe test. For if previously they could not comprehend how the children by themselves could cross those vast wilds and deserts separating that region from the Nile and Fashoda, then at present they could not at all understand in what manner "the little Pole," as they called Stas, not only accomplished that but appeared before them as the leader of a caravan, armed with European weapons — with an elephant bearing a palanquin, with horses, tents, and a considerable supply of provisions. At the sight of this, the captain spread out his arms and said every little while: "Clary, I have seen a great deal but I have not seen such a boy," — and the honest doctor repeated with no less astonishment: "And he rescued the little one from slavery and saved her!" After which he hastened to the tents to see how the children were and whether they slept well.

And the children, having appeased their thirst and hunger and changed their clothes, slept as though slain, during the whole of the following day; the people in their caravan did the same. Captain Glenn tried to question Kali about Stas' deeds and adventures during the journey, but the young negro, opening one eye, only answered: "The great master can do everything," — and again fell asleep. It positively became necessary to postpone questions and explanations for a few days.

In the meantime the two friends conferred over the return journey to Mombasa. They had, as it was, penetrated farther and explored more territory than they were commissioned to; they decided, therefore, to return without delay. The captain indeed was lured very much by that lake unknown to geography, but a regard for the health of the children and a desire to return them as quickly as possible to their afflicted fathers prevailed. The doctor insisted, however, that it would be necessary to rest on the cool heights of Kenia Mountain or Mount Kilima-Njaro. From there they also decided to send news to the parents and summon them to come to Mombasa.

The return journey began, after due rest and baths in the warm springs, on the third day. It was at the same time a day of parting from Kali. Stas persuaded the little one that to take him farther with them — to the ocean or to Egypt — would be selfishness on their part. He said to her that in Egypt, and even in England, Kali would be nothing more than a servant, while when he assumed the government of his nation, he, as king, could spread and establish Christianity, soften the savage customs of the Wahimas, and make of them not only a civilized but a good people. The same thing he repeated in substance to Kali.

At the leave-taking, however, a multitude of tears were shed of which even Stas was not ashamed, for he and Nell had passed with Kali through many evil and good moments and not only had learned to appreciate his honest heart, but had conceived a sincere affection for him. The young negro lay long at the feet of his "Bwana kubwa" and the "Good Mzimu." Twice he returned to look at them for a while, but finally the moment of separation came and the two caravans started in opposite directions.

It was only during the journey that the narrative of the adventures of the two little travelers began. Stas, at one time prone to be a trifle boastful, now did not brag at all. He simply had performed too many great deeds, he had undergone too much, and was too developed not to understand that words should not be greater than acts. There was, after all, enough of deeds, though related in the most modest manner. Each day during the scorching "white hours" and at evening during the stops there glided before the eyes of Captain Glenn and Doctor Clary pictures, as it were, of those occurrences and incidents through which the children had passed. So they saw the kidnapping from Medinet-el-Fayûm and the awful journey on camel-back across the desert — and Khartûm and Omdurmân, resembling hell on earth, and the ill-boding Mahdi. When Stas related his reply to the Mahdi, when the latter tried to induce him to change his faith, both friends rose and each of them warmly shook Stas' right hand, after which the captain said:

"The Mahdi is not living!"

"The Mahdi is not living?" Stas repeated with astonishment.

"Yes," spoke out the doctor. "He choked himself with his own fat, or, in other words, he died of heart trouble, and the succession of his government has been assumed by Abdullahi."

A long silence ensued.

"Ha!" said Stas. "He did not expect when he despatched us for our destruction to Fashoda that death would first overtake him."

And later he added:

"But Abdullahi is still more cruel than the Mahdi."

"For that reason mutinies and massacres have already begun," the captain replied, "and the whole edifice which the Mahdi reared will sooner or later tumble down."

"And after that who will succeed?"

"England," the captain answered [1]

In the further course of the journey, Stas told about his journey to Fashoda, about the death of old Dinah, of their start from Fashoda to uninhabited regions, and their search for Smain in them. When he reached that part where he killed the lion and afterwards Gebhr, Chamis, and the two Bedouins, the captain interrupted him with only two words: "All right!" after which he again squeezed his right hand, and with Clary listened with increasing interest about the taming of the King, about settling in Cracow, about Nell's fever, of finding Linde, and the kites which the children sent up from Karamojo Mountains. The doctor who, with each day, became more and more deeply attached to little Nell, was impressed so much by everything which threatened her most, that from time to time he had to strengthen himself with a few swallows of brandy, and when Stas began to narrate how she almost became the prey of the dreadful "wobo" or "abasanto," he caught the little maid in his arms as if in fear that some new beast of prey was threatening her life.

And what he and the captain thought of Stas was best evidenced by two despatches, which within two weeks after their arrival at the foot-hills of Kilima-Njaro they expressly sent to the captain's deputy in Mombasa with instructions that the latter should transmit them to the fathers. The first one, edited carefully, for fear that it

---

[1] The reign of Abdullahi continued for ten years. The decisive blow to the dervish power was delivered by Lord Kitchener, who almost totally annihilated them in a great bloody battle and afterwards ordered the Mahdi's tomb to be razed.

should create too astounding a sensation, and forwarded to Port Said, contained the following words:

"Thanks to boy, favorable news about children. Come to Mombasa."

The second, more explicit, addressed to Aden, was of this purport:

"Children are with us. Well. Boy a hero."

On the cool heights at the **foot** of Kilima-Njaro they stopped fifteen days, as Doctor Clary insisted that this was imperative for Nell's health, and even for Stas'. The children with their whole souls admired this heaven-kissing mountain, which possesses all the climates of the world. Its two peaks, Kibo and Kima-Wenze, during daytime were most frequently hidden in thick fogs. But when in fair nights the fogs suddenly dispersed and from the twilight the eternal snows on Kima-Wenze blushed with a rosy luster at a time when the whole world was plunged in darkness, the mountain appeared like a bright altar of God, and the hands of both children at this sight involuntarily were folded in prayer.

For Stas the days of worry, uneasiness and exertion had passed. They had yet before them a month of travel to Mombasa and the road led through the charming but unhealthy forest of Taveta; but how much easier it was to travel now, with a numerous caravan well provided with everything and over familiar trails, than formerly to stray in the wilderness with only Kali and Mea. Besides, Captain Glenn was now responsible for the journey. Stas rested and hunted. Aside from this, having found among the implements of the caravan a chisel and hammers, he was in the cooler hours engaged in chiseling upon a great gneiss rock the inscription

"Jeszcze Polska nie zginela," [1] for he wished to leave some trace of their sojourn in that region.

The Englishmen, to whom he translated the inscription, were astonished that it never occurred to the boy to perpetuate his own name on that rock. But he preferred to carve the words he had chosen.

He did not cease, however, to take care of Nell and awoke in her such unbounded confidence that when Clary asked her whether she did not fear the storms on the Red Sea, the little maid raised her beautiful, calm eyes and only answered, "Stas will know what to do." Captain Glenn claimed that truer evidence of what Stas was to the little one and greater praise for the boy no one would be able to pronounce.

Though the first despatch to Pan Tarkowski at Port Said had been worded with much care, it nevertheless created such a powerful sensation that joy almost killed Nell's father. But Pan Tarkowski, though he was an exceptionally self-controlled person, in the first moments after the receipt of the despatch, knelt in prayer and began to beseech God that the intelligence should not prove to be a delusion, a morbid chimera, bred from sorrow, longing, and pain. Why, they had both toiled so hard to learn that the children were even alive! Mr. Rawlinson had despatched to the Sudân whole caravans, while Pan Tarkowski, disguised as an Arab, had penetrated with the greatest danger to his life as far as Khartûm, but all was futile. The men who could have given any news died of smallpox, of starvation, or perished during the continual massacres, and of the children there was not the slightest clue. In the end both fathers lost all hope and lived only on recollections, in the deep conviction that

[1] "Poland is not yet lost." The title of the most popular Polish national march. — *Translator's note.*

here in life now nothing awaited them and that only death would unite them with those dearest beings who were everything for them in the world.

In the meantime unexpected joy, almost beyond their strength, fell upon them. But it was linked with uncertainty and amazement. Neither could by any means comprehend in what manner news of the children came from that part of Africa, that is, Mombasa. Pan Tarkowski supposed that they might have been ransomed or stolen by some Arabian caravan which from the eastern coast ventured into the interior for ivory and penetrated as far as the Nile. The words of the despatch, "Thanks to boy," he explained in this manner: that Stas had notified the captain and the doctor by letter where he with Nell could be found. Nevertheless, many things it was impossible to unravel. On the other hand, Pan Tarkowski understood quite clearly that the information not only was favorable, but very favorable, as otherwise the captain and the doctor would not have dared to awaken hopes in them, and above all would not have summoned them to Mombasa.

The preparations for the journey were brief, and the second day after the receipt of the despatches both engineers, with Nell's teacher, were on the deck of a great steamer of the "Peninsular and Oriental Company," which was en route for India and on the way stopped at Aden, Mombasa, and Zanzibar. At Aden awaited them the second despatch: "Children are with us. Well. Boy a hero" After reading it Mr. Rawlinson walked about almost out of his senses from joy, and, squeezing Pan Tarkowski's palm, he repeated: "You see, it was he who saved her. To him I owe her life." Pan Tarkowski, not desiring to display too much weakness, answered only, setting his teeth, "Yes! The boy acquitted

himself bravely," but when he retired to the privacy of
his cabin he wept from happiness. At last the hour arrived
when the children fell into the embraces of their fathers.
Mr. Rawlinson seized his recovered little treasure in his
arms and Pan Tarkowski long clasped his heroic boy to
his bosom. Their misfortune disappeared as pass away
whirlwinds and storms of the desert. Their lives were filled
anew with serenity and happiness; longing and separation
had augmented their joy. But the children were surprised that the hair of their "papas" had whitened
completely during the separation.

They returned to Suez on a splendid French steamer
belonging to the "Messageries Maritimes Company,"
which was full of travelers from the islands Réunion,
Mauritius, Madagascar, and Zanzibar. When the news
spread that on board were children who had escaped
from dervish slavery Stas became an object of general
curiosity and universal praise. But the happy quartette
preferred to lock themselves in a great cabin which the
captain gave up to them and spend there the cooler hours
in narrations. Nell, too, took part in them, chirping
like a little bird, and at the same time, to the amusement
of all, beginning each sentence with an "and." So, sitting
on her father's knees and raising to him her beautiful
little eyes, she spoke in this manner: "And, papa, they
kidnapped us and conveyed us on camels — and Gebhr
struck me — and Stas defended me — and we came
to Khartûm and there people died of hunger — and Stas
worked to get dates for me — and we were at the Mahdi's
— and Stas did not want to change his religion — and
the Mahdi sent us to Fashoda — and afterwards Stas
killed a lion and all of them — and we lived in a big tree,
which is called Cracow — and the King was with us

— and I had a fever — and Stas cured me — and killed a wobo — and conquered the Samburus — and was always very kind to me — papa!"

In the same fashion she spoke about Kali, Mea, the King, Saba, Mount Linde, the kites, and the final journey until their meeting with the captain's and doctor's caravan. Mr. Rawlinson, listening to this chirping, checked his tears with difficulty, while Pan Tarkowski could not contain himself from pride and happiness, for even from these childish narratives it appeared that were it not for the bravery and energy of the boy the little one ran the risk of perishing, not once but a thousand times, without help.

Stas gave a more specific and complete account of everything. And it happened that during the narration of the journey from Fashoda to the waterfall, a great load fell off his heart, for when he told how he shot Gebhr and his companions, he hemmed and hawed and began to look uneasily at his father, while Pan Tarkowski knitted his brow, pondered a while, and after that gravely said:

"Listen, Stas! It is not allowable for any one to be lavish with death, but if anybody menaces your fatherland or puts in jeopardy the life of your mother, sister, or the life of a woman entrusted to your care, shoot him in the head and ask no questions. Do not reproach yourself on that account."

Mr. Rawlinson immediately after the return to Port Said took Nell to England, where he settled permanently. Stas was sent by his father to a school in Alexandria, where his deeds and adventures were less known. The children corresponded almost daily, but circumstances combined to prevent their seeing each other for ten years. The boy, after finishing school in Egypt, entered the Polytechnic in Zurich, after which, having secured his diploma,

he was engaged in the construction of tunnels in Switzerland.

When ten years had passed, Pan Tarkowski retired
from the service of the Canal Company, and he and Stas
visited their friends in England. Mr. Rawlinson invited
them to his home, near Hampton Court, for the whole
summer. Nell had finished her eighteenth year and had
grown into a maiden as charming as a flower, and Stas
became convinced, at the expense of his own peace, that a
man, who had completed twenty-four years, could nevertheless still think of ladies. He even thought of beautiful
and dear Nell so incessantly that finally he decided to
run away to whatever place his eyes would lead him.

But while in that state of mind, Mr. Rawlinson one day
placed both of his palms on Stas' shoulders and, looking
him straight in the eyes, said with an angelic benignity:

"Tell me, Stas, whether there is a man in the world to
whom I could give my treasure and darling with greater
confidence?"

The young couple married and remained in England
until Mr. Rawlinson's death and a year later they started
upon a long journey. As they promised to themselves to
visit those localities in which they had spent their earliest
years and afterwards at one time had wandered as children, they proceeded first of all to Egypt. The state of
the Mahdi and Abdullahi had already been overthrown,
and after its fall England, as Captain Glenn stated, "succeeded." A railroad was built from Cairo to Khartûm.
The "sudds," or the Nilotic obstructions of growing
water plants, were cleared so that the young couple could
in a comfortable steamer reach not only Fashoda but
the great Lake Victoria Nyanza. From the city of Flor-
ence lying on the shores of that lake they proceeded by a

railroad to Mombasa. Captain Glenn and Doctor Clary had already removed to Natal, but in Mombasa there lived under the solicitous care of the local English authorities the King. The giant at once recognized his former master and mistress and particularly greeted Nell with such joyful trumpeting that the mangrove trees in the neighborhood shook as if they were swept by the wind. He recognized also old Saba, who outlived almost twofold the years usually allotted to a dog and, though a trifle blind, accompanied Stas and Nell everywhere.

Here also Stas learned that Kali enjoyed good health; that under the English Protectorate he ruled the entire region south of Lake Rudolf, and that he had introduced missionaries who were spreading Christianity among the local savage tribes.

After this journey the young couple returned to Europe and, with Stas' venerable father, settled permanently in Poland.

THE END

CPSIA information can be obtained
at www.ICGtesting.com
Printed in the USA
LVOW01*0613200616

493300LV00007B/69/P